HIGH TENSION

HIGH TENSION

THE RECOLLECTIONS OF

HUGH BAILLIE

Illustrated

HARPER & BROTHERS PUBLISHERS

NEW YORK

TO THE REPORTERS OF THE FREE WORLD

This Book Is Dedicated

All the characters and incidents in this book are real; and all descriptions of people living or dead are real, as are the quotations attributed to them. The opinions are the author's.

CONTENTS

Sixteen pages of photographs may be found in four groups following pages 34, 66, 98 and 130.

PREFACE

THIS IS a story of men in crisis—men whom I encountered during forty years of reporting for the United Press. Included are some of the most infamous villains of history, beneath the weight of whose evil mankind is still laboring. Some are remembered as glamorous heroes. Others held the headlines for a space, and then were seen no more. Some were guilty of mistakes which cost them their lives . . . and many other lives, too. There is nobody in this book whom I didn't see personally—frequently when their deeds, or misdeeds, were making history.

The reporters are a great breed. Without them, you wouldn't know what was going on in the world. Or in the next block, for that matter. I am proud to be one of this breed, and appreciative of the opportunities the work gave me to be in on the battle, the murder, the sudden death or whatever else was transpiring worth reporting. During the years, I have held a lot of jobs in the United Press—from chairman down—but I was A REPORTER all the way.

I must acknowledge the assistance given me in preparing this book for publication by Martin Mayer, author of *Wall Street, Men and Money* and *Madison Avenue, U.S.A.* I have learned that there is a difference between writing a book and batting out a dispatch for instantaneous distribution, publication and broadcasting. For instance, in the book you often put the kick in the last paragraph and lead up to it gradually. In the news dispatch, you put the kick in the first paragraph and append the facts to support it.

There is no bibliography, because I saw and heard all this stuff myself.

HUGH BAILLIE

New York, 1959

HIGH TENSION

Chapter 1

CITY OF ANGELS

LOS ANGELES in 1910, when I went to work for the *Record*, was a tough boot camp for a young reporter. News was local and violent, and you weren't supposed to miss any of it. If getting the news meant putting yourself in trouble, that was your business and nobody felt sorry for you. It was an asset for a reporter to know where to carry a gun so he could get at it fast (the right place is down the front of your pants, not at the shoulder), or how to hold a stiff arm to conceal a maul up your sleeve while out on door-smashing police raids. During five years as a reporter on the *Record*, I was jumped twice, once with some success.

With six newspapers in town, jobs were not hard to get, by today's standards. But once you had the job the easy part was over. I was nineteen years old when I started out, but that didn't entitle me to any special consideration. By the same token, my age didn't deprive me of any chances. There was no prejudice against youth. I was never a cub reporter, because there weren't any cubs in Los Angeles. If you couldn't do your job, you were fired out of hand—but once you had demonstrated that you could handle a story you were on a level with the old timers. You could fight for your share of the front-page stuff. From the beginning, I liked to consider myself the bull goose of the staff, and to go after more than my share. Often enough, I got what I went after.

The city I covered for five years was a world to itself. Los Angeles was growing fast—it was heresy to say anything else (and, besides,

1

anything else would have been untrue). All mankind was divided into two categories, "boosters" and "knockers," and if you weren't a booster you could get out. There was no place for you. The typical Angeleno read his newspaper mostly to find out what was happening at home. We told him—without worrying too much about whether the news was or wasn't "fit to print."

There was always a local story worth writing about, if you just looked around you. In those days, for example, Los Angeles had a high opinion of its own morality, and enforced that opinion by means of rigorous laws which made unlicensed romantic dalliance a very chancy thing. So we had interesting criminal trials. We had a balmy climate's share of balmy eccentrics. Prophets wandered down through the canyons, bearded to look like picture-Bible illustrations of Christ. "Advertising dentists" parked their trucks along the main streets, and illuminated the platforms by flaring gasoline torches. Behind these ghastly footlights, terrified drunken bums would sit in the dentist's chair, waiting for their free extraction, while the pitchman flourished his forceps, praised himself and sold his services to the open-mouthed crowd. Most of the movies still came from "back east," but in Hollywood the new age was dawning. I went out on location to see the wooden scaffolding of the sets and mingle in the commissariat on the lot with the crowds of extras dressed as Ku-Kluxers during the filming of D. W. Griffith's *The Clansman*—later called *The Birth of a Nation*. Like everybody else, they were whistling "Alexander's Ragtime Band."

We had enough crime to make headlines, but not so much that people were bored with it. Nearly every reporter got some police experience. Every man who covered the sheriff's office was a sworn deputy, with power to arrest. (During a fight in the press box at an automobile race, two reporters tried to arrest each other. One of them was me.) Covering police, many reporters carried guns. I did. Deputy sheriff badges weren't worth much, because anybody could buy one at a pawnshop, but the guns gave us a certain security against reprisals from punks and hoods. And a police badge was worth cash money: by putting your finger over the word REPORTER, which ran across the middle of the shield, and flashing the badge at a streetcar conductor, you could ride for free.

Covering the police beat, six of us (one from each newspaper) would sit in a narrow room beside the entrance to police headquarters, breathing in the perfume of disinfectant which filled the building and waiting for the "fast call buzzer." When the buzzer sounded, it meant the wagon was going out on a job, and would take one reporter, so the next man up would dash out to cover for everybody. You made yourself useful when you went with the police. They didn't have sirens in those days, they had bells; and the reporter sat beside the driver and rang the bell as the wagon rattled through town. When you arrived, you got out and lent a hand, which usually consisted of holding one end of the stretcher. The police patrol was the ambulance too, and on the way to the hospital the stretcher would hang like a hammock from leather loops. You sat by the head of the stretcher and tried to get the occupants' stories. They'd taken poison and jumped out the window; they'd be lying there with compound fractures and full of poison, and they'd expire while you were taking their final statements.

I saw a lot of dead and dying people as a kid reporter in Los Angeles. I remember the coroner kneeling astride the body of a friend who had blown off the top of his head with a revolver. As he went through his friend's pockets he kept saying, in an aggrieved voice, "Why'dya do it, Claude? Why'dya do it?"

Meanwhile, the girl for whom he had done it lay quietly dying of his bullets, on the next stretcher.

Then there was the young girl who had shot her choirboy lover, and failed to shoot herself. She sat on a hard chair in the jail and whined at me, "He ain't dead, is he? Please say he ain't dead?" But I'd seen him, and he definitely was dead.

One day there was a crackpot loose in the police chief's office—a seamy fellow named Carl Warr, who jumped from a car and bolted in past the officers on guard, wearing a mask with goggle eyes and carrying a box with a glass window which revealed sticks of dynamite. He demanded that the chief fetch to his office several of the richest men in Los Angeles, so he could "dictate terms." Warr said his bomb was constructed to explode the moment he took his finger *off* the trigger; if anyone shot him or knocked him out, we would all be killed. The rich men of Los Angeles, of course, were not to be lured in this manner, but a number of people at police headquarters —patrolmen, detectives, and reporters including me—wound up in the office and were told to stay. Outside, the neighborhood was evacuated, and people trudged through the streets dragging trunks, or loaded down with household goods, as if a fire were sweeping the area. The vigil with Carl Warr lasted several hours, until a county detective named Sam Browne lost his patience and clipped the would-be bomber at the base of the skull with a sap. The fuse on the bomb began to sizzle as Warr fell; Browne grabbed the box, held it high over his head and ran to the street, yelling at the top of his voice. The crowd in the chief's office suddenly dispersed out doors and windows. Browne smashed the box in the gutter and it burst. The dynamite rolled harmlessly down First Street hill.

I saw Warr again, a few minutes later, in the receiving hospital. Somehow, he had got himself badly beaten up. He was chained to a bed while two plain-clothes men vigorously tickled the soles of his bare feet with lead pencils, to make him tell where he got the dynamite and who had driven him to headquarters. This was the first time I ever saw a man tortured by the police. Warr groaned and writhed, and never told; and the only offense they could pin on him in court was illegal transportation of dynamite.

The Los Angeles police at that time had some reputation for third-degree methods, not all of it deserved. Some of it was the fault of the men in the pressroom, which had a window over the sidewalk. Every once in a while, after an important arrest, we would stage a show for the benefit of the pedestrians. One reporter would slam a telephone book on a table, making a loud, soggy slap, while another groaned in mock agony and still another shouted, "Confess, you son of a bitch! Confess!" Another game in which a few of the gun-toting reporters indulged themselves—briefly—involved shooting at a clock on the wall of our room. This sport came to an end one day when a soft-spoken police lieutenant pushed open our door and said in a gentle voice, "Boys, I wish you would stop shooting at that clock. The bullets have now gone through the wall, and they're passing among the people on the stairs."

Newspapers were not stratified and compartmentalized in those days, and if you were a reporter you were supposed to be able to report anything you saw. I'd been hired originally for the sports desk, and I never wholly left it. The fact that I'd covered the police beat the day before didn't bar me from covering a fight the next night. Prize fighting was illegal in most parts of the country then, but it was legitimate in Los Angeles. I saw the double knockout of Ad Wolgast and Joe Rivers, who went down on the canvas together, to the confusion of the crowd. Referee Jack Welch was not confused, though: he picked up Wolgast and counted Rivers out, on the grounds that Wolgast was the champ and thus entitled to the preference. He also thought Wolgast landed first. There were no judges to add up score cards and vote on decisions; instead, the bell sounded, the referee lifted the winner's arm, and that was that. I saw Johnny Kilbane take the featherweight title from Abe Attell in twenty artistic rounds. At one point the referee, Charley Eyton, had to stop the fight, call for a towel and massage the grease off the wily Attell.

Boxing was rough work then. Nobody would have thought of stopping a fight just because one of the men was bleeding. Handlers carried lancets to reopen puffed black eyes. Ringside weight was made when the pugs stepped on the scales stark naked, in the presence of the crowd. Women were not allowed in. (Once, at Jeffries' Vernon Arena, a girl dressed in men's clothes was discovered among the spectators. The story about *that* was bigger than the story about the fight.) The punishment a fighter received was not entirely restricted to the ring, either. One morning Joe Rivers weighed in at the downtown offices of Uncle Tom McCarey, and the scale showed him a trace over the agreed numbers. There was a forfeit for failure to make weight, and his handlers weren't paying it. They stretched him out on the floor and gave him a massage with handfuls of brown wrapping paper until the ounces were off him. I saw that, too.

Demonstrations of flying machines figured as sporting events, and thousands of people would come out to Dominguez Field to sit in wooden grandstands and watch the unbelievable boxlike crates rise into the air. At one of these meets, Archie Hoxsey took a Wright biplane more than 11,000 feet up into the sky for a new world's record. The next day a little puff of wind tipped the biplane over, and it spun down to crash in a cloud of brown dust. It was a long run to where Hoxsey had crashed, including about a hundred yards across a plowed field, but I got there in time to see them pull him out of the wreckage, and to cling to the back of the ambulance as they carried his body to the hospital at the other end of the field. Other aviators played other risky games with this new toy. Lincoln Beachey used to rock the planes and wobble the wings as he took off, to make flying look even more dangerous than it was. One day Beachey had three wrecks and walked away from all of them. After the third one, Glenn Curtiss, who had made the planes, greeted him sourly with the words, "You're the crackup kid, aren't you?" I went out to the Bolsa Chica Gun Club one day, and saw Hubert Latham hunt ducks with an Antoinette monoplane and a twelve-gauge shotgun. He sat in the open cockpit of the flying kite, head and shoulders exposed as though he were sitting in a bathtub, chasing flights of ducks and shooting them down. It did not occur to me that I was watching a primitive preview of future wars.

We had automobile races, too, in those days when the streets still carried an authentic whiff of horse manure. They were held out in Santa Monica, where the Grand Prix and Vanderbilt Cup were run through suburban streets on a course eight and a half miles long. Cars were already getting up around a hundred miles an hour on the straightaways, and there were accidents every time. I remember one corner on the Santa Monica course, a ninety-degree left turn, which was so certain to produce a smash that we stationed a reporter and a photographer there for the entire four hours of the race. I covered the story myself from a wooden pressbox right over the mechanics' pits, gasoline fumes rising slowly all around us, reporters smoking cigarettes and flicking ashes into the oil-soaked earth.

Among my sport stories which got on the wires back East was a baseball miracle—an unassisted triple play by a center fielder in a game between Vernon (later Hollywood) and Los Angeles. With Angels on first and second, Walter Carlisle raced in from center to pick a line drive off his shoetops, turned a somersault to regain his feet, continued in to touch second (two outs), and then ran down and tagged the runner who had been on first. It was hard to believe if you hadn't seen it yourself, and many papers thought it was a gag. Eastern sportswriters were suspicious of all world's records coming out of California then—why, we even had sprinters who were clocked at less than ten seconds for the hundred-yard dash, which was then regarded as impossible. But a ball park full of people had seen Carlisle's bit of magic, and it's in the record books today.

Covering baseball games was no soft berth in those days before Los Angeles even dreamed of becoming a major-league town. Ballplayers were tough, oblivious to the value of good public relations, and willing to beat up a reporter who had written something they didn't like. My sports editor, Ed O'Malley, wrote a column which he called "The Sporting Miscellany" (we called it, of course, "The Sporting Misery"), and used his editorial privilege as a crusader's lance. The morning after he'd battered an athlete with his prose he'd send me out to interview the man and get his reaction. I used to carry a piece of lead in a sock when I went for those interviews. To get to the press box in the old Washington Park, you had to walk across the playing field, and it was nothing unusual for me to feel baseballs buzzing about my ears as I crossed in front of the screen.

Then there were one-shot events, like a review of the Pacific Fleet. We had the whole Armada outside Los Angeles harbor one day— the battleship *Oregon*, the cruiser *California*, three or four destroyers, some supply ships and a single submarine. That was it. The feature of the review was a dive by the submarine: it went down on one side of the *California* and came up on the other. Later they renamed the *California*, called her the *San Diego*, and she hit a mine and sank during the First World War. Naval exercises in the Pacific were just a pageant, then: nobody thought there were any dangers from which the Pacific Fleet might protect us, back in 1910.

We had the elections, local elections on the grand style, complete with arrests of candidates for violation of the vice laws, and national elections which brought us the orators from the East. There were no microphones and loudspeakers then, and you had to produce a big voice if you wanted to be heard. I watched Teddy Roosevelt bellowing at the crowd and waving his big hat, and I covered a speech by the senior La Follette in Philharmonic Auditorium. He spoke for two hours, charging back and forth on the stage; he never stood still for a moment. He must have covered a couple of miles. This was hot work. After an open-air speech in which his voice was audible over all Fiesta Park, a block square, William Jennings Bryan received us reporters in his hotel room, dressed only in his long underwear, which he always wore when he had to make a speech. It was wet with sweat. He doffed the long johns and concluded his press conference in the bathtub, predicting the election of Wilson and discoursing on foreign affairs while he lathered himself vigorously with soap and a sponge.

If news was short, there were always a few recurrent events which could be picked up and played big for a day or two. There were Holy Rollers in a tent temple with a tanbark floor, yelling in tongues and snorting, jumping and wrestling with "The Spirit." Local and visiting radicals made speeches to small but excited audiences of anarchists, and sometimes got run out of town during a bomb scare. Emma Goldman and her boy friend, Dr. Ben Reitman, came through on a lecture tour, and Reitman went down to San Diego, where he was tarred and feathered. I was at the railroad station when he came back. He had left us nattily dressed in the approved Eastern style, wearing a broad-rimmed hat. He returned in dungarees, with blobs of tar and tufts of feathers sticking to him, and fell into Emma Goldman's arms, crying, "Oh, Emma, they twisted my testicles!"

Periodically, the police would raid a Chinese fan-tan joint (always a possible opium den). We usually found the room deserted, although the phonograph might still be playing Chinese music. The denizens had vanished into the warrens of Chinatown. Whenever we happened to catch one or two, they knew nothing. You can't find anything blanker than a silent Chinaman.

If all else failed, a reporter could always go out on the roads and look in on the convicts of the chain gang, and rip off a story protesting the inhumanity of the county prison system.

But the most important single source of big stories, when I was a working reporter in Los Angeles, was the Superior Court, where crime and vice cases played to standing-room-only audiences. Local courts in the West had not then reached the heights of English-style refinement which were customary in the East. Judges did not wear bombazine gowns, and they entered their courtrooms without much in the line of an Oyez! They were not regarded as a superior species of humanity, and any good court reporter counted at least a few judges among his friends. It was an informal atmosphere. If a lawyer didn't like something a reporter had done, he did not write a letter to the editor or complain to the judge. He grabbed the reporter by the lapels and clarified his position.

The informality of the courtroom atmosphere made the legal drama something that could appeal to everybody. The crowd loved the show, and sometimes—especially when a case involving a lady's virtue was on the docket—people would line up on the street outside the old Hall of Records, waiting three or four hours to get inside and see the doings. The only limit on the number of people allowed in the court was the physical capacity of the floor space. For a really interesting case, the public would pack the aisles and stand along the walls.

Lawyers never had a better stage to play on than the Superior Court of Los Angeles in those days, and a few of them took advantage of their opportunities, with high-flying oratory, showmanship, tear-jerking and even violence. District attorneys and even defense lawyers were public figures, half actor and half politician, and everything they did was news. And they knew it.

One man in particular stood out in the way he managed the courtroom and aroused the crowd—Earl Rogers. Since he was not held down to the counsel's table and the well of the court, he wandered around the aisles, even sitting on vacant seats—when there were any —to continue his cross-examination from amidst the audience. He could stare down a witness, shout down a judge, utterly distract a jury from even the plainest piece of evidence. Usually, his clients were local criminals or violators of the local vice laws. Some pretty high-class murderers, too. Once, however, he represented a national figure, a man whose very name was news all over the country. This trial, the most important in Rogers' career, was also my first big assignment, the first time I was ever on the working end of a national news wire. In 1912, when I was twenty-one years old, the Los Angeles *Record* loaned me to the United Press for three months to cover the trial of Clarence Darrow, who had been indicted on charges of trying to bribe a Los Angeles juror. Sitting in the defendant's chair himself, the great attorney for the defense had hired Earl Rogers to be his lawyer.

Chapter 2

ROGERS AND DARROW

THE TRAIN of events which carried Clarence Darrow into the dock at Superior Court started on October 1, 1910, in a dynamite blast which wrecked and burned the building of the Los Angeles *Times*. The bomb went off in the early morning, and twenty-one men who worked the overnight shift were killed in the explosion or in the fire which followed. The *Times* itself, appearing that morning as a single sheet printed in another plant, had no doubt about the nature of the criminals. Its headline proclaimed:

UNIONIST BOMB WRECKS THE TIMES

The editorial which accompanied the story was a bitter exhortation:

Oh you anarchic scum, you cowardly murderers, you leeches upon honest labor, you midnight assassins, you whose hands are dripping with the innocent blood of your victims, you against whom the wails of poor widows and the cries of fatherless children are ascending to The Great White Throne, go look at the ruins wherein are buried the calcined remains of those whom you murdered.

There was, in fact, no question that labor agitators had set the bomb. Los Angeles in 1910 was the scene of a war between capital and labor, a war which makes even the most violent of today's strikes look tame. Mayhem in the picket lines, limbs twisted out of joint, sabotage and explosions were commonplace. I heard them discussed openly in labor meetings. The bombing of the *Times* was an episode

—the worst episode—in that long and vicious war. In 1910, Los Angeles was an "open shop" town, and an active Merchants' and Manufacturers' Association was fighting to keep it so. Nobody played a larger role in this fight than General Harrison Gray Otis, who owned and ran the *Times*, the most puissant anti-union force on the coast. By striking at Otis, these bomb-minded friends of labor had hoped to hit the whole anti-union employing community of Los Angeles.

State and federal authorities joined the Los Angeles police in hunting for the individuals who had planted the bomb, and the Los Angeles district attorney hired William J. Burns, the most famous living private detective, to help in the search. In April, 1911, six months after the bombing, the Burns Agency found its quarry. In Detroit, Burns' son Raymond arrested James B. McNamara and Ortie McManigal of the International Bridge and Structural Iron Workers. Less than a week later, McManigal made a confession implicating McNamara in the *Times* holocaust and in many other, similar crimes. He said he and "J.B." had for years served the union as professional dynamiters, traveling up and down the land blasting non-union building jobs. And he said that they committed their crimes under the instruction of J.B.'s brother, Joseph J. McNamara, secretary of the union. Both McNamaras and McManigal were bundled out to Los Angeles and lodged in the county jail to await trial. I went out to have a look at them in their cells. J.B. was a ferret of a man, small and nasty; his brother J.J. had the benign expression of a pale priest whose thoughts were always on spiritual matters.

The arrest of the McNamaras raised the bombing from a vulgar matter of murder to a question of public policy. Their union was no fly-by-night anarchist bunch; it was an affiliate of the American Federation of Labor, which had often denounced violence and was supposed to stand for the peaceful settlement of labor disputes. On the McNamaras' insistence that they were innocent, Samuel Gompers, president of the A.F. of L., came to their support, and hired Clarence Darrow to defend them. A McNamara defense fund was established, and contributions to it rolled in from workingmen all over the country, who were convinced that the McNamaras had been railroaded out to Los Angeles to be lynched. There could be no neutrality in the McNamara case: you saw the brothers either as murdering dynamiters or as martyrs to "Labor's Cause."

So, in the late summer of 1911, Clarence Darrow stepped off a train into Los Angeles, the hero of all those who believed in the innocence of the McNamaras. I met him at the train, representing the Los Angeles *Record*, a pro-labor paper committed to the proposition that the McNamaras had been framed. Because my paper was on his side, Darrow singled me out for special favor.

Darrow brought a stately presence into the arena. He looked rather like our notion of a Roman Senator. He was a tall, homely, stooped man with a deeply lined face, who always seemed to be grieving about something. His eyes were set deep and hooded; you found him looking at you when you least expected it. His brown hair was long and lank, with a forelock that kept falling in his eyes, and he dressed sloppily. His clothes hung on him in folds and drapes, and there were soup spots on his tie and his vest. But when he spoke, you listened. He expected it, and talked in the leisurely manner of a man who knows he won't be interrupted. I've seen chairmen of the board of big companies who have much the same manner. At fifty-three, he was already a man of international reputation, the Great Defender of the downtrodden and oppressed.

From the moment I met him, I knew I was in the presence of an actor who would never forget his public role, never remove his make-up. He was carrying the weight of the world on his shoulders, and his gestures were calculated to express his reactions to his burden. He could shamble, or stride vigorously, as the occasion demanded, use his smile as a gesture of gratitude or as a formal grimace. He could weep at will—real tears. He didn't laugh.

During the months immediately after his arrival, I saw Darrow frequently and asked him questions about every aspect of the case. He never gave so much as a hint that he had doubts about the innocence of the McNamaras: they had been framed, and he would prove it. Meanwhile, he tried to soften the sense of outrage that people felt when they thought about the crime itself. There was no *murder* here, he said, because whoever had set the bomb had not intended to kill anybody. The *Times* building had not been blown down—it had burned up. The fire, true, had started from a dynamite explosion, but the bomb had really been a very small one, set off in

"Ink Alley" inside the building to scare Otis rather than to destroy his plant. Labor had no entrenched position in the law of those days, and its friends theorized that it was entitled to certain "belligerent rights." Darrow never mentioned the fact that twenty-one men had died in the bombing, and that his clients had been indicted on twenty-one counts of murder. He tried to give the impression that the Macs were honest and ardent labor organizers made the victim of an employers' plot, and to keep people's minds off the fact that there was a crime involved. Later, when he summed up in his own defense, he was to call the bombing an accident. Darrow had a great appreciation of the importance of public opinion—he used to call it a "spiritual weight." And he used me, I later realized, as a sounding board for his approach, to hear how well his ideas were being received. I thought he was doing fine, and I told him so.

Exactly when Darrow first found out that the McNamaras were guilty is a question nobody but Darrow could ever have answered. Maybe he knew it before he came: he wouldn't have had much reason to talk about "labor's belligerent rights" if his clients were innocent. Anyway, he let J.B. go on trial for murder in October, 1911, a year after the bombing. Then he wrangled for weeks about the selection of a jury. By November only five jurors had been seated. Meanwhile, the tension of the McNamara case built up all across the country. Labor mass meetings and parades for the McNamaras were an almost daily occurrence; people took to wearing buttons reading "MCNAMARAS NOT GUILTY." And Darrow was the hero of the hour.

A few weeks later, he was a hero no longer. In the last weeks of November, a hard-eyed, hard-boiled private detective named Bert Franklin, Darrow's chief investigator of prospective jurors, kept what he believed to be a clandestine appointment with George Lockwood, a member of the jury panel, on the corner of Third and Los Angeles streets. It was a busy, crowded corner on which to attempt such monkey business, as we all saw later, during Darrow's trial, when the jury traipsed over to look at it. While plain-clothes policemen watched from all sides, Franklin passed Lockwood a $500 bill, and showed a roll of $3,500 more which Lockwood would receive after he voted to acquit the McNamaras. Franklin had been trapped:

Lockwood had tipped the district attorney on the detective's first approach, and had set himself out on the corner as bait. Franklin was arrested on the spot, and was promptly bailed out by the Mc-Namara defense fund. Two days thereafter Darrow made a deal with the district attorney. The McNamaras pleaded guilty and escaped the noose. J.B. got life; J.J., fifteen years.

The news that the McNamaras had confessed carried an emotional jolt hard to recapture after all these years. I was in the editorial room of the Los Angeles *Record* when the flash came screaming over the United Press wire: "MACS PLEAD GUILTY." The editor of the *Record,* who had gone all out in defense of the McNamaras and had complete faith in their innocence, collapsed at his desk. All across the country, people who had been taken in by the McNamara agitation looked for someone to blame. Darrow was the obvious choice. He was denounced everywhere as a bungler if not a traitor, and his friends deserted him in a body.

Darrow himself was hurt and frightened. In a way, the McNamara result was a triumph for him: he had got the brothers off with relatively light sentences. As he told the story, J.B. had confessed while Darrow was preparing him for trial, and Darrow had then opened negotiations with the district attorney to see if he could save his clients' skin. These negotiations (in which Lincoln Steffens, the "muckraker" and professional friend of labor, took a major role) had been well under way on the day Franklin attempted to bribe Lockwood. As Darrow explained it, the Franklin debacle had nothing to do with him, or with his decision to have the McNamaras cop a plea.

As Franklin explained it, however, Darrow was the culprit in the attempted bribery of Lockwood and in another attempted bribery of another talesman, Robert Bain. Franklin in January, 1912, pleaded guilty to the attempt, paid a fine, and swore that Darrow had given him the bribe money and directed all his actions. On January 29, 1912, Darrow was indicted separately for the Lockwood and Bain attempts. Released on $20,000 bail provided by the still-functioning McNamara defense fund, Darrow issued a statement proclaiming his innocence and requesting the public to withhold judgment. But anyone could see he was deeply worried.

Worried enough, it soon developed, to hire Earl Rogers as his defense counsel—though Rogers was as little like him as could be. Darrow was a shabby man with an afflicted look; Rogers was "tall, dark and handsome," and a sharp dresser—a howling swell, as we said in those days. In an age when many men of some distinction thought it no harm to go without a shave for a day or two, Rogers was always neatly barbered, his face glowing, his black hair well trimmed. At a time when it was no disgrace to be seen in baggy pants —and defending a client who came to court every day in the same dirty old suit—Rogers would appear in cutaway coat with braided edges, fawn waistcoat, spats, boutonniere, lavish cravat and bat-winged collar. Politically, the two men were on opposite sides: Rogers had, in fact, acted as a special district attorney investigating union "conspiracies." Darrow had made his reputation defending the poor and oppressed; Rogers had made *his*, which was only slightly less considerable than Darrow's in the Los Angeles area, by defending rich criminals, prominent citizens accused in vice cases, and the like.

Darrow was as much an actor as Rogers, and as skilled at putting across a point by the use of his personality. But he always *seemed* to have scored his point by pure logical argument, and you had to watch him carefully to see that he was acting. Rogers' acting was obvious and flamboyant. He generated electricity. Often, his theatrics overwhelmed the point he might be making with them—but, even more often, the Rogers act made jurors forget whatever points the prosecution had tried to hammer home.

Rogers played his voice the way a musician plays a church organ. He could make it full-throated and menacing, or gentle and beguiling. He had bright blue eyes spaced rather widely apart, and he could use them as penetrating searchlights when he wished—or dull them with counterfeit indifference. He wore a lorgnette on a long black ribbon, and would hold it to his eyes and stare through it at a witness, leaning into the box to face the man down. When the lorgnette had served its purpose, he would twirl it on the ribbon and shoot it into the breast pocket of his coat. He never missed the pocket. As a feat of juggling, this was fascinating in itself, and frequently the jury paid more attention to the stunt than they did to the witness and what he was saying. Having restored the lorgnette to its resting place, Rogers might ask the next question from *behind* the witness stand, or turn his back on the witness and shout the question at the audience in the courtroom, or coo it at the members of the jury. He put on quite a show; everyone liked it except the prosecutors—and, in this case, Darrow, the client. Darrow was obviously embarrassed. He deplored any circus tactics except his own more subtle shenanigans.

As a cross-examiner, Rogers was always at his best with expert witnesses—especially doctors. He knew more about medical argument than any doctor I've seen on a witness stand, and he could run rings around medical authorities when it came to gunshot wounds. One of his favorite techniques was to ask a hypothetical question that went on and on, sometimes for as long as an hour. While the witness was trying to figure out how he could answer it, Rogers would retire to the hall outside the courtroom and pace up and down, smoking a cigarette. Meanwhile, of course, he had managed to put in the record his views of the situation.

Rogers was wonderfully resourceful, never at a loss for a question or an answer. During the course of the Darrow trial, he often absented himself from the courtroom for several days without an explanation. Rumors would fly about, that he was boozing (Rogers was known as a considerable drinker, though I never saw him under the influence in court), or that Darrow had failed to pay an installment of his fee and he had refused to continue until the money arrived. Once I telephoned him at his home to ask him why he was staying away.

"Well, Baillie," he drawled, "I tried to give myself an enema yesterday and by mistake I used sapolio instead of soap. I'm very sore and I won't be able to come back to court until I'm able to walk without it hurting so damn much."

It was the perfect answer: it didn't tell me anything I could use, and it virtually prevented me from guessing at his real reasons. You could trust Rogers to have an excuse nobody had ever used before.

In addition to Rogers and Darrow, two other lawyers worked for the defense: Jerry Giesler and Horace Appel. Giesler was Rogers' assistant, a young man who kept the papers in order and made sure Rogers had whatever he might need in the line of document or argument. He spoke rarely, though in other trials Rogers put him to excellent use, relying on his talents as a tear-jerker to move juries after all else had failed. Later Rogers' own mantle was to descend on Giesler, and today he is the defense attorney of choice for Holly-wood stars or other Los Angeles magnificos who get into trouble.

Appel was an entirely different sort, a Mexican Jew with a vast command of accented English, who could goad the district attorney and his staff almost beyond endurance with his easy contempt. He, too, was a brilliant cross-examiner, but on this team he acted mostly as backstop, objecting to the prosecution's objections to Rogers' conduct of the trial. At one point he infuriated assistant district attorney Joe Ford with a snide reference to Ford's personal habits. "I'm seeck and tired," he said, "of these gum-chewin' objections."

All in all, the case had a fascinating cast of characters. But it was more than a show; it was news, an important story all over the country and front-page material in Los Angeles for twelve weeks—weeks which also saw the Balkan War which opened our Age of Wars, the nomination of Woodrow Wilson, and Teddy Roosevelt's bolt from the Republican party. The mighty Darrow, caught personally in the toils of the law, drew ace correspondents, giants of journalism, from newspapers in Chicago, New York, and Washington, and even from newspapers in Europe. The story was so big that the press associations could not risk the usual, somewhat slower, process of reporting, by which a correspondent sat in a courtroom and ran out every once in a while to call in his story. The Darrow trial required direct, immediate coverage, with a telegraph wire brought into the courtroom itself, a reporter to cover the story and a Morse man to tap it out into newspapers all over the country.

The United Press did not have a big enough staff in Los Angeles in those days to take a man from his usual duties and assign him full-time to the Darrow courtroom. So the association asked the Los Angeles *Record*, a UP client (and a Scripps paper, which meant that it had the same corporate ownership as the press association), to lend reporter Baillie for the job. At the age of twenty-one, two years out of art school, I found myself consorting with—and competing against—the great reporters of the time. I looked upon them with mingled awe and cockiness; despite my respect for their persons and accomplishments, I was young-son-of-the-West enough to regard them as a bunch of overdressed dudes. I couldn't imagine them riding in a police wagon, not with those spats on their ankles. At the same time, I was thrilled to be among them as an equal. I suppose that's what you'd call ambivalence; anyway, it's what I felt.

I scribbled my dispatches in pencil on yellow pad. As I finished a paragraph—or even a sentence—I tore off the sheet and handed it to the Morse operator at my elbow. (Since he could send it as fast as I could write, he often read over my shoulder and got the sentences on the wire before I could hand him the sheet.) When the going in court got too fast for writing, I dictated my story directly to the operator, whispering in his ear. The transmitter, or "bug," was enclosed in a soundproof box, from which the operator's hand never emerged. My Morse man was George Carse, one of that great school of press telegraphers who were as good reporters as the men who fed them the stories. When he thought I might be missing something, he'd nudge me with his elbow to make sure I was on the ball. Sometimes, I suspect, he took over and sent the story out by himself, without waiting for me to write or dictate anything.

The amount of material we sent varied each day, depending on the activity in the courtroom. From an early point in the trial, the strategy of the two sides was obvious. District Attorney John D. Fredericks and his assistant Joe Ford were out to prove, via Franklin, Lockwood, and the common sense of the situation, that Darrow must have been behind the attempted bribery—and, meanwhile, to surround the bribe itself with the odor of the McNamaras' crime. Fredericks kept referring to "the bum" which was detonated in Ink Alley to destroy the *Times*. Darrow and Rogers were out to plant the seed of suspicion that the prosecution witnesses were engaged in a plot against the great defender of labor—and to diminish the apparent importance of the attempted bribery. In this second goal, they were helped by the fact that, before Franklin gave Lockwood the bribe, Darrow had offered in negotiations with the district attorney to have the McNamaras plead guilty. If the McNamaras were going to confess, anyway, the bribery would seem an aberration rather than a crime.

But the day-to-day incidents which developed out of these strategies were often so exciting that they obscured the purpose of the trial—which was, simply, to find out whether or not Clarence Darrow was guilty of jury bribery. The most spectacular sessions came during Rogers' cross-examination of William J. Burns, who had been put on the stand to tell about the McNamaras and the bombing of the *Times*.

When Rogers first pulled his lorgnette on Burns, the great investigator started visibly. Rogers placed his face very close to Burns' face, and glared at him through the glasses. Burns was a formidable figure himself, a powerful, stocky man with a full head of wavy auburn hair and a full, old-fashioned auburn mustache. He was taking no bullying from Rogers; he appealed to Judge Hutton to protect him from the lorgnette. Later, Rogers managed to rouse Burns' temper, and involved him in a shouting argument. During the course of the argument, Rogers accused Burns of coming armed to court, with a gun in his pocket and a sword-cane on his arm. Judge Hutton, at his wit's end, fined both men for contempt of court and adjourned session to the next day. At the end of that day in court, it would have been hard indeed for a juror to remember what the trial was about.

Burns' attitude toward Rogers, when they were not in court, was that of a man who deplored the carryings-on of a well-bred hoodlum. Surrounded by reporters, the investigator would stand in the corner of the corridor and look sadly in the direction of Rogers. As a matter of fact, the two men knew each other well. They had worked as allies in the investigation of the *Times* dynamiting itself, when Rogers acted as a special deputy district attorney. But they were both men who insisted on controlling the situation, and in this case they were quite genuinely angry at each other. On one occasion, after court adjourned, they got into a brief fist fight in the hall. More shoving than slugging—but it made quite a story.

Another courtroom brawl involved Darrow, Appel and district attorney Fredericks, whom Appel had provoked into the charge that Darrow's unchanging stare was an attempt to hypnotize a witness. In the excitement Fredericks threw an ink well which narrowly missed Giesler. He was seized by Martin Aguirre, the one-eyed bailiff, who in his day had been a real shooting Western sheriff. As Aguirre held the district attorney in a firm grip, Appel went on badgering:

"I say that heepnotism is not recognized in a court of law! Anyway, I object to the questions wheech are being interpolated here from time to time by the deestrict attorney! They are eemproper. They are eerrelevant and eemmaterial, never asked in a court of justice before. They are eentended to degrade the weetness and his attorneys!"

Rogers' most serious and difficult cross-examination came, of course, when Franklin was the witness. He kept Franklin on the stand for days and days, striking at him from all directions, but basically with the argument that the detective was an untrustworthy paid informer and framer. Finally, he directly charged Franklin with perjury. Franklin looked unblinkingly ahead with his marble eyes, which were like those of a caged lion and never seemed to focus on anybody. He replied:

"I never was afraid to go to the penitentiary, and I'm not afraid to go there now."

Darrow himself took over the cross-examination on occasion, with effects far different from Rogers'. He would drop soft questions on the witness like water on a stone, wearing his antagonist away until a contradiction emerged—at which point he would raise his voice slightly, only slightly, to call attention to his victory. Rogers pranced all over the courtroom during a cross-examination (if the seat next to me was vacant, I might find Rogers in it, asking questions of a witness while he read my dispatches and attempted to edit them). But Darrow stayed in one place, bent over the table, looking alternately at his notes and at the witness, his haggard, gloomy expression doubly effective because of the very real peril he was in.

As the weeks passed, Darrow looked worse and worse. The courtroom was close and stuffy in those summer months, and he felt it. His hair hung down the back of his neck. He lost weight, accentuating the bagginess of his clothes, and he became more and more round shouldered. Both his head and his lower lip thrust forward more despondently than ever, his face grew longer and the rest of him seemed to shrink. In fact, he looked guilty. His appearance obviously disturbed Rogers, who began to argue with him—often within the hearing of others in the courtroom—about the way he looked. It was Rogers' theory that Darrow should seem jaunty and confident, though the gates of San Quentin yawned before him.

I talked to Darrow regularly throughout the trial, and he told me of his disagreements with Rogers. He never made an optimistic statement about the result of the trial. He was increasingly glum and grim; he felt mortified and resentful, heartbroken and trapped. He believed that his friends had joined his foes, that they seemed ashamed of knowing him, that they had turned against him because he had thrown in the towel in the McNamara case. Darrow burned when he sensed that some of those whom he regarded as associates felt privately that he was guilty as charged. He told me he thought that even Rogers believed him guilty. He didn't approve of Rogers' dramatics in court. He didn't like Rogers anyway. And he certainly didn't think that he should put on an act of buoyancy to impress the jury. Instead, he thought he should look as he felt—bitter, and gravely concerned.

And, undoubtedly, he was right. I felt that his shambling, worried demeanor wove a skein of sympathy between him and the jury. And I'm certain that the jury had decided to acquit him even before all the evidence was in. I knew how they were going to vote a week before the trial ended.

My foreknowledge had a real, not a mystical source. Every day when the jury went out to lunch they walked down a narrow aisle between the press benches; and the reporters, including me, studied their faces to see what could be seen—if anything. The last few days, juror F. E. Golding caught my eye, several times running, smiled, and then shook his head negatively. I pondered what to do about it, and then decided to do nothing: I couldn't very well send out over the UP wires a story to the effect that one of the jurors had given me the headshake to signify acquittal.

In my own mind, though, Golding's shake gave an air of anti-climax to the final summings-up. Assistant district attorney Ford opened for the prosecution, and made a virulent attack on Darrow, accusing him of responsibility for the *Times* bombing itself, because he had taught that there was no such thing as a crime. Ford wore thick glasses which made his eyes look big and black, and gave him a disconcerting stare. Then Rogers and Appel spoke. And on August 14 Darrow closed his own defense. It was quite an occasion. My dispatch from the scene read:

More than 1,000 spectators who had fought and struggled with bailiffs
in a narrow corridor for two hours listened as the defendant slowly rose
and advanced to the jury box. A thousand others had fought and struggled
to get in, only to be disappointed. . . .

The bailiff shut the doors in the faces of the crowd. Women fainted, and
men gasped for breath. Reserves were called from the sheriff's office to
quell the crowd, and clubs had to be drawn before it could be handled.
Finally the mob surged into the room and filled all the standing space.

Before this audience, Darrow roused himself from his lethargy
and delivered one of his greatest summations. He used a homespun,
gallus-snapping delivery. For a day and a half he held the courtroom in his hand; even the court stenographers cried at parts of his
oration. After he had finished, district attorney Fredericks summed
up for the prosecution, and took another day and a half.

On Saturday morning, August 17, Judge Hutton delivered his instructions to the jury, which retired at slightly after 9:30. Most of
the people in the courtroom relaxed, convinced that there would be
a wait of hours, perhaps days, before the verdict arrived. I thought
otherwise, and stayed in my chair, with the wire clucking away at
my elbow.

My diary for August 17, 1912, carries the following notation:
"Darrow found Not Guilty at 9:50 A.M., first ballot. The jury was out
fifteen minutes."

After the verdict had been announced, Judge Hutton stepped from
the bench and cried, "Hallelujah! Hallelujahs will go up all over the
world because of this verdict!" He hurried to Darrow, to shake hands
and clap the recent defendant on the back. A party of jurors, labor
leaders, defense witnesses, newspapermen and spectators formed in
the well of the court. It was like the locker room of the winning team
after the last game in the World Series. Men embraced. Men and
women embraced. There were tears and cheers. People tried to lift
Rogers to their shoulders, but he backed against the wall and planted
himself on his feet, shaking hands with both hands, with all comers.
People came rushing in from the street to join the jubilee, and the
bailiffs made no effort to control the traffic; in fact, the bailiffs were
participating in the hoopla themselves. Darrow was swamped with
well-wishers. I kept struggling into the crowd, getting quotes, mak-

ing notes, and then shoving back to the wire to send another add on the story. During one of my forays I ran into juror Golding, who grabbed my hand and asked excitedly, "Did you get my signal, little cub?" I told him that I had indeed, and he went on to say that the verdict had been generally agreed on, a week before. Foreman Manley Williams said the jury had not debated the testimony at all, merely taken their vote and come back to report the results.

The district attorney and his staff had slipped away from the celebrations almost immediately, and when I had milked all I could from the story in the courtroom I went upstairs in the Hall of Records to talk with Fredericks. Though I had seen him every day during the trial, and he was the political glad-hander type who always waved a greeting to anyone he'd ever seen before, he knew me as a reporter for the *Record*, a pro-Darrow paper, and therefore beyond the pale. "Who are you?" he said sourly.

I obligingly identified myself as Baillie of the United Press, and then he remembered me. Fredericks was a dour individual who seemed to have no glint of humor. He looked a little like Senator Kefauver, and he went after his objectives in the same unwavering way. Darrow was still his objective. This acquittal had involved only the Lockwood indictment. Down in the courtroom, it was generally assumed that the evidence in the Bain case was much the same, and that Fredericks would drop it or Darrow would force him to drop it with the claim of double jeopardy. Actually, Fredericks said, the Bain evidence was considerably different. Bain had accepted a bribe, and told the district attorney's office about it, weeks before Darrow began the negotiations to plead the McNamaras guilty. Anyway, Fredericks was determined to press the case.

Forty-eight hours after the celebration in Judge Hutton's courtroom, on what was probably the darkest day of his life, Darrow faced Fredericks once again in the Hall of Records, and before another judge pleaded not guilty to a charge of bribing juror Bain. He had expected to be on his way to Chicago; instead, he had to apply himself to preparations for the second trial, which opened before Judge Conley, in a different courtroom, on January 20, 1913.

The second Darrow trial was a tedious anticlimax after the first one. Rogers was still Darrow's leading counsel, and he started off in his star-spangled manner, but the antagonism between the two men was now too great. Rogers soon lost interest, or fell ill. Sometimes he would sit in court for hours, slumped down in his chair, saying nothing. Finally he disappeared from the case altogether, leaving Darrow's defense in the hands of a far less colorful attorney from Salt Lake City.

Despite what Fredericks had said, the evidence in the Bain case was virtually the same as the Lockwood evidence. The principal added starter for the prosecution was Ortie McManigal, the McNamaras' partner who had turned state's evidence. McManigal's presence was interesting to me, because I had got to know him fairly well during his nearly two years in the county jail. He was a trusty in the jail, and easy to interview. I'd come in the barred gate, check my gun in the cage, step behind the grating and halloo for Ortie, who would presently appear with his broom. Ortie was a plump, cocksure wise-guy, one of the most likeable dynamiters I ever knew.

Later, it fell to my lot to run Ortie out of town. One day, shortly after he had testified against Darrow, I looked for him in the jail and didn't find him. Jailer Gallagher denied any knowledge of where Ortie might be, wouldn't talk about Ortie and walked away from me when I began asking questions. Then I got a tip that Ortie had been released and was working as a painter in a Hollywood studio, under the name of Brown. Naturally, I went right out and asked for Brown, and Ortie emerged from the scaffolding of the outdoor sets, cocky as ever—but with his mustache gone. He looked me in the eye with an impish, arrogant air.

"Hello, Ortie," said I.

"You're wrong, young feller," said he. "My name is Brown."

"Oh, come off it, Ortie—I know you!"

"I'm sorry, but you don't. I never saw you before in my life."

I said, "You're Ortie McManigal. You're the guy that turned in the McNamaras. I've been talking to you nearly every day in the county jail. What's the idea of the disguise?"

"Nope," said he, still fresh. "You're all off. My name is Brown, I'm a painter, and I've been working here for six months. Now, skiddoo."

I said, "Hell, Ortie, if you're hiding out, you won't be hiding out much longer, because this is a story, and it's up to me to go to the phone and call it in."

"Adios," said he, and strutted away. But when I came back the next day for a follow-up story, he was gone. And nobody at the studio had ever heard of him—so they said. In 1915, Ortie reappeared as a witness in another dynamiting trial, and then he disappeared for good. Years later, I learned that he had gone to Honduras, and returned to Los Angeles under the alias of W. E. Mack. As W. E. Mack he was hired by the county to be a watchman, complete with badge and gun, in the Hall of Records, where Darrow had been tried. And when W. E. Mack retired on April 12, 1944, he received a scroll of appreciation from the Board of Supervisors, honoring "duty so long performed with integrity and honor." So help me.

While Ortie was interesting to me, however, he didn't have much to contribute to the Darrow trial—he'd been securely in jail all the time the alleged bribery was going on. So far as tales of bribery were concerned, the Bain jury heard much the same story as the Lockwood jury. But without Rogers at center stage the story must have been more impressive. The Bain trial resulted not in an acquittal but in a hung jury, split eight to four for conviction.

Darrow left the courtroom as soon as the disagreement had been announced, and walked back to his office, a group of reporters behind him. He slumped through the streets, glancing neither right nor left but staring fixedly ahead. At his office he received a small group of us, and scolded me particularly for some of the headlines that had appeared in the papers. Well, you couldn't blame him for being edgy and quarrelsome. He'd been crucified twice, and he still wasn't free: the state had the option to try him again on the Bain charges.

Shortly after the Bain disagreement, however, the district attorney decided to drop the case. Darrow wasted little time in leaving Los Angeles. When he left, he seemed a beaten man. He was fifty-five, but looked much older, haggard and tired. The McNamara defense funds—some of them squandered in defending Bert Franklin—had run out early in his own trial, and he was virtually bankrupt. It seemed the end of a great career.

Rogers, on the other hand, was riding high. He was a dozen years

younger than Darrow, and the Darrow trials had been no discredit
at all to him. Between the two Darrow defenses he had conducted
one of his most flamboyant actions—the successful defense of Guy
Eddy, city prosecutor and author of the "Eddy Rooming House Law."
By the terms of this law, any man and woman who occupied a room
together in a public hostelry—and this went for anything from the
lowest fleabag to the swankiest hotel in town—were subject to arrest
if they couldn't produce a marriage license. And the charge against
Eddy, suitably, was that he had engaged in amorous dalliance in
his office at police headquarters with a young lady who was applying
to him for a job. Four sleuths, peeking through peepholes they had
bored in his door, broke in on him while he was with the young lady,
and claimed to have seized him red-handed. He was haled before
Judge Curtis D. Wilbur (later to be Secretary of the Navy) and held
for trial. Eddy claimed he had been framed by the underworld. We
wolves of the press were at Eddy's heels from the moment of his ar-
raignment, and thereafter throughout his trial. The story looked bad
for Eddy, but Rogers got him off, by demonstrating that the young
lady was over twenty-one (in the original charge she was supposed
to be a minor), and that the alleged location of the "crime" couldn't
be seen through the peepholes in the door, anyway. And oh, what a
circus he staged!

A few years later, Rogers was to top even the Eddy case in defending chief of police Charles E. Sebastian, candidate for mayor on
the Reform ticket, who was alleged to have wrought his will on a
middle-aged lady in the presence of her younger sister at a rooming
house next door to Central Police Station. The Sebastian trial on some
days put the World War off the front pages of the Los Angeles
papers. Rogers won it for Sebastian, and Sebastian thereupon won
the election for mayor—though he was later forced out of office when
the Los Angeles *Record* published some letters of his relating to the
incident for which he was tried. The letters revealed that he had at
least sighed for the lady in the case, deeming her preferable to his
wife—"the old haybag."

But Rogers was, in fact, nearing the end of the road. He had always
been a heavy drinker, and now he was forced to commit himself to
a sanitarium for a cure. (Later his family attempted to commit him

again, against his wishes, and he conducted one of his last great trials in his own defense. The high point of his cross-examination, according to people who were present—I was already gone from Los Angeles—came when he had his daughter, Adela Rogers St. Johns, on the witness stand. He leaned over her and said softly, "You don't think I'm crazy, do you, honey?"—and she replied, "No, Papa," and wept.) A decade after the Darrow trials, at the age of fifty-two, Rogers was dead, another alcoholic corpse in a cheap rooming house.

And Darrow's greatest days were still before him. His vitality returned, and he went on to his most spectacular triumphs, in the Leopold-Loeb, Massey-Fortescue and Scopes cases. Today he is part of the history in the history books, largely because of the cases he tried after his escape from Los Angeles.

Darrow was, in the flesh, a great man. He gave you that psychic impact, that showed when you came into his presence, the way great men, good or evil, always do. But great men make mistakes, too. Darrow, like some others, had come to feel that the rules which bound ordinary people were not binding on him. My impression was that he had few scruples about the procedure to be used in winning, so long as he personally believed that the cause was just. The Bain jury left undecided in the records the question of whether Darrow was or was not guilty of jury bribery, but I never had any doubts on the subject. In my opinion Darrow was guilty—on the evidence, which included his presence across the street, as a spectator, while Franklin was passing the money to Lockwood; on his attitudes and appearance during the trials; and on the basis of my private conversations with him. Only Earl Rogers in 1912 and four jurors in 1913 saved the Great Defender from ending his career prematurely, within what he called in his closing address to the jury "the gray, dim walls of San Quentin."

Jerry Giesler always believed him innocent, and the walls of his office in Beverly Hills today have pictures of Darrow and Rogers hanging on them.

Chapter 3

MIGRATIONS WEST, THEN EAST

WHEN I took over the UP wire at the Darrow trial, at the tender age of twenty-one, I was carrying on a family tradition: my father David G. Baillie had covered his first big story at the age of twenty-one. Born in Scotland, he had studied for the ministry at the University of Edinburgh and worked on the Dumfries *Standard*. He came to New York in 1887, shipping on the S.S. *Devonia*, which had a rough crossing and arrived no less than sixteen days late, after having been given up for lost. Crowds lined the waterfront as it steamed up the Hudson to the Anchor Line pier. My father debarked (there was no nonsense of passport control or red tape in those days), took a hansom to the Astor House, and flipped a British gold sovereign to the cabby. Then, armed with the exclusive story of the *Devonia* crossing, he went and sold his services as a reporter to the New York *Tribune*.

A working press tradition came down to me on the other side of the family, too. My mother's father, John B. Hays, was dean and president of the New York City Hall Reporters' Association. (Until recently, a crayon portrait of him hung in the City Hall pressroom, but some member of a much younger generation seems to have taken it down, probably with the idea that nobody still remembers who this distinguished old gentleman might be. The picture was drawn when he was younger than I am today, but those were the days of whiskers. If anyone knows where that drawing is now, I'd like to hear from him.) Grandfather Hays was "Major Hays" to everyone of any importance in New York—and it was an honest military title, won in the field with the Union Army.

While working for the *Tribune*, my father held a second job, as literary secretary to his fellow Scotsman Andrew Carnegie. The closest I ever came to *not* being a newspaperman, I suppose, was the day Carnegie offered to pay my father his salary in stock. But my father preferred coin of the realm. My father's main duty for Carnegie was to keep the busy steelmaster abreast of the news by making digests of newspaper dispatches and magazine articles. He also "ghosted" articles and speeches when required. During the course of his work, he came to know many of the nation's industrial leaders—men like Frick and Schwab. They never frightened him overmuch.

Some years later, my father took me to meet Carnegie. I remember him as a jolly little old Santy Claus with sparkling blue eyes, apple cheeks and a snow-white beard which grew bushy, not trimmed to a point the way you see it in his pictures. He told me about Skibo Castle, his recent travels, and his conversation with the king. It was my first wide-angle view of the world.

My first trip to Washington was on McKinley's inaugural train from Canton, Ohio, where my father had covered the new President's "front-porch campaign." We all lived in Canton during those summer and fall months. I remember the delegations marching up behind the bands to hear McKinley speak, and ripping the pickets from the candidate's fence for souvenirs, after the speech was over. McKinley was an avuncular gentleman whose visitors, as I remember it, called him "Major." He used to dandle me on his knee. His wife was a frail woman in a wheel chair. I asked her why all those pictures of McKinley were on the walls, and she replied, "Because he's a dear good man and I love him!"

There is a group picture of the newspapermen who covered McKinley's campaign, and I'm in it, among the reporters—aged five. On the train heading for Washington, my big young ears picked up a piece of one of that era's biggest stories. My father was talking with McKinley about the possibility of war with Spain, and McKinley said, "But, Mr. Baillie, we have no *casus belli*."

You could use Latin with my father in perfect confidence that he would know what you were talking about. In fact, you could have

spoken to him in Hebrew and Greek, too: training for the ministry
at the University of Edinburgh was good and thorough. One of my
father's triumphs as a newspaperman came from his knowledge of
Latin. Robert Louis Stevenson had come to town, and had refused
to receive reporters. My father went to the hotel, took one of his
calling cards and scribbled on it the message "Civis Edinburghensis
sum" (I am a citizen of Edinburgh). Then he sent the card up to
Stevenson—who returned word that Mr. Baillie should come right
in for his interview.

Both my father and my grandfather liked to take me along with
them on their assignments, whenever practical, and among the other
personages of the period whom I met while a small boy were Grover
Cleveland and Teddy Roosevelt; Chauncey Depew; "Boss" Platt, in
his Amen Corner at the Fifth Avenue Hotel, dictating New York
politics; Joe Jefferson, in costume as Rip Van Winkle; the Shakes-
pearean Robert Mantell, with big cigar sticking out of King Lear
whiskers, talking broad Scots backstage; Mark Twain; Admiral
Dewey; and General Nelson A. Miles, the old Indian fighter. Once, I
remember, I was taken to Menlo Park, to meet Thomas A. Edison in
his laboratory. The place was littered with all sorts of shabby-looking
gadgets, and in my childish impudence I referred to it as a "junk
shop."

"What's he say?" yelled Edison, cupping his hand behind his ear.

All this was highly educational, and the education stayed with me.
Having watched my grandfather and father in action, I had no fear
of the great when I became a reporter myself. I never held a qualm
about crashing in on anybody. I knew it could be done, because I'd
seen it done.

Then the whole family migrated to California—father, mother,
brother and I; grandmother, uncle, aunt and canary bird from Ayr.
This was past the days of the covered wagon, but well before the
days of the airplane. Our train took seven days to cover the distance.
In our tourist car, you boiled your own coffee on the big-bellied
stove by the door.

In the new world of Los Angeles my father resumed his career
as a political reporter, and I returned to my often-interrupted education. In 1907 I entered the University of Southern California as a

"special," which meant that whatever I did they weren't going to give me a degree—I hadn't met the academic requirements for matriculation. Nevertheless, though it took me forty-two years, I finally got a degree—an honorary LL.D. awarded at a special convocation in 1950. While attending classes at U.S.C., I also studied at the Los Angeles School of Art and Design, with the aim of becoming a newspaper cartoonist. And it was as a prospective cartoonist that I made the rounds of the Los Angeles papers in 1910, looking for a job.

Though I didn't know it then, this was a waste of time: Los Angeles had more than its share of good cartoonists, and I was nowhere talented enough to break into that league. The situation was pointed up by the editor of the *Examiner,* who grinned at me and said, "Sure, Gus Herriman just moved East. Maybe you can take his place." Since Herriman and his Krazy Kat were the champions of the business, the suggestion was obviously a sarcastic boot to a greenhorn with a bundle of amateurish drawings under his arm. When I showed my drawings to the editor of the *Record,* he said, "No job for a cartoonist. We've got a cartoonist. But if you can cover baseball, I'll put you on sports for a couple of weeks."

I stayed longer than a couple of weeks; in fact, I worked on the *Record* five years, almost to the day. It was the razzle-dazzle paper of Los Angeles, more likely than any other to carry a screaming headline across all eight columns of the front page. As often as possible, that headline was supposed to be a story you couldn't find in any other paper in town. We were sensational partly because we were a relatively small and struggling operation, and partly because that was the way George Young (not to be confused with the Hearst editor of the same name) liked to see a paper run. He had a staff of a dozen or so reporters to cover the news and find the stories for the headlines.

There was almost nothing connected with the editorial end of a newspaper that I didn't do for George Young. In addition to being a sports reporter and a police reporter, I was entertainment editor for a while, legman and rewrite man. I wrote a column of the news in blank verse, which I signed, "Jim Frothingham," and another column of "Broadway" news called "The Town in Review" and signed by "The Reformed Office Boy." I'd go out and cover stories in the morning, come back and sit in the slot in the afternoon, breathing that wonderful atmosphere of printer's ink and oil-soaked wood, then run out to Long Beach to chase the pictures at night. I was absolutely fascinated by my work, and Young was a man you could learn from. I remember once I asked him why a certain prominent citizen of Los Angeles came into his office so often to help supply inside information for a political crusade that was virtually Young's private affair. Young opened his safe and produced a Rogue's Gallery photograph of the gentleman, front-and-side, with prison number in the usual place below. "I guess," Young said, "it's because he doesn't want me to run this on page one."

Young's tactics did not add to the popularity of his staff at either end of the social scale. The respectable elements of Los Angeles were shocked by his concentration on the seamy side of life, and men who made their living on the seamy side hated the publicity. One night while I was working for Young, two strangers followed me off the streetcar and tried to work me over with a sap on the lonely road that led to my home in Eagle Rock. A single blast from my revolver, however, and they turned tail, while the sound of the shot re-echoed in the hills. The next day when I came in, Young was in the composing room making up the paper. I told him about the attempted attack, and added that I thought I could write a pretty good story about it. Young rubbed his hands gleefully and said, "Go ahead, Hugh, and we'll put it in the next edition. This edition, the one I'm rolling now, leads off with a story about me being arrested for criminal libel. These two gentlemen"—and he waved his hand in the direction of a couple of plain-clothes men standing by—"have come to take me into custody."

So that day one edition of the *Record* carried the banner "RECORD EDITOR ARRESTED," and the next edition bore the screaming headline "RECORD MAN BLACKJACKED." That was Young's idea of the tempo at which a newspaper should be run. (And he was easily acquitted on the libel charge.)

The biggest single job I did for Young was an exposé of the Los Angeles vice crowd, which I wrote under the pseudonym "John Danger." This series of stories was stimulated originally by an article in *Smart Set*, "Los Angeles the Chemically Pure," written by George Jean Nathan. Young, who knew just how far from chemically pure Los Angeles really was, decided to use the article as the kick-off for a big *Record* crusade. He sent me off to research and write a series on Los Angeles vice and crime, and began running "boxes" on the front page—"John Danger Is Coming to Town!" "In New York, Jerome [the District Attorney] Used Axes! John Danger Is Not So Crude!" The boxes were a big hit; after the first week, there was scarcely a DANGER sign in town that didn't have a little "John" written in front of it. One of the local burlesque houses called its new show "John Danger." Circulation zoomed.

The idea that John Danger was coming from out of town gave me some protection as I went gathering material. And I looked too young to be the flesh and blood behind such a well-publicized name. As final protection for me, Young had agreed not to run any of the John Danger pieces until I had finished all of them and was off the crime beat. But he couldn't hold his water. The day after he received my story about dope peddling in Los Angeles, he put it on the front page of the *Record*.

The center of the cocaine trade in Los Angeles, as I found it, was the rear room of a big downtown candy store near several schools and theaters. Because the store sold the biggest chocolates and sundaes in town, it had a clientele of sweet-toothed innocents at the front counter. I went into the store with a dope pusher, a punk conspicuous for his mouthful of gold teeth, and bought a packet of cocaine. Then the pusher and I dropped into the back room of a saloon, where another addict joined our party. He broke up the crystals in their paper wrapping, placed the powder neatly between his thumb and forefinger, and snuffed the cocaine up each nostril. From the saloon my pusher friend and I went to a rooming house on Franklin Street, where we found ourselves in a crowd of hopheads who were "cooking" the cocaine in teaspoons over open gas jets, then pouring it into hypodermic needles and taking their jolts in the arm. The room was so hot and the atmosphere so thick that the members of this club went about their party games dressed only in BVD's.

The problem with this story, from my point of view, was that Mr. Gold Teeth knew perfectly well who had gone with him from candy store to saloon to rooming house. John Danger had been identified to the people who wanted most to know who he was. One three A.M., as I was sitting in the Saddle Rock Restaurant on Spring Street, waiting for a steak, Mr. Cold Teeth took a seat on the stool beside me. He ordered a steak for himself and muttered out of the corner of his mouth, "I know you, you son of a bitch. And the boys are outside."

Spring Street at three in the morning was usually about as empty as Wall Street in New York on Christmas Day, but when I looked out the window I saw several gentlemen outside, eyeing me curiously. I dawdled over that steak for quite a while, listening to Gold Teeth tell me what they were going to do to me. Finally, with a sigh, I paid my chit, took the .32-20 Colt Army Special out of my pants, and moseyed into the street. With me moseyed my bodyguard, a proved fighter from the *Record* circulation department, who carried a flat automatic. The reception committee quietly disappeared. That was one of the advantages the 1910's had over the 1950's: today, in a similar situation, if the boys really wanted to get you, they'd just cut you down in a dark alley.

In 1915, when I had been on the *Record* five years, I was making thirty dollars a week—a good salary for a twenty-four-year-old reporter in those days, when the president of a small railroad might earn five thousand a year. It was more money than the *Record* paid any other man on the staff. I was beginning to feel that I had no future on the *Record* (as a matter of fact, the *Record* itself had no future; it's been dead for years). The Los Angeles offices of the United Press were just across a partition from the *Record* newsroom, so the UP and I knew something about each other, in addition to my work on the Darrow trial. I'd met Roy Howard, who ran the UP show, on one of his visits to Los Angeles. Howard would come tearing into the UP bureau, and would rip through the "exchanges"—the copies of the client newspapers that came into the office every day. Here he would hunt for UP credits, counting up how many of them there were and how prominently they appeared, meanwhile pronouncing loudly his dictum that "the news report is no good unless it gets printed." Then he would get on the wire and make the fur fly in other bureaus all over the world. Years later, when I was president of the United Press, I did much the same sort of thing myself.

The author and two Presidents: McKinley, whose campaign he watched
with the eyes of a five-year-old while his father (on McKinley's right)
covered for the New York Press; and Eisenhower, with whom he par-
leyed as president of the United Press.

Clarence Darrow: "Nobody who ever knew me could call me corrupt.
I did not bribe the jury in the McNamara case."

Woodrow Wilson: he held informal bull sessions in the club car with the reporters covering his campaign for the League. Below: A photograph taken of the author during that trip.

The author, in shirt sleeves, as New York manager of the UP in 1920.
Probably a posed photo, as three of the staff are wearing their coats in
the newsroom.

At the time, Howard impressed me as a dynamo, and as a flashy and courageous little Easterner, the first man I'd ever seen with the guts to wear spats and carry a cane east of Main Street into our ratty end of town.

Now Bill Hawkins, general manager of the UP, came up to me on a street corner near the office and asked me to go to work in the San Francisco bureau. I took the job, then went to talk things over with the manager of the Los Angeles bureau. He gave me one piece of advice: he said, "They're very strong on loyalty." He was right about that.

Three months later I was back in Los Angeles as manager of the bureau myself, and in 1916 I was in San Francisco again, writing the full news report for the coast wire. At that time the UP had no leased wire across the mountains. The news went out on the UP's own circuit as far as Denver, where it was condensed and sent on to San Francisco over Postal Telegraph facilities. In San Francisco I took these skeletonized dispatches and expanded them into a full news report, which went out on the UP leased wires up and down the Pacific Coast.

I was the last man to handle this job. Shortly before I left the San Francisco office the UP became prosperous enough to carry its own wire from Denver to the coast, so member papers on the Pacific could receive exactly the same service everybody else received. Actually, the papers themselves never knew the difference.

This was an important job for me—more important than it sounds in the telling. It put the news in perspective. Up to this stint in San Francisco, I'd been the reporter of violence—crime and vice and queer doings in the world of sports and entertainment had been my meat. In San Francisco I found myself editing and transmitting the important news of the world, and the crime stuff began to fade.

In the summer of 1916 I was told to move again, this time to Portland, to be manager of the bureau there. When the word came, I asked a favor from Barney Furay, my boss: pay my wife's fare to Portland, too.

"Your wife!" Furay said. "You're not married."

"As of tonight I am," I said.

I finished my day's work in the UP office, the future Mrs. Baillie finished her day's work on the Oakland *Tribune,* and in forty-eight hours we were in Portland as bureau manager and wife. . . .

The big story that year was, of course, the Wilson-Hughes election. Hughes came to Portland on his Campaign Special, escorted by an impressive contingent of correspondents, and I met the candidate himself through Perry Arnold, who was covering his campaign for the UP. We paraded through the streets in the Hughes motorcade to the hotel, where the candidate was receiving the usual delegations and applications for favors. Arnold knew how to get the news of what was going on behind the closed doors, and he proceeded to do so; I helped by being fast on my feet and good at wedging myself into a telephone booth ahead of the opposition. Arnold and the other correspondents impressed me at least as much as Hughes: they were the grandificos of journalism, the men in whose footsteps I would follow if I ever achieved my own ambitions. I watched them with awe.

Not that Hughes himself was anything but impressive. His beard alone would have given him an air of great superiority, and added to the beard were an equally distinguished mustache, a stately walk, and a benign and condescending manner. I had been shocked during the motorcade through the city when an irreverent bystander shouted, "Get his whiskers!" Watching from the pressbox that evening, as Hughes walked down the aisle to the platform in the biggest arena in Portland, I got an impression of Moses leading the Israelites through the Red Sea. The sea in this case was the crowd itself, which jammed the aisle, parted respectfully before the candidate and then closed up again behind him, shouting all the while. His speech was a solid and sober Republican utterance, without oratorical or physical gymnastics. All was calm and confidence. The experts did not believe that Wilson—elected originally in 1912 through a split in the Republican party—stood a chance against this majestic figure.

So great was the faith in a Hughes victory that the New York *World* and other Wilson supporters conceded on the strength of Eastern returns on election night. But the United Press, nonpartisan, of course, conceded nothing. I came to work election day at seven in the morning, and was still in the office, dressed in the same clothes, unwashed, unshaven and unrested, at eight in the evening on Thursday, when the final returns from California clinched Wilson's victory. By the time it was over I had become well aware of my beard. Lots of other Unipressers kept the same long vigil.

Our bureau was housed in the office of the Oregon *Journal*, another Democratic paper, which had followed the *World* in conceding a Hughes victory. The *Journal's* concession had been a news story in the East, during the hours of indecision, and when the results were definite a message from General Manager Bill Hawkins came over the Morse wire. He wanted to know whether anything in a United Press dispatch had persuaded the *Journal* to capitulate to Hughes—and, if not, why the *Journal* had given up. I assured him that the *Journal* was merely accepting the opinion of the *World*. The United Press never elected Hughes.

The Portland bureau in 1916 consisted of myself and a telegrapher, period. Bureau manager was a business job as much as a reporting job, and the manager was supposed to sell the service as well as provide it. Every night, after I'd finished the rest of the work, I would send out half a dozen letters to newspapers in the area, selling the United Press.

One month while I was in Portland the UP held a nation-wide contest among bureau managers, with a prize to the manager who sold the greatest number of new clients. I won it, with a score of eight or nine sales. In an article about me in the *Saturday Evening Post*, Jack Alexander said that it was this feat of salesmanship which first brought me to the attention of the top brass in the UP. Myself, I think that the top brass already knew about me—and that the effect of my victory in the great contest was to worry them about my swelled head. The only extra attention I received as the result of it was a letter from Hawkins, the man who had hired me. He called my attention to the map of the United States on the back of our letterhead, with the UP wire interconnections superimposed over the geography. And he reminded me that the Portland bureau was an insignificant flyspeck of an outpost in what was already a great nation-wide organization, and that I personally was a very small fleck of that flyspeck. (I responded by making three more sales, and sending him the contracts.)

Anyway, the next summons I received to move on—from Portland to Chicago on St. Patrick's Day, 1917—was not delivered out of respect for my executive abilities. Impending war cast a shadow of personnel problems for the management of a press association, and in Chicago the UP needed a fast pony reader—a man who could dictate a news report over the telephone to client papers which couldn't afford the regular wire service. After seven years of reportorial experience, working with eyes, ears, nose, and brain, I found myself prized by the organization mostly for my clear, quick tongue. When I wasn't talking over the telephone to editors, I was working on the desk as a rewrite man.

Still, an order East, in those days, was for some inscrutable reason always considered a promotion. And I didn't know what they wanted me for when I left. My wife and I just got on the train to Chicago. Upon arrival we separated, I to the office, she to look for a furnished room. I asked her to call me and tell me where I lived.

To get to work on time in the Chicago bureau, you had to catch the six A.M. elevator—or walk the seventeen flights up to our office in the old Chicago *Tribune* building. At that early hour of the morning, the elevator operated on a once-every-half-hour schedule, and you were due in before six-thirty. It was a rare day when you got out before six in the evening. When all the other work was done, you had to type the boss's letters. Bureau manager E. T. Conkle was a news agency driver of the old school, and had never learned to use a typewriter. At intervals during the day, he scribbled his correspondence on scratch paper; and when the wire closed, he handed his letters out to members of the staff, to be transcribed on letterheads.

Saturday, everything was different. On weekdays, the UP served only afternoon newspapers, so that you were done when the final afternoon editions went to press. Many afternoon dailies published Sunday-morning papers, however, and we served them, too. Usually, you left your house as dawn was breaking to get to work on Saturday, and staggered home again as dawn was breaking the next morning.

I was summoned away to New York, after only three weeks in Chicago, by another wire from Hawkins. The wire arrived on Friday, and told me to be in New York on Monday, concluding with the comment: "These are war orders, and are to be obeyed as such." We packed and got out. New York was the Mecca, home office. When "NX" appeared on the wire, all other offices hopped to it. Headquarters was where I wanted to be.

Again, the UP had not called me East for my executive abilities: I started on the New York staff as a reporter and rewrite man. I also found myself in line for some hazing, traditional practice for taking the conceit out of recruits from the Pacific Coast offices. Two examples of this hazing were interesting in their own right.

One of them was the routine assignment for new men: covering an electrocution at Sing Sing. I drew a prominent killer for my journey "up the river"—Dr. Arthur Warren Waite, a dentist who had undertaken to kill off all his wife's family to get his hands on their money, and was making good progress toward that end, with several already dead, before the police caught up with him. The credentials required to watch his electrocution consisted of a printed invitation, as if to a dance.

The holders of these invitations—among them an actor, Robert Hilliard, who was working on a play with this sort of scene in it, and wanted realism—went up to Ossining by train for the eleven P.M. electrocution. A few minutes before eleven, the warden called us into his office. There was a big clock on the wall, with a very loud tick. The warden announced that we would wait in the office until eleven, to allow the prisoner every opportunity for a reprieve or delay. At eleven on the dot, the warden took a big hunting-case watch out of his vest pocket and compared it with the clock. Then he closed it with a click, and stood up. He said, "Gentlemen, it is eleven o'clock. We shall now proceed to the death chamber."

So we followed him outdoors, under the stars, and into a small building which stood by itself. There, with an immediacy which was startling, stood the electric chair: tall, gaunt, with its helmet and mask dangling over it on wires; and a team of guards standing beside it. The room was brightly illuminated, the lights reflecting from the whitewashed walls and ceiling. There were three or four rows of "pews" as in a church, and in these we sat. The door clunked shut behind us, with that finality you hear when an airplane door is pulled to and bolted.

The warden then nodded to one of the uniformed guards, who led a small detachment out into the death cells which adjoined the execution chamber. Today, the man scheduled for electrocution is kept in a special cell which opens directly into the death room, but in those days the condemned prisoner walked a "last mile" past the gratings of his friends, with whom he had lived for months. They could see him and he could see them. So they called out their farewells, in voices audible where we sat:

"Good-by, Doc!"

"So long, Doctor Waite . . ."

"See you later, maybe."

To which he replied in a strong and resonant voice:

"Good-by, boys.

"*Au revoir* to you all.

"I hope you all get out.

"So long!"

Then Waite stepped into the room and took a quick look around. He glanced briefly at the electric chair, and ran his eyes over the men in the pews in a slightly amused way—as though he was counting the house. He was tall, dark-haired, completely alert, in full possession of his faculties. He was dressed in a plain gray suit, with one trouser leg flapping where it had been cut to the knee for the electrode. Behind him stood a priest, with the unfortunately appropriate name of Father Cashin, reciting the Twenty-third Psalm.

Waite paused in front of the electric chair and looked inquiringly at the guards, who sprang into action like a well-trained football team running through a complicated play. Almost immediately Waite was in the chair, a big strap over his chest, his arms and legs fastened down, a helmet and mask buckled over his face. Only the lower part of his nose and his mouth were showing. He grinned broadly, showing remarkably fine teeth. And in that instant the warden gave the signal, and the current hit him.

As the warden signaled, Father Cashin stopped reciting the psalm, which struck me as odd—if ever Arthur Waite needed intercession, it was then. Waite was galvanized with electricity, straining forward against the straps.

Another signal was given, and the current cut off.

Waite's body slumped back in the chair. The broad chest strap was quickly unbuckled. A doctor ripped the buttons from Waite's shirt with one finger, and applied a stethoscope. The big strap was replaced, and with a whine of power another jolt hit the slumping body. Up it came against the creaking leather bonds, as if to leap from the chair. This time the dose was longer.

Again, Waite's body crumpled in the chair, hands dangling; and again the doctor examined and signaled for another shock.

As they shot the juice through the man once again, I saw the fists clench. There was a sputtering sound like fat on a frying pan, and a thin pencil of smoke, as from a cigarette, arose from one knee. The smile was still fixed on the corpse, but spittle was now drooling from the corner of the mouth.

After this shot, the doctor formally pronounced that Arthur Waite was dead. The guards removed the straps and carried out the rag doll of a body that had walked cheerfully in only a few minutes before.

Then we heard the noise of the big door being reopened, and we went out to send our stories. It was, all in all, a great piece of theater —but, like some other things in the theater, it was a little too mechanical, a little too cut-and-dried, to be real.

Another part of the hazing was experience in facing infuriated editors. I knew something about this already, of course—but I'd never run into angry big-leaguers like Jack Tennant, managing editor of the New York *Evening World*. As the newcomer from the West Coast, I got perhaps more than my share of these assignments to stand still and take Tennant's tongue lashings—such as, "Where are you stealing your news now?" I came to know his office pretty well. I remember his desk, surrounded by racks of lead piping on which newspapers were hung, and the plaques and ornaments that hung on his walls.

After the *World* was merged with the *Telegram*, many years later, I went in to pay a final visit. I wandered around the deserted rooms, from which all signs of life had departed, and wound up in Tennant's office. The racks were still there, but no newspapers hung on them. There was no Tennant behind the desk. The walls were bare, and the floor was littered with wastepaper. Out in the city room, one of the plaques that had hung on the wall was down with the garbage on the floor: evidently nobody had wanted it. I picked it up and read what it had to say:

> In Memory of
> Gregory T. Humes
> Reporter on The World.
>
> Mortally injured in the Stamford Railroad Wreck
> He thought first of his paper and with indomitable
> Courage sent the news of the disaster.
>
> Born April 12, 1878
> Died June 13, 1913.

For two years I was a reporter and a rewrite man, in New York, then in Washington, then New York again. As always, I was a competitor, and I made my presence known. And in 1919, at the age of twenty-eight, I was promoted to one of the most important posts in the organization—manager of the bureau in Washington, then as now the biggest single source of wire-service news. I was the youngest man in the bureau, which was staffed—again, then as now—by great reporters. When I came down to take charge, they lined up like troops awaiting inspection by a new general, and not liking it very much. I was proud to join this corps d'elite.

One of my first acts as manager was to appoint an assistant manager who could handle the inside job while I went out and covered stories. So, when Woodrow Wilson decided to take his case for the League of Nations directly to the people of the country, over the head of the Senate, I was in position to assign myself to what was—both in significance and in human interest—one of the great stories of this century.

Chapter 4

WILSON

THAT SUMMER of 1917, when I first saw Woodrow Wilson, the White House was cordoned with troops. When the guard changed, the soldiers debouched from a sally port in the State, War and Navy Building, the rococo pile across the narrow street from the executive mansion. There was no music. No colors. Just a column of rather grim-looking youngsters in khaki uniforms and flat-brimmed campaign hats, with bayonetted rifles over their shoulders. You could enter the White House only by special pass, which was inspected first by these suspicious sentries and then by a Secret Service detachment inside the building. Nobody was allowed to tarry, even momentarily, on the sidewalks around the White House—not even to crane a touristy neck at the portico with its big hanging lamp. For behind the portico, somewhere or other, sat the Commander-in-Chief of a nation at war, the prophet of hope for the Allied world, the demigod Woodrow Wilson.

Wilson did seem to be a kind of god in those days. What Herbert Hoover calls his "ordeal" was still ahead of him, and nobody could have seen it coming. In the history books it says of Wilson that he was an earnest, high-minded, dedicated man who thought he could change the world simply by the strength of his leadership and the force and *rightness* of his ideas. And who was, of course, wrong—impractical to the point of foolishness. What the history books forget is how practical Wilson's dream seemed in 1918 and 1919—just because Wilson, the immortal, amazing Wilson, stood behind it. No

43

man in my lifetime has been so adulated by the public—both in his own country and abroad. When you experienced that adulation, as we of the press did when we covered Wilson's speeches and parades, it was impossible to believe that anything this man recommended would ever be refused.

Members of a younger generation have seen this kind of public hysteria over an individual only once—when MacArthur received his hero's reception after his recall from Korea in 1951. And even the MacArthur parades lacked the final note of hopeful frenzy which sounded loud and clear over the Wilson demonstrations. Perhaps it is significant that both MacArthur and Wilson lost what they were fighting for—MacArthur the chance to attack the Chinese Communists in their homeland, Wilson the League of Nations—despite the public acclaim.

When you rode in a parade with Wilson, you traveled in the middle of a cone of noise. Wilson was not a mere man to the people of America: he was a presence. When they saw him, they became a roaring, screaming, howling mob. Sometimes in Washington during the hot summer of 1919 he would sneak out for a drive along Rock Creek Park, hoping nobody would spot him. But, on a street corner, a startled soldier might recognize the President in his unmarked car and call, "Hup! *Wilson*"—and the cheers would start.

I remember when Wilson came to New York on May 18, 1918, to march in a Red Cross parade and make a speech. When Wilson said "march" in a parade, he meant it literally. He climbed out of his official car up in the Sixties alongside Central Park, and walked down the three miles to Washington Square on his own two feet. He wore his high hat and morning coat and striped pants, and carried a small Red Cross flag. Fifth Avenue was absolutely massed with people, though it had just rained and seemed about to rain again. The sidewalks were packed and the police were hardly able to keep the spectators from flowing out and engulfing Wilson. Windows were crowded. There were enthusiasts on roofs. And there was a frenzy of cheering.

I never heard such a volume of human voices, before or since. The sound grew as the word sped down the avenue that Wilson was coming, on foot. It was at its loudest and most intense just as Wilson passed. Right behind the President marched an imposing rank of glittering Allied brass, and behind the generals and admirals—perhaps half a dozen strides off Wilson's pace—came us reporters, a straggling line of unmilitary men wearing rubbers and carrying umbrellas. So we, too, passed through this deafening climax of noise, block after block, mile after mile, all the way down the avenue. It was like being under Niagara Falls. It was solid and stunning. And there was nothing artificial about it. No cheerleaders. The populace was beside itself. If there were any words uttered, I didn't hear them: the sound was just one prolonged roar, massive and full, like a steady bass chord on a great organ, shaking a church. There was no music to march by—no brass band could have made itself heard in that bedlam.

Wilson walked rapidly and gaily down this canyon of people and sound, flourishing his high hat, waving his flag, looking far up at those frantically brandishing handkerchiefs out of high windows. At his heels were the Secret Service agents, watching the huge crowd as best they could, and knocking down the bouquets which were tossed at the President, with all the agility of baseball fielders. At one point in the march, just below St. Patrick's Cathedral, they fielded a man— a man who had run out of the crowd, laid hands on Wilson's shoulder and slewed him halfway around. As quickly as you could see what was happening, the Secret Service men seized him and threw him bodily back into the crowd—which straightaway set about killing him. An ugly thing, to see a mob on Fifth Avenue trying to beat a man to death.

Men and women fought to get a hand on the interloper. His derby fell off, exposing a bald pate, and immediately it was asplash with blood as a woman began hammering him on the sconce with the heavy handle of an umbrella which she wielded like a baseball bat. Then the man made another trip through the air. This time he was grabbed by the cops, which saved his life. They tossed him into the nearest car—open, as most cars were in 1918—which just happened to be the United Press vehicle, following with the others along the curb, slowed to a walk to match the President's gait.

I dropped back from my position in the parade and climbed into the car. I was immediately aware of the perfume of bourbon which permeated the person of the man who had grabbed the President. The cops were busily going through his pockets, but all they could find was a book of Liberty Loan coupons.

"What's your name?" I screamed at him above the din. He couldn't hear, what with the ovation and the recent pummeling he had endured. So I yelled it again and again in his ear. Finally he gave me a bleary look, and replied, his lips to my ear, "My name is Daniel Boone. And I only wanted to shake him by the hand. . . ."

Most remarkable of all, Wilson never let the Wilson-worship turn his head. Undoubtedly, the incredible echoing, roaring cheers of the crowd strengthened his belief that he could remake the world over the opposition of the European governments and the United States Senate. But he was always a stubborn man (he once told me that he had never even *thought* of compromising with his Congressional critics on the League of Nations issue), and he probably would have been equally stubborn without the overwhelming applause. Behind the rather frosty exterior, he remained throughout the period of his world leadership a very human sort.

I had seen the frosty exterior first, when I was a reporter in the Washington bureau and attended one of his small but very formal press conferences. What you saw there was his severe manner, his long Covenanter countenance, his cold and challenging eye. And he could be brutal to anyone he didn't respect. An Irish-American politician, Jeremiah O'Leary, wired Wilson in 1916 to announce that he could not support the President in his race for a second term, because of Wilson's stand on the Irish question. Wilson's reply was crushing:

"I would feel deeply mortified to have you or anybody like you vote for me. Since you have access to many disloyal Americans and I have not, I will ask you to convey this message to them."

But Wilson also had a private manner, open to all those around him who he thought were intelligent, mentally honest and fairly well informed (whether they agreed with him or not). You never felt with Wilson that he was looking down his nose at you—as you often felt with F. D. Roosevelt. Wilson was a great believer in mental aristocracy. He didn't really think all men were created equal, any more than the signers of the Declaration of Independence did (if they thought their Negro slaves were "men"). He could be sarcastic, and he'd fox you at the drop of a hat. But he never tried to win an argument by ridicule. It would not have occurred to him to ask a reporter to put on a dunce cap and go sit in the corner, or to pin an Iron Cross on the jacket of a columnist whose writings he found distasteful. He wouldn't waste his time on anyone he had catalogued as a boob—whether the man was rich or poor, high or low. But if he had accepted you into his circle, he could be friendly and patient, listening to your opinions and replying earnestly with his own.

He loved the theater, especially vaudeville, and I used to see him often in an upper box, enjoying the show. The curtain rose as soon as he was seated, and if possible the performance was pushed through without intermissions. He laughed heartily at the jokes. Though he attended serious plays as well as comedies, he preferred something with fun and music in it. He could do a pretty good buck-and-wing himself.

Never a stuffed shirt, he had little patience with the oratorical bores who came to him as heads of delegations—but he was unfailingly courteous. His answers were sometimes so artful that the meaning of what he had said didn't dawn on the people in the delegation until they were outside. Like many men who enjoy acrobatics in language, he had a taste for limericks. One that he once threw out at us ran:

> For beauty I am not a star,
> There are others more handsome by far.
> My face, I don't mind it,
> For I am behind it,
> It's the people in front that I jar.

He never said whether or not his limericks were original, but I'm sure he wrote a number of them himself.

Wilson's clothes were, of course, very proper at all times. He rarely appeared in public without the morning-coat-and-striped-pants outfit that would be a mark of extreme formality today. But he never regarded formal dress as a straight-jacket. A tall, lean man, he looked comfortable and casual—even natty—in diplomatic costume. I have a picture of him on the back platform of a train at eight in the morning, dressed in the full regalia, complete with top hat. But his hands are in his pockets, and his air is free and easy as you please,

So, armed with humor, directness, conviction and popular support, Wilson went to Versailles to write the just and enduring peace that would establish his cherished (and, to my mind, mistaken) principle of "self-determination," which has created vast swarms of small nations and vastly increased our national headaches. Three months later he was back in America for a visit, already disappointed by the deviousness of Old World diplomacy and the growing opposition of the new, Republican-controlled Congress. He landed in Boston, and I went up there to cover his speech at Mechanics Hall. He attacked on both fronts at once, warning Congress that America would "break the heart of the world" if it rejected the Treaty and the League—and warning the European heads of state that he would go directly to their people for support if they attempted to sabotage his program for a just peace. The people, he said, "are in the saddle, and they are going to see to it that if their present governments do not do their will, some other governments shall."

At this meeting, by the way, Wilson was introduced by the Governor of Massachusetts, a nasal Yankee who had recently become a national figure by breaking the Boston police strike: Calvin Coolidge.

Eight days later, the President was on his way back to Europe. Shortly before he left, he said to a group of us reporters, "The first thing I am going to tell the people on the other side of the water is that an overwhelming majority of the American people is in favor of the League of Nations." When he returned home again, in the early summer of 1919, he faced the task of proving to the politicians that this statement was true.

It was a hot summer in Washington, but Wilson worked through it, arguing, pleading, debating with the "irreconcilables" of the Senate, singly and en masse. On August 19, the entire Senate Foreign Relations Committee came to the White House for a full-scale conference. I watched them go in—Wilson's implacable foe Chairman Henry Cabot Lodge, whiskers abristle; Borah, who was leading the fight against the Treaty on the Senate floor; Harding, destined to succeed Wilson as President; Fall, later to go to jail over Teapot Dome; Hiram Johnson, who would miss the Presidency by passing up the nomination to run for Vice-President on Harding's ticket; and ten others, all imposing. The committee wrestled with the President for three hours and thirty-five minutes, and what was said at the meeting has never been fully revealed. When it was finished, however, Wilson had made his decision: he would go to the people, over the heads of their Senators, and sell the Treaty on a face-to-face basis.

September 3, 1919, we took off on this campaign. During the next twenty-two days, Wilson was to cover eight thousand miles through seventeen states. He was to make forty formal speeches, all extemporaneous, without an advance copy or even a note—I never saw him use a lectern—and without benefit of television, radio or even loudspeakers (except one, in San Diego). If he'd had radio and television to carry his message and his personality to millions rather than to thousands, the history of the world might have been different. With television, I am convinced, Wilson would have carried the country for the League.

The Presidential train was long, composed of Wilson's dark blue private car, The Mayflower, plus a string of Pennsylvania Railroad compartment cars for the President's personal staff, the Secret Service and the press. The red Pennsy cars looked odd when we got out West. The press corps, which was to keep the world advised of what Wilson was saying and how he was doing, included such magnificos as David Lawrence, James A. Hagerty (whose son is now press secretary to Eisenhower), Joseph Jefferson O'Neill (writing for Henry Ford's news bureau), Edwin C. Hill (later a prominent radio broadcaster), Louis Siebold, and Ben Allen, who was to be killed in an automobile crash in Portland, when his car turned over in Wilson's speeding motorcade. For the press associations, there were J. Jerome Williams of Universal, Jack Neville of INS, Byron Price (later Assistant Secretary General of the United Nations) for the AP . . . and me. I think most of us were on Wilson's side, hoping he would win his gamble—and believing he would pull it off.

Of course, our sympathies found no place in our dispatches. Bill Hawkins had given me special warning in his last instructions before I left on the train. "You always have to be careful," he said, "when you're out on a long trip with one of these crowd-swayers. The first thing you know, if you don't watch it, you will get to feel that you're part of the official party. Remember, you're not. You represent the public. You take no sides." Hawkins also suggested that this trip would be a good occasion for me to leave off wearing woolen vests and caps, and generally to abandon my "Wild-Western ways." But I never got around to it until some years later.

All arrangements had been made in advance by the Secret Service, and they were the same everywhere. The pattern of the trip became apparent very early. We thumped along overnight to Columbus, Ohio, where the President was to deliver his first afternoon speech. Upon arrival, we all jumped from the train and looked for the automobile with our number on it (mine was Number Six; I shared it with three other reporters). Then we went rolling through the streets, in what we soon began to call The Big Parade. It preceded every speech, the way the circus parade used to precede the old-time circus. All we needed was the calliope. Twice a day, six days a week, we rode through rows of shouting, cheering people, to whom all this was fresh and new. To us, it was soon all the same, day after day. Sometimes we even forgot what town it was that the President was "playing" this particular afternoon or evening. Then we would arrive at the auditorium or tent or whatever, and Wilson would usually devote a few moments to pleasing the delegation of local big-shots who were lying in wait for him. Thereupon, onto the platform, with an ovation going on and on, the chairman of the meeting trying vainly to get order—or trying to keep the ovation going, while pretending to call for order. Wilson would speak for about an hour, more or less—he wasn't limited by "radio time." I would keep up with him on the UP wire, mixing a few direct quotes with many indirect quotes. As he neared his peroration, I would work on two separate sheets of paper, one for the lead paragraphs, singling out the most important elements in the speech, the other for the running story.

Because he didn't have to direct his remarks into a mike, Wilson could move around the platform, which he did, though he was never the prowler that La Follette, Hiram Johnson and Bryan were. When he finished, whooping applause—and the crowd rushing for the platform! Sometimes Secret Service men had to lift us reporters bodily out of the orchestra pit and onto the platform, to save us from the engulfing crowd and restore us to the President's party. A quick walk to the cars—often a run, for the reporters—and then back to the train, another trip through walls of shouting. This time we moved at a good clip: it wasn't a parade, it was a getaway. Wilson, however, could not always get away. Even at 11 P.M., local leaders might come aboard his car and keep him from resting.

Between stops for formal speeches, Wilson liked to make informal appearances and brief talks from the rear platform of the observation car. The first of these stops was at Richmond, Indiana, not far from Columbus. The crowd pressed around, stepping over the tracks, pushing to get closer, holding babies up to see, waving hands to be grasped. I mingled with them to hear their comments. Most of the people spoke to one another in hushed tones, as if they had just seen something holy. Many lined up to shake hands. I joined the queue, and saw how it was from their viewpoint. Approaching the President, I became aware of his benevolent and kindly air, like a preacher greeting his parishioners—and then, the gimlet eye of Colonel Starling, whose hypnotic gaze drilled into everybody in line, one at a time. Two other Secret Service men stood on the ground beside the observation platform, and each man on the line had to pass between them. One grabbed my right arm at elbow and wrist, put it up to the railing of the platform so I could shake, then jerked it back and sent me on my way. No chance of a Czolgosz getting near the President here, as he did McKinley, with a revolver wrapped in a handkerchief.

The same Secret Service group that had guarded Wilson in Europe watched over him on this trip. Murphy was the head man. Ferguson was known as "the Doctor" because he carried the first-aid kit. Starling had the X-ray eyes that examined the inner thoughts of everyone who came near the President. Slye was built much like Wilson, and walked almost in lock-step with him whenever he was afoot, making sure that nobody could get a shot at the President from behind. These men were athletes. They would dog-trot for miles, alongside the automobiles, hopping onto the running boards only when the car came to a stretch of open road and picked up speed.

Wilson's workout lasted all day long. He often made his first appearance on the back of the train as early as eight in the morning, and almost every day there were the two parades. We could sit down in our cars; Wilson couldn't. He had to stand in the open all the way, waving to the crowd, bowing and smiling on all sides—while his wife sat beside him, her hand in the small of his back to brace him as he stood. Sometimes he had a local leader in the car, waiting for him to sit down for a good gabble about home politics. Always there was a delegation lying in wait for him at his destination, ready to give him chapter and verse on their problems. Often, these gentry boarded the train as it pulled out, and Wilson would turn from waving farewell to the boiling crowd only to face their interminable yak as he rode to his next engagement.

What Wilson was saying was much the same throughout the trip: "The Treaty was not only intended to end this war; it was intended to prevent any similar wars. The League of Nations is the only thing that can prevent the recurrence of this dreadful catastrophe." But in each place he said it differently, highlighting a different argument. He was not a great orator in the old style. He talked like a college lecturer—which he had been for many years. His voice was not consciously "cultured," nor was it sharp and rasping. He had learned to project an ordinary speaking voice to the back of a big classroom, so it came easily to his to project further, to the back of a big auditorium. Only in San Diego did he have the use of a microphone, and then he didn't like it. This speech was scheduled for Balboa Stadium, a football amphitheater, which not even Wilson could have filled with his unaided voice. The President was instructed to stand on an exact spot designated by crossed chalk marks on the stage, inside a sort of glass screen, and he was told to speak directly into the microphone. His impatience with these arrangements increased as the technicians fussed over him, adjusting the microphone to his height. He stood immobile throughout a prolonged ovation. Then silence fell over the multitude, and all attention was riveted on the speaker, on the great words that would issue from the loudspeakers. In this silence the loud clack of a Morse telegraph key arose from the press seats. That was the only sound. Wilson glared. Then he pointed a long arm and finger at the offending rat-a-tat-tat, and the first words a President ever uttered over a loudspeaker came harshly and well spaced:

"Stop—that—electrical—instrument!"

It stopped.

In addition to the work of the formal speeches, the informal talks and the political conferences, Wilson had to put up with the discomfort of living on a train. Sunday was the only day we did not travel, because Wilson observed the Sabbath. (We of the press, freed from our compartments and the rush of reporting Wilson's speeches, had a Sabbatarian observance of our own. Our first Sunday, in Des Moines, after treating ourselves to our first bath since leaving Washington, we held a party in the hotel, with refreshments, food, singing and hi-jinks. I came out of the banquet room during the festivities and found Wilson spooking around among the desks and typewriters in the anteroom, shuffling his feet through the papers on the floor. I explained to the President what was going on, and invited him to join us. "Well," he said, "I would, if if weren't Sunday. But you fellows go ahead and have a good time." So he continued his pacing, seemingly so preoccupied that he couldn't even hear the laughter and the music.) On the other six days of the week, Wilson was either riding on the hard rails or working on the crowd, all day long. It got to be quite a roast for him.

But he was never less than affable with the press—especially during that first week, when vociferous receptions at Columbus, Indianapolis, St. Louis and Kansas City had given the trip the aspect of a triumphal progress. After his first rear-platform talk, at Richmond, Indiana, he went through the train, greeting personally all the thirty or so reporters who were traveling with him. I remember he came to my door with Murphy of the Secret Service, who introduced me. Wilson smiled affably and said, "What are you writing, Baillie?"

"Mr. President," I replied, "I am writing the story of your speech back there at Richmond, Indiana."

"Aha!" said he, grinning widely. "I'm glad to see you writing it *after*, not *before!*" And, chuckling, he went down the aisle, kidding the other reporters.

During those first weeks, Wilson held several "press conferences" in the club car. These sessions were completely off the record, and the

President treated them as a form of relaxation. They were surely the most informal of their kind ever held—more like bull sesions than press conferences. Wilson would sit somewhere around the middle of the car, with the reporters about him, and we would all gab and argue together—as though the President were one of the reporters himself. We'd ask him the questions that were most agitating the opposition—why was it that "England" was to have five votes in the League of Nations (via her Commonwealth), while the United States had only one; or why we had to commit ourselves to supply troops to an international police force, under Article X of the League. Wilson would answer without palavering or hemming and hawing. He'd reach over and tap you on the knee and say, "Now, look here," and argue nose-to-nose with any member of the press corps. He would never retreat from or agree to modify any section of the Treaty, as he had finally signed it in Paris; and he beat his head against this wall until he died.

During the second week, the physical strain of the trip began to show on the President, and he became more and more worried about developments in Washington. William C. Bullitt testified before the Senate Foreign Relations Committee, and said that Secretary of State Lansing shared some of his doubts about certain aspects of the Treaty. Wilson refused to give us a press conference on Bullitt's testimony, and wired Lansing for an explanation. The Secretary admitted the truth of Bullitt's testimony, and Wilson became furious. Joe Tumulty, Wilson's press secretary, told me that the President felt like demanding Lansing's resignation at once—and would have done so, had he been in Washington. Tension on the train grew noticeably; Wilson, suspicious and much on his guard, looked grave indeed.

Sometimes there was an element of personal nastiness in the news from Washington. One day I got a wire from home office, asking Wilson to reply to an enemy's charge that there was whiskey aboard, and women; and that the Presidential train was in fact a sort of traveling Bacchanalia (this was during the early days of Prohibition, remember). Well, of course there was whiskey aboard—though I don't know that there was any in the President's private car. As for women, I never saw any except Mrs. Wilson. There weren't even any female reporters. I showed the inquiry to Tumulty, who manifested some fine Irish indignation at such peanut politics. After Tumulty got through cursing the man who had made the accusations, I explained to him that his remarks couldn't be transmitted on the wire, and that my office was interested in Wilson's reply, not his. Joe tried to get a statement from the President, but Wilson wouldn't dignify the charge with a denial.

One day Tumulty dropped in at my compartment for a chat, and suddenly said, "Baillie, do you know that that man back there has had a terrible headache for a week?" This was important news—but it would hardly have done for me to dispatch a bulletin that Tumulty said Wilson had a headache. At the first opportunity, I asked the President. His reply was that the headache had passed. But it hadn't.

By the time we reached Seattle—the halfway point of the trip, where we were all going to get a couple of nights off the train—those of us who had traveled with the President from Washington could see evidence of wear and tear under his dashing and cheerful front. Seattle provided a break in the routine, including two novel incidents —one in which the President deliberately and very neatly trapped the press, the other in which the press nearly drowned the President.

A group of local leaders in Seattle were still debating their position regarding the League, and wanted to get Wilson on record with a few explanations. A closed-doors session was scheduled at the President's suite in the Hotel Washington, and we reporters camped outside, ready to collar the delegates as they emerged and squeeze some information out of them. Suddenly, to our surprise, a Secret Service man threw open the double doors and invited us in. There sat the President, facing a portentous-looking group which viewed us with some hostility.

"These are the gentlemen of the press," Wilson explained courteously to the local leaders. "I have asked them to be seated at the side of the room, and observe and take notes on everything that is said here."

A great deal was said. Wilson was asked important questions, and replied frankly. We wrote rapidly, and I was tensing up for the dash to the typewriter at the end when the President remarked casually, "Of course, everything that has been said here is in confidence. And"

—he threw a stern look at us newspapermen—"I will expect my friends of the press, who have been my guests here, to observe that confidence."

So not a word could be written. If Wilson had not invited us in, some description of this meeting, gathered from the lips of the guests, would have appeared in the papers. Now there could be nothing at all. By letting us in, the President had locked us out of the story.

At Seattle, also, the President was scheduled to review the Pacific Fleet, gathered in Puget Sound for the purpose. The Navy had arranged to have Wilson and Secretary of the Navy Josephus Daniels, and their wives, proceed to the reviewing ship—the old battleship *Oregon*—in an admiral's barge. The reporters would be herded into a whaleboat which was to be towed out by a launch.

This didn't suit me at all. My assignment was to stick to the person of the President. Neither did it suit one of the other reporters who had the same instructions—Pierce Miller, of the Associated Press. We decided that, arrangements or no arrangements, we would go out with the President and Secretary Daniels. David Lawrence put his head into our huddle, and said he would go with us.

The President's barge was to leave from one dock, and the reporter's whaleboat from another; so our first step was to get past the local police who were guarding the President's dock. When Messrs. Wilson and Daniels and their wives went down the ramp to the dock, Messrs. Baillie, Miller, and Lawrence went, too. We walked boldly, shoving the Seattle policemen aside, and they made no objections; maybe they thought we were Secret Service agents. But the admiral's barge wasn't at the dock: the timetable was off. Another barge was hastily brought up, with a nice covered cockpit aft for the guests, and a smaller cockpit up front for the bluejackets who ran the craft. Between the two was a beautiful flush deck with neat coils of rope, all very shipshape. The Presidential party was gingerly handed into the stern cockpit, and the barge was shoved off. Nobody noticed us intruders. As the barge moved away, the three of us leaped nimbly onto the flush deck and squatted down, trying to make ourselves as inconspicuous as possible.

Instantly our weight caused the barge to heel violently, which nearly dumped us into Puget Sound. We scrambled to the other side

—and she rolled in that direction.

"Trim the ship!" yelled Commander Percy Foote, Daniel's aide, jumping up in the rear cockpit.

By this time we had heeled to port again. Water slopped into the Presidential seats. Wilson's high hat fell over one eye. He grabbed for something to hold onto. The bluejackets forward looked around.

"Get those men off there!" roared Foote.

The sailors reached back, laid hold on us, and hauled us down beside them. They didn't say a word. What was being said by the President's party, I have no idea.

More was to come. With the navigating crew looking toward the stern and pulling us down, to restore the equilibrium of the boat, we shot out at gathering speed past the end of the dock—and banged into the whaleboat carrying the less audacious press, which was making its way around the wharf. Collision! More shouts! Barefooted sailors with boathooks scrambled forward and fended off the whaleboat. And thus we three reporters went off to the *Oregon* with the President, jammed in by the mariners, who were now beginning to frown on us . . . but they never spoke.

We could see an animated and angry conversation in the luxury cockpit in the stern. Commander Foote looked grim. The President and the Secretary and their ladies had been well doused with the chill salty waters of Elliott Bay.

Since we were off the timetable, and our barge flew no Presidential insigne, we arrived at the ladder of the *Oregon* when nobody was expecting us. The officer of the deck, telescope under arm, demanded to know who we were.

"The United States!" announced Commander Foote.

"Why, he's fifteen minutes early!" said a surprised voice.

There was a great squealing of bosuns' pipes from the deck as sideboys were assembled to man the gangway. First off was us. Up the ladder we scrambled, and made ourselves scarce—though not so scarce that we didn't have a good vantage point from which to see the President come aboard. This he did with dignity restored. Then just as he reached the top of the steps the first BANG of the twenty-one-gun Presidential salute cracked out. It sounded as if it was almost in his ear. He started visibly, and stepped onto the deck with top hat slightly askew, mad as hell.

Shortly thereafter, the whaleboat with the respectable press came alongside, and was waved off. Round and round the *Oregon* went the whaleboat, with the men in it gesticulating and yelling. We couldn't hear what was said, but it was probably adequate to the situation. One of Wilson's assistants, Thomas Brahany, used all his powers of persuasion on their behalf, and finally convinced the officers of the *Oregon* that it would just make a further embarrassment for the President, over the long run, if they refused to accept the passengers in the whaleboat, who were going with him all the rest of the trip.

Then the review began. The fleet, under Admiral Hugh Rodman, was to pass the *Oregon* in column, while the ancient battleship steamed slowly in the opposite direction. With a great clanking of chains, the *Oregon* got going. Down past her came first the smaller vessels of the fleet, then the cruisers, and the battleships *Idaho, Mississippi, New Mexico, New York,* and *Texas.* Each ship was dressed . . . the crew standing in a long rank from stem to stern, pennants and flags flying. Bugles sounded. The strains of "The Star-Spangled Banner" came across the water from each ship as she passed. Each ship fired twenty-one guns, creating large clouds of smoke.

Wilson and Daniels stood up forward on the *Oregon,* in a sort of pulpit specially constructed for the occasion.

But this review was not destined to run smoothly. A swarm of rubberneck boats—"See the Review, 25¢"—appeared on the sea lane, loaded to capacity with cheering thousands. The fighting craft had to slow, to avoid running into excursion boats. Some of the ships overlapped. And the twenty-one-gun salutes, bugles, national anthems began overlapping, too. Great clouds of smoke rolled over the scene, which began to look like my conception of a Civil War battle. . . .

The review over, we returned to the dock—this time with our compatriots in the whaleboat—to be greeted by newsboys whose papers carried headlines proclaiming that "Eastern journalists" had nearly pitched the President into Puget Sound.

Leaving Seattle, Wilson seemed recovered from his extreme fatigue. The sendoff was again through canyons of cheering people, and a crowd at the railroad station assembled behind the barrier, as close to the train as they could get. Wilson appeared for them on the rear platform, responding individually to those who called to him, carrying on conversations with the men and women jammed against the gates. As the train pulled out, he stood on the platform, waving his top hat at the rapidly disappearing crowd. Then, as we learned later, he returned to his private car and caved in.

At a lunch in Portland he was deeply depressed by the news that Ben Allen, whose arguments in the club-car bull sessions had pleased and amused him, had been killed by an accident in his speeding motorcade. (All Presidents drive fast.) And the news from Washington was bad. Senator Hiram Johnson was following him around the country, speaking where he had spoken, dissipating the aura of enthusiasm he built around the League.

San Francisco . . . Oakland . . . On the way from San Diego to Los Angeles we of the press had a memorable session with the rolling bones. After finishing our stories on the President's speech, a number of us retired to the diner for a steak supper, and somebody broke out the dice. Dice games on an "expense-account economy" can be quite sensational, and the news spread through the train. The off-duty waiters tumbled out of their bunks and came to join the throng, eyes sticking out at the stacks of bills. I lost eighty dollars myself, and retired. Then the Secret Service joined the game, and cleaned out the rest of the press corps. . . .

We spent most of that night on a siding at Del Mar, and pulled into the old LaGrande Station of the Santa Fe early in the next morning. The usual pretty girls were waiting in their starched dresses, carrying their tiny flags, making a singing and cheering corridor through which the President was to walk to his automobile; the committee chairmen were ready with their addresses of welcome; the streets were already banked with waiting spectators. But, for the first time on the trip, the President wasn't ready. The train backed away into the yards, and everybody had to wait an hour.

Meanwhile, all sorts of rumors flew about. The Los Angeles chief of police and one of his lieutenants boarded the train and sought me out, because they remembered me from my days as a police reporter. They took me aside and asked me to confirm that Wilson was dead. I made a quick check (anything was possible) and assured them that the rumor was untrue—the President was just a trifle late with his shaving and dressing. Still, it had never happened before.

Wilson scored another personal conquest in Los Angeles, but it was clear to all of us that he was spending his energy fast, getting down to his last reserves. Though he maintained his posture of faith and cheerful enthusiasm, his confidence in success had begun to wane. He withdrew himself from the reporters on the train, and discontinued the club-car press conferences. And he began to say strange un-Wilsonian things. At a night speech in the packed Mormon Temple in Salt Lake City, he told a slightly odd-ball joke (about the old maid at the county fair who refused to go to the sideshow where the man "could see through a one-inch board"—on the grounds that if he could see through a stick of wood he could certainly see through her thin dress). It was out of character, not so much for Wilson the man, but for Wilson the glorious crusader.

At Cheyenne, sticking to his schedule, he took a dusty automobile ride to review troops, the press tearing along behind him. In Denver there was one of the noisiest of his parades, culminating in roaring cheers which filled the lobby of the Brown Palace Hotel, rising tier on tier through the open center of the structure, up to the suite where the weary man had sought rest and quiet. But he was still making the effort to look jaunty.

The next speech was in the afternoon at Pueblo, Colorado. Sitting on the platform before he was introduced, he gazed down at the newspapermen in the orchestra pit and said loudly to us, "I expect you men are getting tired of this traveling circus, aren't you?" His voice was audible in the first few rows of the expectant audience. To these people, many of whom had come a difficult way to hear him, everything about the spectacle was bright and shiny new. At that moment, Wilson sounded like an actor tired of his role, fed up. Those who heard him were surprised and shocked.

But he rallied. There was nothing jaded or bored about that Pueblo speech. It was one of the longest of the trip, and one of the most emotional and persuasive of his life, bringing out his full resource of noble rhetoric. It was here that he took upon himself full responsibility for the declaration of war:

"Again and again, my fellow citizens, mothers who lost their sons in France have come to me and, taking my hand, have shed tears upon it—not only, but they have added, 'God bless you, Mr. President.' Why, my fellow citizen, should they pray to God to bless *me*? ... I ordered their sons overseas. I consented to their sons' being put in the most difficult part of the battle line, where death was certain, as in the impenetrable difficulties of the forests of the Argonne. Why should they weep upon *my* hand, and call down the blessings of God upon *me*? Because they believe their boys died for something that vastly transcends any of the immediate and palpable objects of the War. They believe—and they rightly believe—that their sons saved the liberty of the world. They believe that, wrapped up with the liberty of the world, is the continuous protection of that liberty by the concerted powers of all the civilized world. ...

"There is one thing that the American people always rise to, and extend their hand to, and that is the truth of justice and of peace. We have accepted that truth, and we are going to be led by it; and it is going to lead us—and through us, the world—out into pastures of quietness and peace such as the world never dreamed of before."

He finished this speech looking as spirited and as certain of himself as he had at any time during the trip: he had been revived by his own oratory and by the emotional response of the crowd. I filed a story about how well he looked when he returned to the train. But in fact he was seriously ill. He was never to make another formal speech; those words about the "pastures of quietness and peace" were to be his last words from any platform.

Later that day we pulled off onto a siding at a place called Baxter, Colorado, at that time a switchtower. Tumulty told us the President and his wife were going to take a walk, and we should stay behind. The President's personal physician, Dr. Grayson, said he would "cover" for us, and tell us if anything happened.

So I reluctantly remained aboard and watched as Wilson, with Mrs. Wilson at his side, disappeared up a country road—followed by Dr. Grayson in his admiral's uniform, and the Secret Service agents. An hour passed. Automobiles on a highway paralleling the tracks recognized the Special by the red Pennsylvania Railroad cars and halted, despite efforts to shoo them away. It was nearly two hours before the hikers reappeared, very dusty. The President was striding along, his wife was keeping up, the Secret Service operatives and White House retainers were lugging fruits and vegetables which had been bestowed on them by the astonished ranchers who had glanced up from their work to find the President of the United States dropping in for an informal call. (Throughout the trip, incidentally, well-wishers had loaded the Wilson party with food—far more than was necessary to supply the President's private galley. Mrs. Wilson always sent the surplus back to the diner where we ate, and the usual opening gambit when we sat down to a meal was, "What is Mrs. Wilson offering today?")

This walk on the country roads built up my story that Wilson had returned to his finest fettle, and I sent off a few bulletins on the subject to back up my previous dispatch. But I was 100 per cent wrong. The walk had been Grayson's last, desperate attempt to snap his patient out of an intense mental weariness and despondency.

The next morning we halted on the outskirts of Wichita, Kansas, where a speech was scheduled. Everything seemed the same as usual. The automobiles were lined up on the road alongside the train for the parade to the hall. There was the customary committee of welcome . . . the bunting, the flags, the girls with flowers. We waited and waited, concerned but less disturbed than we might have been without the memory of the delay in Los Angeles. This time, however, the President was not to appear. A White House attaché came out to the reporters who were standing alongside the train and distributed a mimeographed "handout" which said tersely that the President was ill, the rest of the trip had been canceled, and we were returning to Washington forthwith.

This was September 26, 1919. Washington was seventeen hundred miles away. A pilot engine appeared, sending up a plume of smoke ahead. We reporters ran up and down the tracks, looking for telephones from which to send our stories. I finally yelled a watchman into letting me into a factory which had been closed for the day, so the employees could go to town and hear Wilson's speech.

At eleven that morning, the Presidential Special started the long road home.

For forty-eight hours the train rolled toward Washington, stopping briefly en route in the principal rail junctures—where we of the press had a chance to file our stories, and the crowds had a chance to ogle the President's train, if not the President himself. Apparently many of them refused to believe Wilson was sick. They would surround the President's car, and hoist each other up to press noses against the window panes and try to peer inside. The blinds had to be drawn in The Mayflower every time the train stopped, to protect the ailing President from the boisterous crowd. Secret Service and local police chased them away, but they kept infiltrating back.

Dr. Grayson stayed awake throughout the journey, and so did we, keeping what seemed like a death watch. As we grew more and more tired, we began to play weary-man's hi-jinks in the club car. At one point we convened a mock trial, and chose a "King of the Boll Weevils" (boll weevil being Tumulty's favorite epithet for people who bothered him). The obvious candidate was the functionary who had been in charge of filing copy for us along the route. We roused him from his sleep and did a war dance around him, after which Tumulty crowned him with a circle of baling wire. It was the comic relief in a tragedy which involved us all.

We reached Washington at 11 A.M., Sunday, September 28. Wilson, making a last, game effort, walked from The Mayflower to his automobile unaided. He looked stooped and shrunken, a far different man from the debonair and rakish Wilson who had climbed into the train twenty-five days before. But he stepped along gallantly: no wheel chair for him. At the end of the automobile trip he walked from the car into the White House, whence he was not to emerge until March, 1921, when he rode in a car beside the new President to Harding's inauguration.

The next day, a dozen of us who had been on the trip went to the White House for tea with Mrs. Wilson. She apologized for her husband's inability to join us: he was still too tired from the trip. Later, in her memoirs, she wrote that Wilson had spent that afternoon prowling like a ghost between his bedroom and his study, unable to rest. But we were not told about that.

Nor were we told when, four days later, at six in the morning, Wilson fell unconscious in his bathroom in the White House, having suffered a stroke which paralyzed his left side. There were no three-a-day medical bulletins from the White House in those times, telling you everything about a sick President's physical condition, down to the state of his bowels. The air of mystery surrounding Wilson's disappearance within the White House was so thick that all sorts of rumors were abroad—he was dead, insane, comatose. One rumor cited the bars Teddy Roosevelt had put up outside the windows of the room he used as a nursery for his children—that room, people said, was the one where Wilson was kept, and the bars were to make sure he didn't jump out. One of my bosses came down from New York about this time, to survey my arrangements for covering Washington. In the course of conversation he asked me, "Suppose Wilson was running around nekkid on the second floor of the White House, and nobody could ketch him—how would you find out about it?" To which my answer had to be that there wouldn't be any way to find out about it—for all I knew, and for all the public knew, the President was running around "nekkid" all the time.

But, though we didn't know the truth about the President's health, we knew that he was sick—and that his great effort for the Treaty and the League had failed. So far as America was concerned, the Treaty and the League had been destroyed, and Wilson had been destroyed with them.

Chapter 5

TOP JOB

MY COLLECTION of Presidents must be among the largest in the world. Man and boy, I have met eleven men who were or had been President of the United States—every one of them since Cleveland. Cleveland and McKinley I saw while under the wing of my father, but all the others have figured more or less prominently in my own career, as newsmakers whose speeches and actions were part of the scene I was covering.

I came to know Teddy Roosevelt near the end of his life, while I was a staff reporter in New York. He was headquartering at the offices of *Outlook* magazine in New York, trying to get permission from Wilson to raise a division to fight in France. Roosevelt had frequent press conferences on the subject. He banged his desk with clenched fist as he denounced Wilson's veto on his plans—a veto which he unhesitatingly ascribed to "politics." I was intrigued by Roosevelt's energy, the gnashing and flashing of the famous teeth under the straggly mustache, and the electric vitality that built up as he slugged away. But he did not prevail—even though one of his high command in his mythical division was to be John L. Sullivan. John L. was always at T.R.'s shoulder. An immensely wide man, with snow-white hair and mustache, he was long years beyond his heavyweight championship. He kept an unblinking stare in his expressionless face, and he still looked as if he could lick any man in the place—with pleasure.

Later I made a number of trips out to Sagamore Hill, Roosevelt's house in Oyster Bay, to inquire about letters from his sons at the front. The first time I came I was shown to the trophy room, to wait until Roosevelt came in from chopping wood. All around were mementos of T.R.'s fabulous career—including the mounted heads of beasts he had slain in Africa. Through the window, I saw him returning to the house, coming across the porch with an ax over his shoulder, wearing rough, woodman's clothes. I proceeded to the front door, which he threw open with such violence that it whacked into me. He laughed, and roared, "*Whom* have we hiding behind the door?" Then he produced the letters from his sons, and read them to me with great pride, illustrating them with gestures. He also threw in a number of asides of his own—none of them complimentary to Wilson.

One day we got a tip from Fred Ferguson, a resourceful correspondent at the front: "Watch Oyster Bay for news." I went out to Roosevelt's house and he showed me the War Department telegram, containing the news which always went first to the next of kin. One of his sons had been killed. He was a graven image, without visible emotion of any sort, as he repeated to me the words of the official message.

In January, 1919, I flashed the death of Roosevelt himself. The lead I wrote was very brief. It said:

"Oyster Bay, N.Y., Jan. 6—T.R. is dead."

He was only sixty-one years old.

I watched both the birth pangs and the funeral of the President who followed Wilson. As manager of the Washington bureau, I headed the UP delegation to the Republican convention in Chicago in the summer of 1920. The nomination seemed likely to go to either Governor Lowden or General Wood, but there were several dark horses in the field, among them Senator Warren G. Harding of Ohio. He had been an obscure Senator, and he seemed an unlikely choice. His supporters put out a brochure which was distributed in the press gallery. It bore the title, "Who Is Warren G. Harding?" When I got my copy, I thought, "I'll bite. Who is he?"

But the convention deadlocked, apparently hopelessly, between Lowden and Wood. Toward the end of one morning session, after it had become apparent that neither of the front runners could win

Moscow, 1935: the author and Doletzky, head of Tass, who would soon commit suicide as the OGPU came to pick him up.

The Duke and Duchess of Windsor, on their way to greet the press:
"Here I go," she said brightly, "to have my appendix out."

"Traitor" Pierre Laval, twice premier of France, who bragged, "The Pope says that next to God he depends on Pierre Laval."

Neville Chamberlain, angry and confident: "There will never be a successful air raid on London. We have an impenetrable barrage."

the nomination, the presiding chairman, the venerable Senator Lodge, called a huddle on the platform. I saw the Republican leaders all putting their heads together. So I climbed up, and put my own head in among theirs. And I heard them plan to adjourn the convention and hold a private session in a local hotel room, where they could quietly agree on a nominee. Just at this point a reporter from another press association saw me, and scrambled up onto the platform . . . followed by two or three others. Senator Lodge saw what was going on, and began waving his gavel.

"Get off this platform, sir!" he said to me.

I don't know why he picked on me—maybe it was the loud silk shirt I was wearing.

I stood my ground and said, "Senator, I will get off the platform when those other reporters do the same."

But his attention was focused on me. He called on the sergeant at arms to throw me off. Now, the words "sergeant at arms" conjure up a picture of a large, muscular, altogether formidable fellow. But this particular bearer of the title was very skinny, and wore glasses. He seized me by the elbows from behind. I whirled around, and my right fist narrowly grazed his chin. There ensued quite a commotion, in the course of which somebody from the UP box reached over, grabbed me by the ankle, and yanked me down. Otherwise there would probably have been no United Press representation at the next session.

Immediately after the scuffle the Senator banged his gavel and announced that the session was adjourned until late that afternoon. And I climbed back up on the platform. There was another huddle around Lodge, but this time, since the meeting had "arisen," so to speak, there was no reason why I should not be up there—or the other reporters, either. We stood around listening, and heard the leaders complete their arrangements for their private "convention."

When I returned to my seat I was accosted by Arthur Brisbane, who was writing a daily running story on the convention for the Hearst newspapers. He wanted to interview *me*. I gave him a few vital statistics, and found myself all over his column. He was particularly pleased with my return to the platform after I had been booted. "Young Hugh Baillie," he wrote, "is back right where he was, getting news. He is a good reporter." That was the high point of that convention for me.

The high point of that convention for history came a few hours later, when the Republican leaders chose Warren Harding for the nomination. The decision was made in what Raymond Clapper of UP Washington bureau called "a smoke-filled room" in the Hotel Blackstone, originating a phrase which is now in the language. Harding's nomination then went through as arranged. The action of the convention on the next ballot had less animation than a puppet show: the chairman of delegation after delegation rose to his feet as if pulled by strings, and cast his votes as ordered.

President Harding was a pleasant, country-squire type, who frequently smelled of whiskey. He resumed the Presidential press conferences, which were scantily attended. I stood in the circle around the President's desk, where friendly hunting dogs shoved against your legs; and Harding, his hands shoved down into the front pockets of his gentleman-farmer pants, answered questions as best he could. The truth was, he didn't know much. On one occasion, talking about an international situation, he gave us an answer which contradicted what Secertary of State Hughes was saying elsewhere at the same time. After this episode, Harding went into his shell, and hardly ever said anything of consequence again.

Two years later, Harding lay desperately ill in San Francisco, and the UP ran a special telephone line up to Plymouth Notch, Vermont, where Vice-President Calvin Coolidge was vacationing with his father. I was general news manager then, working out of New York, waiting to hear the news that Harding was dead and receive from Plymouth Notch the story of Coolidge's accession. But Harding took a turn for the better, and someone suggested that the time had come to kill the special telephone line and save the expense. Luckily, someone else said, "Let's leave it in one more night." That night, Harding died, and Coolidge at the other end of our private line became President. His father swore him in by the light of a flaring oil lamp. Paul Mallon yelled the story to me over the barbed-wire telephone line, and the connection was so bad I could hardly hear him. But we captured enough to make a story that is still one of the classics of press-association reporting.

Then I hurried to Washington, to prepare to meet Coolidge. I bedded down in the Willard Hotel, which was to be used as a temporary White House until after Harding's funeral, and while I slept they installed telegraph instruments in my bedroom. I awoke to the clattering of Morse signals, and spent most of the next twenty-four hours in my pajamas, running news coverage from my bedroom.

That day, Coolidge came down to Washington and held his first press conference as President. I put on some clothes to cover it. We didn't get much out of him; in fact, we never got much out of him. He was a dry man, very stingy with words (though there was something seething underneath, and, like Wilson, he was to die of a stroke). Reporters have a trick of asking the same question again, rephrased, if the answer was unsatisfactory the first time around. That never worked with Coolidge. When it was tried, he would pause lengthily, looking every inch the quizzical suspicious Yankee, and then say with a twang, "My previous answer covered that." And so it did—at least, you had to be content with it.

Nevertheless, the press corps mostly liked Coolidge; he was affectionately known as "the little fellow." He was a poker-faced practical joker. All his associates were "Ol' Man" This-or-That— Secretary of the Treasury was "Ol' Man Andy Mellon," and the Secretary of the Navy, "Ol' Man Denby." When he retired for the night, he put on a long nightgown down to his feet.

He liked to take long walks around Washington, window-shopping. He said it "rested his brain." In those days it was possible for the President to stroll through the streets without causing traffic jams, but "Ol' Colonel Starling" of the Secret Service always went with Coolidge for safety's sake. To Coolidge all meals were "supper," and he liked to prepare them himself. His carefulness with money soon became common knowledge, and the source of innumerable jokes. Once he went so far as to travel in a mere drawing room instead of a Presidential private car, and to eat in the diner with the rest of the folks. He was given to cryptic remarks which could be interpreted several ways—and he was not likely to explain what he'd meant— but when he said, "I do not choose to run," he meant it.

Coolidge has a special place in the history of the United Press, for he was our guest of honor when we celebrated our twentieth anni-

versary with a banquet in the Cascades Room of the Hotel Biltmore.
(He told UP president Karl Bickel that he thought it would be pretty
expensive, what with eleven hundred people there, and he was right:
the bill came to nearly $18,000.) He was somewhat concerned about
the fact that the other speaker at the dinner was to be the humorist
Irvin S. Cobb. "You never can tell about these funny fellows," he told
Bickel. "I always think they are dangerous. They don't care what they
do to a man, as long as they get a laugh out of it." But Cobb stayed
away from politics and did not rib the President, and when it came
Coolidge's turn he made a major foreign policy address with nothing
parochial or Yankee about it at all.

Hoover's relations with the press when he was President were, if
possible, even more distant than Coolidge's. He conducted his press
conferences strictly according to rules. Questions were written on
slips of paper and submitted in advance. If Hoover felt like answering them, he did. If he didn't feel like answering a question, he would
crumple up the piece of paper and throw it in the wastebasket. You
didn't follow up verbally on your written question, unless it was to
make sure that you had the meaning of the President's answer crystal
clear in your mind. You didn't press Hoover: it wasn't done. And, of
course, you never quoted him directly without special permission—
that was a tradition, which Eisenhower was the first President to
break.

After Wilson's collapse, in short, there was hardly any spectacular
excitement around the White House pressroom, until the arrival of
F. D. Roosevelt. There has been no surcease from excitement since.

By the time Roosevelt became President of the United States, however, I was no longer just one of the boys in the pressroom. I was well
on the way to a presidency of my own—that of the United Press.

If a young reporter of today were transported by a time machine
back into the New York offices of the United Press as they were in
the late 1910's and the 1920's, he would feel himself surrounded by
a rude society. His physical surroundings would have none of the
quiet modernity to which he has become accustomed. The floor was
concrete, not linoleum tile, and it was littered with paper (we may
have had wastebaskets, but we didn't have to use them). The ceilings

were not soundproofed. The illumination was not scientifically perfect. There were no teletypes clunking out their news at a mechanically even rate—instead, there were Morse men, sending stories at a speed to match the urgency of the copy. You could tell when big news was breaking by the sudden speeding up of the Morse signals, and tension would rise throughout the office. Everybody wore a vest, with shirt sleeves rolled up above the elbow. Many men smoked or chewed cigars, and hardly anybody ever smoked a pipe; pipes were the mark of a ruminative and meditative animal, out of a place in the high-pressure operation of a news service.

No attempt was made to run the office in a quiet, decorous way, keeping the newsroom suitable at all times for the earnest inspection of a visiting study group. Then, you might find the president screaming at the general news manager to get that lead out or he will get a new boy. You might hear the news manager saying to an editor who'd had the temerity to talk back in front of the staff, "What's the matter with you? Your face is as red as a spanked baby's ass! You are pissing on the story of the day!" Nobody was embarrassed about yelling "FLASH!" at the top of his voice when big news came in: that was our business. All this is gone now, and many people would say things are better as a result. I would not be one of them.

Anyway, it was this atmosphere to which I returned after the elections of 1920, to be first New York manager, then assistant general news manager, then general news manager of the United Press. The day started at eight o'clock with a call to Bill Hawkins (at Dobbs Ferry 431—a number I will never forget) to tell him what seemed to be coming up. Then for most of the day I was responsible personally for what went out on the UP wires. And I was supposed to know it all—everything that was happening in the world from Capetown to Timbuctu to Whatever.

My worst day in any of these three jobs came in 1922, when I found a dozen telegrams from Henry Wood, our Rome bureau manager, waiting for me on my arrival at the office. Half of them offered the code message we had arranged for the death of Pope Benedict XV: SEND TRUNKS IMMEDIATELY. The rest carried the message: UNSEND TRUNKS IMMEDIATELY. There were a dozen of them divided half and half between the two messages, because Wood had instructions to send his signal over all available cable routes, to make sure we caught whatever line was moving fastest on that day. None of the telegrams carried a time slug, because they were supposed to be private cables, not press-association dispatches (there was always a blanket censorship on news of a Pope's death). I decided that the only reasonable explanation of the two sets of telegrams was a false report of the Pope's death, which Wood at first accepted and then disproved. So the UP sent no story.

The other news agencies, however, were taken in by the rumor, and three hours after I had decided not to announce the Pope's death I began receiving client complaints—why didn't the UP have the story when AP and INS did. One of the men in the office, in fact, urged that we take the word of our competitors over my deduction from Wood's cables, and proclaim the Pope deceased. I told him that if we hadn't sent the story at eight we certainly wouldn't send it at eleven, after everybody else had carried it. Meanwhile, I cabled urgently to Wood in Rome—and received no answer. I stood in the newsroom throughout that morning and early afternoon, sweating from the top of my scalp down the length of my body to my feet. And late in the afternoon the news arrived that enabled me to stop sweating: despite the near-universal mourning of the newspapers which carried the reports from the other press associations, the Pope was still alive.

In 1923, Karl Bickel, who had just been made president of the UP, called me aside one day after work and said, "Hugh, if you want to get to be head of this outfit, you've got to know something about the business side." Every president of the UP had been both a newsman and a businessman. Howard had started the tradition. He worked both sides of the street from the beginning, getting interviews and signing clients wherever he went. And there was no secret about the fact that I was ambitious, thought I could run the UP someday, and wanted the chance. What Bickel said made sense. But I'd never thought of myself as a businessman—except for occasional forays I'd always been a reporter, and proud of it. Bickel finally persuaded me by suggesting that I go on the road as a salesman for three months, and if I then decided I didn't like it I could always return to the job of general news manager. On January 1, 1924, I stepped down from the top spot on the news-gathering end of the UP and went out as a salesman. I felt terrible. And my feelings were not helped by the fact that my desk in the newsroom was immediately taken over by a colleague who regarded his new position as permanent. Whatever Bickel had intended, my bridges were burned. Bickel had gone off on a trip around the world, getting news and signing contracts, and I was on my own.

I was as welcome in the business department as a case of smallpox. I had a reputation: I was a competitor. I was such a goddamned competitor a lot of people didn't want me around. When you're a competitor, the guy at your elbow is always your rival, and sometimes he doesn't like that. I meant trouble, hubba-hubba, and there are plenty of people who would rather lead tranquil lives. And, obviously, if I made good as a salesman, I was going to be promoted fast.

The territory assigned me was the Old South. This was a tough area where the AP was well dug in, and most publishers were not at all interested in switching. (Nobody wanted me to have easy going and get a swelled head. Later, when I was business manager, I browsed through the files and read all the letters people had written about my swelled head.) Many of the hotels on the route were antiquated. The first thing the Negro bellhop offered the salesman was a flask of white mule streaked with fusel oil, and the services of a commercial blonde. This was a big switch for me, coming from the world of Clarence Darrow and Woodrow Wilson, the War and Big News. I didn't like it. But I had to get the contracts or get out. All I needed to sell the service, I felt, was a knowledge of what it was and of the men who made it. By God, I knew the product and I believed in it. So I traveled the red-dust roads and the rattly trains, and forced my way in on the uninterested editors. And early in 1924, I got a big break.

At that time the UP night wire terminated in Atlanta, Georgia. We had no clients in Florida. If we could sign Miami, we could run the wire all the way down, and sell "drops" on it to all the papers between Atlanta and Miami. So I went down to Miami and made my pitch to Olin Kennedy, editor of the *Herald*. I'd known him in California, in the old days. He listened and said, "No. Too expensive."

So I went over to Miami Beach and put in forty-eight hours of lying on the sand. As I was about to leave town, I called Kennedy to tell him that I'd be back, trying to sell him again. He said, "Where have *you* been? I've been trying to get hold of you for two days." He had passed on my sales talk to publisher Frank Shutts, who had okayed the deal, despite the costs. And new salesman Baillie found himself with the triumph of the year for the UP sales force—a new territory opened up, with a dozen new clients for the service.

That September, I became sales manager; and, in 1926, business manager. I had no responsibility for the news side of the UP. But I kept my eye on it all the time, and covered stories as a reporter whenever there was a story anywhere near me. When client newspapers had a complaint about coverage, I'd investigate personally if I could, and come back to New York to criticize and denounce. Sometimes I'd sit on the receiving end of the client's service, to see firsthand what he was squawking about. Pretty soon NX (New York) would begin getting messages from the client—but signed by me, not by the editor.

Then, in 1931, the news report came once again under my direct supervision. I was made executive vice-president, obvious heir apparent to Bickel whenever he should choose to step down. And it was in this role, as the upcoming president of the UP, that I went to Europe in 1932 to check on our personnel, offices and transmission facilities in the places whence the big stories of the next decade were to come.

Chapter 6

GERMANY: VON PAPEN AND HITLER

"GERMANY MUST have her place in the sun," said Chancellor Franz von Papen, and then smiled at me urbanely over the corner of his massive desk in the Wilhelmstrasse. "Germany must have a place among nations as a moral, political and economic equal. Germany will battle relentlessly to wipe out the discriminations imposed on her by the treaty of peace. The Versailles Treaty's moral discrimination against Germany as exemplified by the war-guilt lie and the seizure of our colonies must be abolished. . . . This business of treating us like the Portuguese must stop!"

The date was July 27, 1932, and it was the first time that the head of a German government had talked so openly for publication. He spoke in English—without an accent. The meeting had been arranged by Fred Kuh, our Central European manager, who was the only other person present in the room. It was my first exclusive interview with the head of a foreign state, something which was to become a specialty of mine. And it was one of the most important interviews I ever had. On my arrival in Berlin, in this summer of the Hitler-Hindenburg election, Kuh had told me that war was probably no more than five years off, but it seemed difficult to believe. Now here was Von Papen, in official terms, threatening it himself. "Fair warning," I thought. "They're telling us what we have got to do, or else." The story that came out of the interview—with its big headlines about "Germany's place in the sun"—transmitted that warning to everybody. But people (especially Americans) weren't taking such stories seriously, in 1932.

Von Papen was not at all what you might have expected. He had been military attaché in Washington during the World War, and had been kicked out by Woodrow Wilson after he was implicated in the Black Tom explosion and other acts of murderous sabotage. He was a lieutenant colonel in the Prussian army, and a baron in the Prussian aristocracy. The cabinet which he headed had assumed emergency powers and declared a "state of siege." The day I called on him, Von Papen had unceremoniously dismissed four cabinet ministers from his government. He seemed to be virtually the dictator of Germany.

But he didn't look like any of this. He wore a lightweight gray-flannel summer suit with a loosely knitted black tie, not a uniform —and horn-rimmed glasses rather than a monocle. The glasses sometimes hung from one ear, down to his neck. His office was that of a prosperous businessman—a large, wood-paneled room, severely plain, with heavy German chandeliers and a few paintings in that 1920's modern style that Hitler was soon to condemn as decadent. Von Papen's manner was studious, even professorial, without a touch of the stiffly formal heel-clicking Junker about it. His attitude toward my questions was one of easy tolerance; he seemed to feel that he was teaching a rather backward student some facts—which the student ought to have known already—about a fairly simple subject. (Though there was a rasp in his voice when he spoke to Kuh in German, as he did several times during the course of the interview. Later I learned that he had been denouncing Kuh for some dispatch which his government disliked. Kuh came right back at him every time.) His answers to my questions seemed disarmingly candid, with no diplomatic hemming or hedging. But what he was saying, beneath the foxy, rather simian expression, bared the German teeth for the first time since the Treaty of Versailles.

He talked about German internal politics, too. If he believed what he said, he did not think that the Weimar Republic was in any danger from the Nazis. He thought there was a possibility that after the elections the "Hitlerites," as he called them, the Nationalists and the Catholic party might form a coalition government. Certainly there was no thought of suppressing the Social Democratic opposition.

"Why," he said, "even the German Communist party won't be suppressed or outlawed, after the election, no matter what the outcome."

Perhaps Von Papen was just old-fashioned—up until this summer nobody had thought of Hitler as a really serious menace. On my previous trip to Germany, in 1930, I had found Hitler almost universally regarded as a crank or a fanatic whom the solid Germans would never accept as their leader. He was a strange little man in a trench coat and fedora hat, who went around making ranting speeches with a persistent cadence that seemed to mesmerize an audience. (It often struck me, listening to him, that in other circumstances and with another purpose in life he would have made a first-class revivalist preacher of the Billy Sunday school.) The breathless attention with which his audiences listened to him—an attention reinforced by brown-shirted musclemen who would make short work of any heckler—added a striking element of fear and even horror to his movement. The roaring choruses of "Heil!", led by Hitler's professional cheer leaders, came from hard-eyed, intense and obviously dangerous young men. But when you looked at Hitler's chief lieutenants, the men closest to him, his importance seemed to shrink. Goebbels the unsuccessful newspaperman, Ribbentrop the champagne salesman who had married the boss's daughter, Goering the First World War pilot and drug addict—who could believe that Germany would follow them? But Fred Kuh thought Germany very well might follow them, and he knew the catastrophe that would inevitably result. Kuh had a habit of being right. He was a studious, quiet type with great ability at developing sources. His forecasts were so accurate throughout the 1930's that whenever people asked me about the European situation I found myself replying, "Fred Kuh says . . ."

Berlin in 1930 was a peaceful place, on the surface. You sat around the Eden Roof and enjoyed champagne with a whole peach in the glass, or took a chair at a café in the zoo and talked politics of a peaceful variety. My German friends argued with me that they had now proved their good intentions toward the rest of the world, demonstrated that they'd learned the lessons of the war, and ought not to be "ground down" by the reparations and other penal provisions of the Treaty of Versailles. But they argued in a civilized manner: they weren't savage about it yet.

There was a veterans' organization, the Stahlhelm, which was supposed to be menacing—but you didn't see much much of it in 1930.
I tried to pick up a *Stahlhelm*—a steel helmet—as a souvenir for my
son, and I had to chase all over town before I could find one. Shopkeepers looked displeased when I asked about it. Finally, I located
my helmet, in a fancy-costume bazaar. At the Potsdam palaces the
guides were war veterans in pot hats and shabby clothes, with an
apologetic attitude toward Germany's past military glories. They explained that they had been *forced* to serve in the Kaiser's army. The
Treaty of Versailles had limited the new army to 100,000 men—although it was generally believed that these were all student officers,
cadres for a future expansion. They certainly had that appearance.
Groups of them went around Berlin, ogling the historic sights—
handsome blond boys, looking extremely competent in their tightly
belted cadet uniforms with short jackets. But there was no goose-
stepping, no jack-booting, no overt sign of militarism.

Two years later much of this tranquillity had disappeared. Von
Papen's "state of siege" was far less visible than the words imply.
The term invokes an image of barricades, barbed wire, and machine-
gun emplacements at strategic locations; but nothing of this sort was
in evidence. The only sign that special precautions had been taken
was the fact that policemen patrolled their beats two by two, rather
than singly. Fred Kuh said that these big, brawny cops were actually
soldiers, concealed in different uniforms. Far more noticeable than
the state of seige was the election. The Berlin through which I drove
to meet Von Papen was hung with flags, swastikas in some parts of
town, the hammer and sickle in others. The flags were as common
as posters and pictures of the candidates during our own election
campaigns. They seemed about equally divided between the Communists and the Nazis, in the Berlin of 1932.

On my own that summer, I walked about somewhat circumspectly,
because the chance of getting involved in a free fight were pretty
good. The Nazi members of the Reichstag—107 of them—had
marched out in a body, declaring their contempt for parliamentary
institutions, and Hitler had announced that henceforth his party
would "fight it out on the asphalt." The Storm Troopers were ugly,
and they roamed the town looking for trouble. They marched in

military formations, like soldiers, wearing brown shirts and the characteristic German jack boots—and carrying guns. The Communists also had gangs, called the Red Front, for street fighting, but they and the other anti-Hitler parties lacked the disciplined ardor of the Nazis. They put up a good fight sometimes, but they couldn't muster enough united strength to keep Hitler's mobs from spilling their blood all over Berlin.

In this atmosphere, Von Papen's optimism about the future of the German Republic seemed less than justified. And, in fact, he had little attachment to the Republic. He was an intriguer, not a politician. He probably felt no great affection for Hitler, because he was a Prussian gentleman and Hitler was an Austrian upstart—a man who couldn't even speak German without an accent. But when Hitler came to power, Von Papen was ready to serve him. The next time I was to see Von Papen was fourteen years later, in the dock at Nuremberg, where he was on trial for his life as a war criminal. But, being crafty, he had never signed any of the genocide orders, which is what convicted most of the Nazi leaders. Von Papen was acquitted.

When I came to Berlin again in 1935, Hitler was solidly in the saddle, and the stories of his evil filled the newspapers of the world. Hitler himself, however, had become relatively unapproachable: he had not received the press in some time. So, from the day I arrived, I went hunting for an exclusive interview with the Fuehrer. My guide and mentor on the hunt was Fred Oechsner, who had taken over our Berlin bureau when Kuh moved to London, and who was to remain in charge of it until the war closed us down in Germany.

The chance to get these interviews was one of the many reasons for my trips abroad—especially after April, 1935, when I became president of the United Press. The arrival of the head man from the home office gives the correspondent on the spot an advantage over his competition. The president of a world-wide press association gets special treatment—high priority—on the ground that what he writes will automatically receive a bigger-than-usual play in the newspapers. I was never under any illusion that the big-shots I interviewed saw me because they had some interest in the personality of the man who was president of the United Press. To them, I was simply a chan-

nel—somebody who could get their views onto the front pages of
newspapers throughout the world.

But, important as they were, these exclusive interviews were
merely useful by-products of trips which had a more urgent purpose.
The successful operation of a news agency, with correspondents scattered all over the globe, requires a *mystique*, something that will inspire each individual in the organization with enthusiasm, resource-
fulness, an intense competitive spirit and a common loyalty. The
good press-association man gets his viscera entwined in the organization. He takes its triumphs and defeats *personally*, wherever he
is and whatever he's doing. If the outfit suffers a reverse in Vienna,
he feels the pain in Portland, Oregon—or Portland, Maine—or Hono-
lulu. Conversely, a triumph in London, say, elates him in Chicago.
If he takes the attitude that "you can't win 'em all," there's no place
for him in a press association.

That *mystique* must be generated from the top. It's part of the job
of the president of the United Press to travel around the world, carrying an evangelical fervor, and leaving some of that fervor behind him
when he departs. Meanwhile, of course, he also picks up a firsthand
knowledge of how events are going in all parts of the world. He
learns how to judge the relative importance of the thousands of
stories that pour into his New York office, what the trends are and
where they're leading. Soon he begins to *feel* the news that's coming
up, and he moves his agency's correspondents onto the scene of tomorrow's big stories. That's what you need more than anything else
when you're president of a news agency—a kind of second sense, a
prescience, which smells tomorrow's news.

The man on the spot, of course, does most of the job of educating
the boss about local conditions, and sets up the big interviews: he
knows the labyrinths. In Berlin in 1935, Oechsner decided that the
approach to Hitler should be made informally, through Foreign Minister von Ribbentrop, who had just concluded a naval treaty with
Britain, allowing Germany to build up its fleet, and seemed to have
Hitler under his particular wing. That night Oechsner and I and our
party went to the opera, to hear *Die Meistersinger*, always one of
Hitler's favorites. Between the acts we strolled the corridors. It was
a glittering show, many of the men in dress uniform complete with

medals and orders, the women lavishly gowned and bejeweled. And along came Ribbentrop, looking down his nose at everybody—a pompous fellow in a specially designed "ambassador's uniform" with highly polished boots. When he stopped to talk with us he stood ramrod stiff, arms folded, chin high. He had a broader English accent than anyone in England. Oechsner introduced me to him and announced my desire to interview Hitler. Ribbentrop looked me over with a cold blue eye and said that it would be very difficult. But he made an appointment to see us, for further discussion.

Hitler and his party occupied the state box, the Fuehrer in white tie and tails, no medals. Mrs. Goebbels sat at his right, a beautiful woman with honey-blond hair, wearing a dark green velvet evening gown and a great mink cape. At his left sat Mrs. Rudolph Hess, a far less elegant figure who rarely came to these affairs and looked as though she would rather be home. Hess sat behind Mrs. Goebbels, and Goebbels behind Mrs. Hess. Hitler spoke to nobody, and nobody spoke to him.

Because this was "Goebbels' Opera House," Goering was not in the state box. He occupied the box beside it, dressed in a pale violet uniform which sported, as usual, a double-chested mass of medals. His fat wife sat beside him in a pale violet gown to match his uniform. She was tricked up in furs, ribbons and furbelows, and she looked a fancy rag bag. At another theater, known as "Goering's Opera House," the seating arrangements were revised to give Goering and his wife the honor of sitting with the Chancellor.

Our seats were in the second tier of boxes, so we looked down on the Hitler party. The Fuehrer's wide expanse of white shirt front gleamed in the glow from the stage. It occurred to me that Hitler wasn't very closely guarded. His shirt would have been an easy shot from where I sat. But, of course, this was a hand-picked audience, well screened in advance.

Between the acts, Hitler emerged from his box and stood just outside its doorway, in the corridor. He remained in this one place throughout the intermission, an unsmiling unanimated figure with a pasty complexion, a chopped mustache and a lock of hair over one eye. People clustered around him, and several were introduced. Men and women alike followed a fixed ritual—a stiff bow, then the Nazi salute, then a formal hand jerk.

Two of the ladies in our party ran up the grand staircase to get a better look at Hitler. He immediately detached his attention from those around him, and gazed at the American women intently, looking them over while they were looking him over. "It's your gown," said Dorothy Oechsner to my wife. "That's what he's inspecting so carefully. He's interested in fashions, especially American. Prefers them to the French."

Hitler was a master of the "sliding eye." He could glide his glance from face to face without focusing on anyone, and without letting anyone catch his eye. But while he was sizing up the ladies' dresses he concentrated his roving stare on them for a considerable period. Then he turned his back abruptly, and re-entered his box.

Ribbentrop kept us waiting for an hour at our appointment to arrange for the Hitler interview—and then refused to arrange it. He said patronizingly, in his most High Church manner, "Sorry, the Chawncellor can't see you. Can't see you," he repeated, with a rising, veddy-British inflection. He then put me through a mill of questions, about why the United States was so hostile to Germany, why nothing had been done to punish Magistrate Brodsky (Brodsky had recently released some rioters who had torn down the swastika from the S.S. *Bremen* when it was in New York), why the American press was "allowed" to print such malignant lies about Germany. I told him that Brodsky was a local New York justice who could hardly be removed for exercising his discretion in a disorder on the New York waterfront. And I told him the American press was "allowed" to print the news, because it was a free press. Which gave me the opportunity to ask him why there was no free press in Germany.

This question he condescended to answer. "In Germany, Mr. Baillie," he said in his most oily tones, "we were at five-minutes-to-twelve from Bolshevism. Had the clock struck, this would be a Communist country today. We had to take action, and we have had to keep taking action. If we had a free press today, these criminals would still be writing subversive articles."

Oechsner cut in here to point out that Ribbentrop was complaining about the treatment Germany received in the American press, while refusing an opportunity to let Hitler tell his side of the story in the

American press. The position was contradictory. But Ribbentrop
did not rise to the bait. He bowed us out, with contemptuous deference.

The next day, Oechsner and I took our campaign into different
territory, meeting with Dr. Goebbels at his headquarters in the Ministry of Propaganda at the old Palais Leopold. Goebbels had none of
Ribbentrop's pomposity (or fluency in English). He hobbled around
his desk as Oechsner and I entered, and greeted us with a big smile.
But he, too, treated us to a discourse on the sins of Magistrate Brodsky, and again I went through my explanation. When I had finished,
he began an exposition of the benefits the Nazis were bringing to
Germany. I told him that if Germany wanted to get her story in the
American papers, the statements would have to come from Hitler
himself. Goebbels seemed surprised that Hitler had turned down
my request for an interview. He said he was having lunch with Hitler
that day, and would take it up with him personally. I told him that
we would draw up a list of questions which I would ask the Fuehrer,
and send them to his office at once.

Oechsner and I then hurried back to the hotel and drafted ten
questions, which I proceeded to memorize—so I wouldn't have to
read off a sheet of paper during the interview, if it ever came through.
The next thing I knew, Ribbentrop was on the phone. He explained
that, after all, he had been able to arrange for me to see the Chancellor at 11:30 A.M. the next day. He did not mention the name of
Goebbels.

At 11 A.M. a big Mercedes-Benz stood in front of the Hotel Adlon,
where I was staying. There were swastikas on stiff metal flags on each
fender. Two large gentlemen emerged from the car, then returned
to it with Oechsner and myself between them. I found myself in
a back seat with a guard at either elbow. If this had been a scene
in a movie, you would have known for sure that I was being taken
for a ride. But the ride was very short—just around the corner into
Wilhelmstrasse.

We didn't go to the Chancellery, however. Instead, we were taken
into the Foreign Ministry, into a small private elevator, and when
the door opened there sat Ribbentrop. He greeted me with a fat,
false smile and said, "I have arranged for you to see the Chancellor.

But no interview, mind you! No interview, Mr. Baillie, I want your word on that."

I replied that Hitler wouldn't be quoted if he didn't wish to be quoted. But I was surprised at the sudden switch.

"Then it's understood," said Ribbentrop, pointing his finger. When I agreed that it was understood, he wheeled on Oechsner. "And you, too, understand," he said sternly. Oechsner just looked at him. Relations between Ribbentrop and Oechsner were cool, to say the least. Oechsner's family had been German originally, and the Nazis undoubtedly regarded him as a German still. He was a vigorous, abrupt, hot-tempered sort who hated the Nazis' guts and they knew it. They'd have loved to put him away with all the other Germans who hated their guts. They kept the Gestapo on him for years, but they could never find any shadow of an excuse for taking action against him. When he returned to the United States, after our entrance into the war, he wrote perhaps the most illuminating of all anti-Nazi books, *This Is the Enemy.*

After Ribbentrop had given us his nasty little farewell, our escort formed again and we were led out into a courtyard across the street, and into the Chancellery. As we walked down the long corridor to Hitler's office, we picked up an entourage, including Dr. Paul Schmidt, the official interpreter, and Dr. Walther Funk, the press chief. (Most government officials in Germany were called "Dr.," then as now.) Funk remarked to Oechsner that he was interested to see we had got our interview after all, and Oechsner replied that we'd thought we had an interview, but Ribbentrop said no. Funk was taken aback. He said Goebbels had arranged it as an interview. The element of office politics was by now, of course, crystal clear, and Funk was automatically on the side of his boss, Goebbels. He suggested that, when the talk was over, I put it up to Hitler to release the quotes of what he had said. This decision would have to wait until the end of the session, however, so I would be unable to take notes.

At Hitler's big door stood a Black Guard (aptly named, thought I), more than six feet tall, with a granite face and eyes that stared blankly over our heads. He was dressed in black from head to foot, and didn't so much as twitch as we walked past him. Then we were in Hitler's office.

As we entered, Hitler arose from a small desk in the corner, tossing a pencil negligently onto the blotter. He strolled toward us, looking me over curiously with sleepy, soft-boiled eyes. Up went the arms of our entourage: "Heil Hitler!" I wondered how Hitler would reply. Would he, too, say "Heil Hitler"? Or would he say "Heil Me"? Instead, he said, simply, "Heil," and raised his right hand—not in the stiff Romanesque salute used by the others in the room, but in a rather casual manner, arm bent at the elbow, palm flat to the ceiling like a waiter carrying a tray of beers. He was dressed simply, in a khaki jacket, black trousers and black shoes. The only decorative touches were the Iron Cross and a swastika brassard. He motioned toward a large circular table over near the wall, and we all took seats around it. Hitler sank into an overstuffed leather chair and looked weary and bored. He spoke a few words of German to Oechsner and to Dr. Schmidt, then nodded to me, evidently giving me the signal to start.

My first question was about his treatment of the German Jews. Schmidt translated it into German, meanwhile noting it down verbatim. And as Hitler answered he made a transcript of the boss's statements, while translating them for me. Clearly a handy fellow, Paul Schmidt. Hitler used him at all his meetings with English-speaking visitors, and he was the official translator three years later at the Munich conference.

Hitler's replies followed the expected course ("To eliminate Communists, we must eliminate the Jews. . . . After the war, thousands of officers, educated men, had to take work as chauffeurs, motormen and street cleaners because the Jews had usurped their positions. . . . The destructive influence of intellectual Jewry in Germany has made itself felt everywhere. For this reason it is necessary to put a stop to this destructiveness, and to establish a clear and clean division between the two races..."). There was nothing excited or dramatic about his manner as he delivered his statements. It was evident that he was an actor who could turn his frenzy on and off at will. When he wanted to be, he was the fanatical screeching demagogue; at other times he could play the role of the relaxed businessman in his office, not very interested in what was going on among his subordinates. He turned his rug-chewing act on and off, as circumstances dictated. Like other tragedians, of course, he could get carried away. But when he came out of his weeping and ranting, he knew what he had been doing, and why.

I soon got the feeling that he knew more English than he wished to admit. He seemed surprised at some of my questions even before they were translated. He would glance at me with an air of amused astonishment, as if to say, "Pretty fresh!" Then he would look from one to another of those around him as the question was translated, his quizzical expression carrying the comment, "How about this!"

As Schmidt translated his answers into English, however, Hitler dropped the bored manner and went into an elaborate pantomime. He added emphasis and fight to Schmidt's words, shrugging his shoulders, widening his eyes, jerking his head, jabbing his finger, glaring and laughing. It was a startling performance—the flat voice and weary air while speaking, and then the peppy acting job while the interpreter spoke. I've interviewed many men in my time, but I've never seen anything else like it.

Hitler answered questions about the German Army ("Germany is a major power of the first rank, and has a right to possess an army of the first rank... we are arming only for purposes of defense"), and about the German colonies ("stolen from us under the shameful terms of Versailles. . . . As long as a single German is left alive, we will never relinquish claim to so much as a square mile of our lost colonies"). He made his strongest statement when talking about the Bolshevik menace. "Russia," he said, "is less than an hour by plane from the German frontier. Do you understand the importance of this, in America? Germany is the bulwark of the West against Bolshevism, and in combating it we will meet propaganda with propaganda, terror with terror, and violence with violence."

When I had reached the end of my memorized questions, Hitler looked at me with a slight smile, and then indicated the end of the audience by rising. I said good-by with the words: "Thank you, Mr. Chancellor, for receiving us and answering my questions. What a pity we can't circulate your answers! It seems too bad to bury them with me."

Hitler looked surprised, and made no response. I added, "I propose to put down these questions and answers as well as I can from memory. Then perhaps you would be willing to read them over and decide whether I can publish them as an interview."

Hitler's expression was more puzzled than ever. He glanced questioningly at his associates, and then threw out his hands and shrugged in a gesture eternally French. He said he would leave it all to "the Ambassador," by which he meant Ribbentrop.

It was all very different from my preconceived idea of Hitler—first the weary air, then the pantomime, finally the French shrug. I got the impression that here was a man who, contrary to popular misconception, was easily swayed, and could be persuaded into this or that mistake without too much effort. He was a provincial. He had never been out of Germany and Austria (his birthplace) until he went to visit Mussolini in Italy. What lay behind the high seas was a mystery to him. I felt that his predominant evil genius was Ribbentrop. He had been a wine salesman in Canada. He had traveled in Great Britain, where he was later to be ambassador. And in the contest among the sycophants to be first at Hitler's ear, Ribbentrop was usually up front. Drawing so much of his information by hearsay, especially from Ribbentrop, Hitler hadn't the remotest realization of what he would be up against when he pulled the trigger.

Leaving the Chancellery, Oechsner and I asked Dr. Schmidt to come with us to the hotel and give us his shorthand Q. and A. "It is impossible," he replied, and scuttled across the Wilhelmstrasse.

So Oechsner and I stepped into the official car for the drive around the corner to the Adlon, where we put down the questions and answers as best we could. Robert L. Frey, my executive assistant, who accompanied me on many of these trips, typed our recollections as we talked, and jogged our memory with a cross-examination. Then we sent our manuscript around to the Chancellery—*not* to "the Ambassador"—and I left for London, where I had business waiting.

Four days later, Oechsner called me from Berlin. Hitler had approved the publication of my questions and his answers as a formal interview—and, for good measure, had ordered Schmidt's verbatim transcript placed at our disposal. Our story of the interview—which led off with the business about "meeting terror with terror"—received enormous play all over the world.

Except, of course, in Russia. I had been in Russia just before this trip to Germany (in my notebooks of the time, I compared the German and Russian military preparations, and wrote a memo in which I commented that "it will be a nice war when they fight it"). When I returned to New York I was visited by the local representative of Tass, the Russian news agency, with which we have an exchange-of-news arrangement. After some hemming and hawing, this gentleman said in a rather embarrassed way that he felt it was his duty to inform me that his principals in Moscow were displeased that I had interviewed Hitler in Berlin right after leaving Russia.

"You mean," I said, "that the heads of Tass think I enjoyed their hospitality and ate their food, and then went outside and threw a rock through the window on my way home."

"Yes, Hugh," he replied. "That's exactly what they think."

Chapter 7

MUSSOLINI: ITALY DEFIES THE WORLD

WHEN I arrived in Rome on Saturday, September 28, 1935, the city was in a war fever of a rather carnival sort. Parades and demonstrations went on constantly, day and night. Mussolini had rejected the proposals of the League of Nations, designed to settle the Ethiopian "dispute"—and unless he was bluffing he had to attack. Nobody in Rome seemed to have any doubts about what the results of that attack would be. Revenge was at hand for the Battle of Adua, many years before, when captured Italians had been castrated by the Ethiopian tribesmen. Anyway, Ethiopia was far, far away—and impotent, so far as any danger of retaliation was concerned.

In the streets of Rome, the Fascisti swaggered in various uniforms, their officers carrying huge swords that banged around their legs and dragged on the ground. At their waists they wore formidable daggers and pistols. In a fashionable night spot, the Quirinale, where there was an outdoor dancing floor, a Fascist officer with guns, daggers and sword, wearing a betasseled hat, bowed low at our table and invited one of the ladies for a dance. How they got around the floor with all that armament was something I could never explain. Another handsome item of uniform on the floor was a golden helmet similar to that worn by the gods of mythology. The red-coated band banged out "The Lullaby of Broadway"—within earshot of the ancient Forum.

As I entered our bureau, the office boy gave me the Fascist salute. Like everyone else in Rome, he seemed to be having a good time.

At the United Press, we had been busy getting our war correspondents on the job. Reynolds Packard went to Djibouti, the French
cable head; Edward W. Beattie went to Addis Ababa; Webb Miller
went to Italian army headquarters in the field. I had already
strengthened our Rome bureau by the addition of Virgil Pinkley,
who knew Italy and spoke Italian, and had good contacts within the
Fascist government.

It was at an alfresco luncheon on the terrace of Pinkley's pent-
house apartment, on October 2, that we first got definite word of
what was to follow. Present at the luncheon were a group of visiting
correspondents, and several attachés from the United States and
British embassies. As we started our meal, Pinkley was called to
the telephone to speak to a high official of the Fascist party. He
returned with word that the "test mobilization"—the euphemism for
the start of the war with Ethiopia—had been scheduled for three-
thirty that afternoon. It was then after two P.M. The guests made
short work of the viands and wine so they could get back to their
offices before the streets became impassable. But there were a few
doubters at the party, including several correspondents who telephoned their bureaus and came back to say, "Take it easy. My office
says it must be a hoax." I called the UP bureau and put through an
order for two open telephone lines to London—our news headquarters for Europe, and the transmission head for the dispatch of
news all over the world—so that we would still have communications if one line were snatched away from us on the grounds that
"you've had it long enough." Today all the UP offices in Europe are
interconnected by teletype—like the American offices. But we weren't
so completely equipped in those days.

The luncheon broke at a few minutes past three, and we all hurried
to our cars, some still arguing that Pinkley's call had been just
another false alarm. At three-thirty, as Pinkley and I reached the
UP office, the air-raids sirens began howling. I shall never forget
the grin of satisfaction that came over Pinkley's mug when he heard
those sirens, right on the dot.

"In a few minutes," reads my diary for October 2, 1935, "all shops
closed, down came the iron shutters. The shopkeepers changed
quickly into their Blackshirt militia uniforms and hurried to their

places of assembly. The man who had sold you souvenirs or leather goods in the morning was now a soldier with a bayonetted rifle. Flags flew everywhere. Billposters were plastering the walls with mobilization orders and signs proclaiming 'Duce! Duce!'

"Crowds were surging, soldiers marching, and presently bands playing, regimented civilians parading, children singing patriotic songs over the radio, Caproni bombers roaring and swooping over the housetops."

In our London bureau, over the open phone, they could hear the incessant, insistent wail of the sirens, and the Capronis buzzing the city.

By evening, Rome was foaming at the mouth.

That night, Mussolini was to appear on his famous balcony at the Palazzo Venezia, and proclaim a state of war with Ethiopia. I went down to the Piazza Venezia, below the balcony, to get as close as possible to the story. As twilight came, the Piazza was a solid mass of people, all staring expectantly up at the balcony. All around the square, the rooms which commanded a view of the balcony had been pre-empted by expert riflemen, who would keep an eye on Mussolini and on the crowd. Candles burned on the roofs and balustrades of the buildings, giving the scene a theatrical lighting. The air was motionless; the flames from the tall candles burned straight up and never wavered.

My wife and I had pushed well up front toward the balcony, and now found that we couldn't get out again if we wanted to. More and more people were pressing into the plaza, coming down the Corso Umberto and the Via Nazionale. Motorcycle columns forced their way into the mob, the men walking their machines, racing the engines, shoving a path. Torchlight processions came down the streets and jammed in, carrying signs which ridiculed Haile Selassie, England, the League, all opponents of Il Duce. The rumbling mumble of the crowd shifted to a steady cadence chant of "DOO-CHAY! DOO-CHAY! DOO-CHAY!" Our arms were pinioned to our sides by the crush. We did not wish to speak English, which might arouse the hostility of those around us; so, since I had no Italian, we said nothing.

Then Mussolini appeared on the balcony, and the crowd gave a roar with a real "Touchdown!" quality. Everybody who could disengage an arm raised it in the Fascist salute, to which Mussolini responded in kind, glaring around over the immense throng. There was a spotlight on him, but a rather diffuse one, to make sure that he wasn't too sharply etched a target for any marksmen in the neighborhood. Hanging from the balcony was a handsome tapestry bearing the arms of Imperial Rome. Mussolini stood on a slightly raised platform which could not be seen from the street. The platform, his uniform and his dramatic gestures on that small balcony all combined to make him seem much bigger than he really was. As he swung his stern gaze this way and that, arm upraised, bathed in an effulgence from the screams and cheers of the hysterical crowd, he looked impregnable indeed.

He delivered his speech in short bursts, interrupted by deafening roars, during which he set his arms akimbo, popped his eyes, nodded, and wagged his head. Sometimes he leaned over the balustrade, resting his weight on hands spread far apart, stared down at the people just below, and flashed a big, toothy grin. Sometimes he leaned far back and gave a mirthless laugh. He was a powerful orator. He used short, simple, graphic phrases and words, speaking to the masses in language they easily understood. In a speech briefer than had been expected, he said that Italy was going to have its rights, and nobody would be permitted to interfere. He defied the world. He said, "We shall go straight ahead with Geneva (the League of Nations), without Geneva, or against Geneva." But it was not so much what he said that made the great impression; it was the tremendous emotional voltage he generated as he spoke.

The crowd kept cheering after he finished, then finally dispersed, slowly. All night there were shouting groups in the streets, and the air was vibrant with patriotic hysteria.

After Mussolini's speech, a telephone call came into our bureau from one of our best sources in the Foreign Office, who said, "In view of Il Duce's words, this is it. You can go all the way." We filed a dispatch saying that hostilities were imminent between Italy and Ethiopia. And the next morning, shortly before eight o'clock, Rome time, the message came in from Webb Miller, our European manager and chief correspondent, who was up at the border with the Italian army: "The Italian invasion into Ethiopia began shortly after dawn today when Fascist legions poured across the Mareb River. More, Webb Miller."

We filed Miller's report, which was one of the great beats of news-service history, by every conceivable means—over all wire routes and via telephone call to our bureaus in London, Paris, Zurich, Stockholm, and Copenhagen. In addition to the direct calls, we put through a call to London via Berlin. From London, Webb's report went over every route to New York, including those over Siberia and through Buenos Aires.

The reason for the duplication of messages was simple. Our job was to be in New York first with the story, and where communications are involved the shortest distance between two points is not necessarily a straight line. Because there were eleven telephone lines between Rome and Berlin (as part of the Axis hookup), we got our dispatch into Berlin in one minute, though it took twenty-seven minutes before we could get to London on the direct line. Later, we would often send wires from Europe to New York via Buenos Aires, because the cable to Buenos Aires was a rather quiet one, and the lines between Buenos Aires and New York carried much more traffic southbound to the Argentine than northbound to the United States.

On this occasion, nearly forty hours elapsed between the time when New York first received Webb's message and the time the last duplicate came trickling in.

In Ethiopia, Mussolini's war progressed rapidly. The Italians bombed Adua, and Beattie in Addis Ababa sent the first news of the bombing. The Negus protested to the League, which began discussing the matter. In Rome, meanwhile, the shops reopened, the tradesmen hung up their uniforms, and the city settled down to enjoy the war and gloat over Italy's defiance of the League, the British—and the Americans, too, for that matter. Some taxi drivers stopped giving change, on the grounds that there was a war on; this led to some picturesque gesticulatory disputes. The sidewalk cafés were jammed with people eating ices and drinking mild refreshments, and talking with great animation. Bill posters dashed around putting up signs: "Il Duce Has Spoken"; "Adua Is Italian"; "Adua Is Ours." The posters proclaiming "Adua E Nostra" appeared so promptly on the Roman columns it was obvious that they had been printed in advance, anticipating that city's fall. If things were dull, the signs might read, simply, "Duce, Duce, Duce," or they might have no text at all—just colored lithographs of Mussolini's visage, with enlarged jaw and piercing eyes peering from underneath the rim of a helmet.

Our office had been working on getting me a session with Mussolini, and the appointment was now fixed for October 4, at 6:30 P.M. Shortly before that hour, an official car—a sporty Isotta-Fraschini— and a bodyguard of three Fascisti appeared at the Hotel Excelsior to escort me; but I had already started to stroll down to the Palazzo Venezia on foot. When I arrived at the entrance to the palace nobody was expecting me, and there was a flurry while I was identified. During this interval the official car caught up with me, its occupants looking rather outraged.

The two sentries at the gates were members of the redoubtable Alpinieri, with baggy pants and long plumes on their heads, carrying rifles which had remarkably long bayonets. They were cheeky and arrogant, and looked quite ready, almost eager, to stick somebody with that needle bayonet. Inside, I found to my surprise that the place smelled like a cellar, reeking of old masonry, dampness and mold.

I was escorted upstairs by a muscular lackey in full livery, including knee pants, which showed off his football legs in their white stockings. I thought he was probably one of the old castor-oil boys, now semiretired to a soft job at the palace. He deposited me in a very small waiting room, the walls of which were covered with large and black-with-age oil paintings. It was impossible to see what they depicted, because you couldn't stand far enough away from any of them to focus on it. Here I remained for half an hour, hearing nothing and seeing nobody. I have no doubt that there were peepholes in the walls, and that I was thoroughly inspected and observed during the thirty-minute wait. If you're carrying a weapon under such circumstances, it's second nature to pat it occasionally. I don't imagine they thought me an assassin, but no doubt they took all the usual precautions.

At last my muscular footman returned and signaled me to follow him. This time the route lay along several lengthy corridors, narrow and redolent of age. Finally the footman stood aside and threw open the double doors of a ballroom. I entered. There was nobody there. Empty. "What kind of a game is this?" thought I. But the muscle man led on. We traversed the ballroom, end to end, and he threw open the opposite set of great double doors. Another ballroom. And this time, at the far end, Mussolini. Alone.

The walls were covered with tapestries—and behind these hangings, no doubt, were concealed guards who kept a bead on the visitor all the time. There were no furnishings except at Mussolini's end of the room. The dictator sat at a long, antique table, with a solitary, tall, massive candlestick beside him. Before the table was a high-backed brocaded armchair for the visitor. Nothing else. The windows were big and square, and right beside Mussolini's chair was the entrance to the balcony from which he made his speeches.

I crossed the acre of bare floor and drew to a stop in front of Mussolini's desk. He did not look up from his paper work; he just let me stand there. In theory, I suppose, I was supposed to become more and more uneasy as he ignored me. Actually, I took the opportunity to look him over. He seemed a different person from the powerful giant on the balcony. He was bald—a fact which he always hid under a field cap when he made public appearances. He needed a shave. He had a rather lardy look. His brown civilian suit was rumpled, and his forehead was furrowed in a deep scowl.

Then, abruptly, as if suddenly becoming aware of me, Il Duce rose, folded his arms high on his chest, reared his head back and popped his eyes until the whites showed over the irises.

"HAH!" he ejaculated.

This was indeed the full treatment: an incredible performance. For a moment I was incredulous. I wondered whether this could be a Hollywood rib, with laughing pranksters ready to emerge from behind the arras at any moment.

But it was real, and after Mussolini had held that famous pose awhile it even began to work. His gaze was anything but benevolent. The pressure of his magnetism was palpable, even in his disarray. I began to feel as if I were up before a judge, guilty of something or other. . . . Finally I broke the ice—or tried to—by explaining that I had come to pay my respects as president of the United Press. He

thereupon lunged at me with "The United Press! Are you favorable
to us?"

I replied that the United Press was neither favorably nor unfavorably inclined toward Italy. Our interest was in presenting the accurate news of the history he was making, through the newspapers and
radio stations we served. When he heard this, his demeanor became
even more challenging.

"Yes, yes, yes!" he answered impatiently, "But—are—you—in—
favor—of—us?"

He emphasized every word with a jab of the finger. His English,
though I later found it to be limited, was not heavily accented.

"Your excellency," I replied, "I will answer that in this way: we
are favorable to you to the extent that we are not unfavorable to
you. It balances."

This was not, of course, a satisfactory answer to him. Like all
dictators he felt that you were either for him or against him. But
my double-talk apparently persuaded him not to press his point. His
manner eased a trifle, and he waved me to the chair.

As I sat down, I became aware that the visitor's chair was very
low, and Mussolini's chair was high up, so he could perch at his
table and look down on you. He handed me a book entitled *Abyssinia
—White or Black?* and recommended that I read it. Then, gradually
his hostility evaporated, or was masked, and he became almost affable. Like a salesman, he launched into a huckstering pitch on all
the blessings that Italian occupation would bring to Ethiopia—including good roads, irrigation, and modern developments. The Italian
people, he said, needed room to grow. They were reclaiming the
marshes in their own country; they could reclaim the Ethiopian
deserts and colonize them. He thought the British were in an indefensible position when they objected, after they had seized so much
of the earth for themselves. He hoped the United States would have
sense enough to avoid becoming embroiled, because there were so
many Italians living there. But then, of course, he said with a sort
of leer, the United States was run by Wall Street and the plutocrats,
and the people themselves had little to say. He, Mussolini, and his
Blackshirts had saved Italy from the Communists; and he felt the
United States should become better acquainted with the Communist

menace before making things so hard for those who had stood up to it, in the chaos after the last war, and had prevented its spread over Europe.

Many of the things he said made sense, but by the time I saw him he had gone way beyond any original goal of saving Italy from the Communists. He was a megalomaniac. While I was talking with him, some of his bully boys were probably beating on some poor devil's solar plexus with a rubber truncheon, just because the victim had expressed a dislike for the Fascisti. Mussolini was against Communists, all right—and if you didn't like Mussolini, that made you automatically a Communist.

"But just what *is* the sentiment of the United States?" he asked me—and then answered his own question, with a sardonic smile and a wag of the head. "Oh, I know! I know! You are for peace."

He nodded sagely. He had a most maneuverable head. He could and did wiggle it in all directions, to emphasize his meanings.

I asked him about the progress of the campaign in Ethiopia, and he replied, "*You* should be very well acquainted with the military situation, through the dispatches of my old friend Webb Miller. He and I were newspaper reporters together, only a few years ago." He dug into a drawer, and came up with a handful of flimsies, which he waved at me. "Here are Miller's dispatches right from the front. I am keeping close watch on everything that is written. We do not want anything but the truth to come out."

As a matter of fact, the Ministries of Foreign Affairs, War, Aviation and Colonies all sent motorcycle dispatch riders to our bureau office every half hour, to secure copies of our dispatches, which ran hours ahead of the official Italian messages. The United Press thus kept the Italian government informed on its own war, during the opening days of the conflict.

Throughout my conversation with Mussolini there were only two of us in the big room—aside from the soundless and motionless guards behind the tapestries, whose existence I assumed but could not have proved. Il Duce went through other parts of his act as we talked, grimacing and batting his eyes, grinning and then turning off the grin abruptly and frowning fiercely. He was a showoff. But as the time passed he became more and more an ordinary man, soft and overweight, with a yellowish skin. At the end of our palaver he threw his arm around my neck and walked me across the ballroom to the double doors, as though we were old pals.

It was the crowd that made the difference—the crowd that screamed "Doo-CHAY!" and offered him limitless adulation. Later, when I read the description of Mussolini hanging by his heels, in Milan, I thought about that. Because the two crowds—the one in the Piazza Venezia in 1935, the other around that Milan gas station ten years later—were in reality the same crowd.

A few days later, we saw some of Mussolini's heroes on their way to war. They were boarding ships at Naples, and they weren't wearing any fancy uniforms or doing any singing. Compared to the gaudy Fascisti in Rome, they looked liked picked chickens, scrawny and undersized. They were morose specimens, with none of the appearance or manner of the student princes in Rome.

We went down to Naples by train, and we had a compartment to ourselves—except that there was one stranger in it. He entered at the last moment, quietly took a vacant space, opened a book and applied himself to reading it. Through the window, Virgil Pinkley signaled to us with finger on mouth to be careful what we said in the presence of this intruder. So we were discreet. All the way to Naples our fellow traveler read his book, and never turned a page. As we neared our destination, I asked him if he would mind our opening the window. He looked up somewhat startled. I think he was not supposed to know any English, but he forgot about that. "Quite all right," he said, and returned to his page.

I saw two of the other major actors in the Ethiopian crisis that year. In Geneva I watched Anthony Eden—"Lord Eyelashes," they called him in the back corridors at the League—as he fought for sanctions against Italy. And in France I talked to Pierre Laval, then Premier of France, later to be executed as a traitor to France.

Laval was taking credit for averting a general European war, and basking in the warmth of world approval. An earthy type, he was built low and squat, close to the soil, and he looked out of place in the Premier's big, ornate private office at the Quai d'Orsay. There

Field Marshal Montgomery and the author at field headquarters. "I should like to capture Rommel," Monty said, "and spend the afternoon across the table from him, discussing his mistakes." The drawings are Montgomery's own battle maps of Mareth and Alamein.

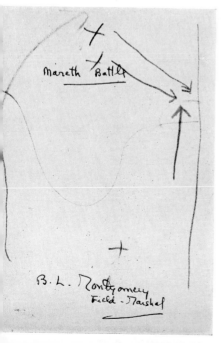

Two aspects of war as seen by a reporter who was also president of a press association. Above, the author entering a field dressing station, after his jeep was caught in a bombardment; right, the author dining with General Omar Bradley at Verdun headquarters.

The Emperor Hirohito. In 1945 he told the author wryly, "We haven't had much time to practice baseball lately."

was no theatricalism whatever in his make-up—he talked in a flatly factual and practical manner and style, even though what he was saying was of massive importance.

He told me with relish how he had acted as a buffer between Mussolini and Britain, eased the crisis in the Mediterranean, and saved the peace of Europe. He said he had been "squeezed hard" between the British and the Italians, but that they had found him "an indigestible morsel." He believed that, as a result, neither the British nor the Italians liked him much at that moment—but their dislike would pass, he felt, when they came to comprehend what they had escaped when, by his efforts, they avoided a European war.

Laval was purring with satisfaction over what he had achieved. Gratification and contentment radiated from him. He was sure he had won a place in history, forever, as a peacemaker. He mentioned that the Pope, in a recent conversation, had said that "Next to God I depend on Pierre Laval." Then he smiled and gestured toward his head as if he were encircling it with a halo, and called my attention to the fact that he had come far up the spiritual echelon since his beginnings as a humble altar boy, drinking up some of the wine after Communion.

Behind his obvious and conscious cunning, he seemed intensely patriotic and eager to serve the best interests of France. And I, for one, think he was always patriotic. When he followed Pétain to Vichy to become Premier of the French government that surrendered to Hitler, he thought he was serving the best interests of France. Like many other experts in 1940, he believed Germany had won the war—and the best thing France could do was adjust to the fact as quickly as possible, and make her own deal. He wasn't happy to see France lose the war (though I suspect he'd have shed no tears over the British losing the war if it hadn't involved France as well). Later, he found he had backed the wrong horse, and he became a scared and therefore willing tool of the Gauleiter in Paris. But it was for his original bad guess, not for his desperate actions at the end, that his countrymen shot him at the stake, as a traitor.

You could say they lynched him, much the way the Milan partisans lynched Mussolini, and you wouldn't be far wrong.

Chapter 8

A HANDFUL OF RUSSIANS

EXCERPTS FROM my diary for the week of November 4–11, 1935:

"Awoke at Warsaw. A dreary-looking city. Cobbled streets, grim stone buildings. The people look shabby, huddled in blankets and hoods.

"All day we poked over the Polish tundra. Saw many farms—thatched roofs, unpainted timbers weathered to a dull grayish tinge; peepholes for windows. Hairy horses drew wains over muddy roads, big droshky collars on them. Some shy at the train—only one train daily. At 6 P.M. we found ourselves in Russia—Soviet sentries with long bayonets. Passport! Passport! Change to Russian train. Clean but antique. Somehow in the transfer all the newspapers and magazines we were carrying in, disappeared. . . .

"Moscow, 11:30 A.M. Bands played, as French and Spanish Communists were aboard. Red flags everywhere, huge photos of Stalin. Busy streets, everybody hurrying, like U.S. People seem to have plenty of zest. Doletzky [head of Tass, the Russian news agency] met us, also Baird [Joe Baird, our Moscow manager]. News photographers snapped us. Put up at National Hotel, clean but museumish. Called at Foreign Office. There's a zip in the air, frosty. In the evening we were guests of honor at a banquet for 100, in the palace of a former rich fur merchant—now the entertainment house of the Foreign Office. I noticed that the waiters were just as obsequious as anywhere else, much more so than most of those in America. . . .

Later visited plant of *Pravda*, official newspaper. Huge. Bed at 3:30
A.M. . . .

"Lunched with Doletzky, another heavy Russian feed, commenc-
ing with vodka. Then Doletzky drove us around the streets of
Moscow. Outside the center, which has been rebuilt in modern style,
and streets widened, the city is an endless and melancholy expanse of
old tumbledown buildings, broken curbs, bumpy cobbles. The crowds
are active and numerous, but the people look shabby—monotonously
so. Concert at night, until 12:30 A.M. . .

"Saw 50,000 Russian troops march through Red Square. Infantry,
cavalry, tanks and artillery. An impressive demonstration. The tanks
raced through the Square at 40 MPH. No airplanes, as the clouds
hung low, but the masses with floats and symbols in incredibly large
numbers marched through the Square for hours. This was the anni-
versary of what is called in Russia the 'October Revolution.' . . .

"With Joe Baird, drove into the country. A drizzly day. Saw several
towns, dismal, muddy, depressing. Decaying wooden houses, some
at crazy angles, moss-grown roofs, mud roads, sodden people.

"Attended opera, *Eugene Onegin,* with Doletzky at the Bolshoi.
We sat in box in what used to be their Diamond Horseshoe. . . . The
audience was most appreciative, in their drab clothing, women in
sweaters. Between the acts there was a break for 'refreshments' which
sometimes consisted of quite a meal. Some of those in the boxes
ate apples and onions during the performance, which was excellent. . . .

"Called on Doletzky at Tass, a formal call. Called on Press and
Publishers' Syndicates, for business sessions. Then drove into country
with Baird, to weekend 'dascha' of one of the U.S. attachés. Muddy
roads, dim lights, barking dogs. Russia. Dined at the Metropole,
decaying grandeur. . . .

"Nobody would think this was Sunday, here in Red Moscow. All
was business-as-usual. Called on Ambassador Bullitt. . . . Strolled
through Red Square and around the Kremlin. Most awesome in the
thin winter sunlight . . . A formal lunch started at 3:30 P.M. Attended music hall. The people seated near us looked at us curiously,
and our guide told us we were too dressed up. . . .

"Visited the Kremlin. Had to wait an hour to get in, despite our special passes, as the red tape was thick. We were followed around by the Superintendent of the Museums, and two soldiers with rifles. . . ."

Virtually everyone I saw in Russia during that whirlwind tour is now dead, and most of them were dead or as good as dead within a year or two of my departure. Molotov, who was one of the least human of the lot, lasted the longest. (He received me in 1935 for the purpose of reading me a long, humorless statistical report on the improvement of highways and schools in Russia under the Bolsheviks.) Nobody had the guts to do anything to Stalin, of course, until after he was dead. I never actually met him, though I interviewed him later by cable, and I saw him on this trip from a distance, while he reviewed the big parade. There were definitely two Stalins on this occasion—one the military figure in uniform with visored kepi and sharp salute as each company of troops marched past, snapped eyes right and uttered their long roaring cheer; the other, the pleasant Papa of all the people, who donned an ordinary cap as the peasants started by, and waved benevolently at the masses carrying banners and riding on floats. It was difficult indeed to learn anything about Stalin in 1935. He made few public appearances, and lived a remote, mysterious life in a palace outside of town. When he passed through the streets he was hidden behind curtains of his Rolls-Royce. And when people mentioned his name, they spoke in awed and hushed tones.

In all of these totalitarian countries, it could be unwise to mention the name of the dictator. We rarely spoke Mussolini's name in Rome, for example; instead, we referred to "Mr. Dean," or "Mr. Deems." But I doubt that the secret police were thrown off the track by our euphemism. We always assumed that everyone who drove us around, or waited on our table, or cleaned our room, was a government agent, who reported back to the authorities everything we said and did. Later I was to receive a detailed confirmation of that assumption, at last so far as Nazi Germany was concerned. In Russia, I was once kept waiting at a government office when I was on my way *out*, after an interview with a very important personage. An attendant escorted

me downstairs to the main lobby, smiled and departed; I took hold
of the doorknob and found that the door was locked. Two soldiers
(one of whom looked Mongolian) appeared and removed me from
the main lobby to a small side room, where I waited while a lot of
telephoning was done. Then the soldiers let me go.

The parade in Red Square, by the way, impressed us more than
it impressed the American military attaché. He was especially scorn-
ful of the tank which rushed through Red Square with a rattling,
banging noise. It was, he informed me, a Christie tank, made in
Rahway, New Jersey—and he had no reason to believe the Russians
would be any good at making or using tanks on their own account. . . .

Four of the most prominent participants in the round of parties
we attended were purged shortly thereafter. One of them was Marshal Tukhachevsky, a man of striking appearance, wearing a number
of the new red-enamel medals which the Communist state had
originated for its heroes. I was told he was the smartest general in
the Russian army . . . but soon he was just a "conspirator," in the
dock, facing a phony trial. Krishtinsky of the Foreign Affairs Commissariat was another, a man in thick-lensed glasses, with a voracious
appetite. I remember him mopping up the ice cream on his plate,
using a biscuit into which had been baked a cabbage leaf. He was
liquidated, too, after recanting his confession and then recanting his
recantation—presumably after he was told what would happen to
him if he didn't. Doletzky didn't live to be tried: he committed
suicide, they said, as the secret police broke into his room to pick him
up.

The most likable of these candidates for imminent disappearance
was the "old Bolshevik" Karl Radek. At the reception given by
Foreign Commissar Litvinov, which presented the usual diplomatic
spectacle of white tie and tails, gold lace, beautiful women, expensive gowns, caviar and champagne, Radek showed up in a soft and
rather soiled shirt, and a loose tie, smoking a smelly hod pipe. I told
him that he seemed to be the only true "old Bolshevik" in the room.

"I vill tell you," he replied, grinning impishly with snaggled teeth.
"I vill still be wearing this attire ven vite ties and vite vests are gone

out of style here." But he was wrong. Soon he was in Siberia, serving what was supposed to be a ten-year sentence, and he hasn't been heard from since.

Ambassador Bullitt was up on all these questions of how well or badly people were doing with Stalin. An aristocrat from an old Philadelphia family, with all the appearance and appurtenances of inherited position and wealth, he was very popular with the Russians: just what they expected of an ambassador from the capitalist West. Bullitt had been an early advocate of recognizing the Soviet government, and as our first ambassador to the Bolsheviki he had arrived with very friendly feelings. By now, he was pretty disillusioned. I sat next to him at one of the banquets and he identified all the guests for me, adding a judgment of their current status. Radek, he said, was "on very thin ice." Speaking of the Commissar for Foreign Affairs, Maxim Litvinov, who had negotiated with Franklin Roosevelt our recognition of the Soviet government, Bullitt said, "I wouldn't trust him with a feather off a dead chicken." He also gave me a piece of personal advice: the Moscow hospitals were terrible, so "don't get pneumonia while you're here. The first-class medicines are only for the members of the party."

One of my most interesting hours in Moscow was spent at Litvinov's office. We got from the National Hotel to Litvinov in a hurry, because the limousine he sent for me (driven by a uniformed chauffeur) was equipped with a special horn. The sound of that horn made the traffic cops clear the way, and made the moujiks jump for their lives, as we raced through the streets.

Moscow was then moving into one of its "popular front" phases, and the pleasant countenance was turned to all the world (except Germany). There was however, some question about the continuing operations of the Comintern, the headquarters staff of international Bolshevik revolution. It was generally believed that the Litvinov-Roosevelt recognition pact had included an agreement whereby the Comintern would be discontinued. I asked Litvinov about this.

"Nothing of the sort," he said. "I had no agreement with Roosevelt concerning the Comintern. As a matter of fact, we have no control over the Comintern, anyway. We don't run it. And the first word I had that it was going to hold a congress in Moscow came from your own Ambassador, Mr. Bullitt. When he told me this, I knew nothing about it, and telephoned Stalin. He said he had heard nothing either, but would call me back. When he did so, he said he had made inquiries and ascertained that Bullitt was right. The Comintern actually *was* going to have an international convention, right here in Moscow."

Litvinov told me this story with a straight face, and I had to mask my incredulity, because one of the gravest breaches of courtesy in Russia is to let the other fellow know that you know he's lying. He may have no doubt about it, but you aren't supposed to show it. That's rude.

Like so many other foreign statesmen, Litvinov asked me to explain why the Americans were still suspicious of the Russians. I told him that one of the reasons was the censorship. Americans believe that any country with a peacetime censorship must have something to hide.

"In a country like Russia," Litvinov replied smoothly in his perfect English, "where everything is controlled by the State, the State must inferentially accept responsibility for the news which goes out through its facilities to the outside world. Therefore, in order to insure that nothing but the truth shall go out, we have a censorship to make sure that the correspondents don't make any mistakes. We never suppress any true news."

Again, I failed to be impolite.

Litvinov was another "old Bolshevik," and in his office he wore a leather jacket and corduroy pants. But he also knew when to put on the white tie and tails—and he knew better than to talk out of turn about the manners and customs of the regime. So he survived—though he died in obscurity, he died in bed. He had a genial demeanor, which he had developed through years of diplomacy in various posts overseas. He was one of the few men in Moscow who had ever been off the Continent. So when we made our adieux they were cordial. He probably knew I didn't believe everything he had said—but, then, he thought I wasn't telling him the unvarnished truth, either. What was important was that the courtesies had been preserved.

Only once did I find myself violating the courtesies—and then it was a matter of simple ignorance. At Russian banquets then as now, it was the custom to drink a wide variety of toasts. I proposed one to Karl Bickel, a former president of the United Press, who was at that time home in the United States, and after the toast I suggested that we collaborate on a cable conveying our greetings to him. The Russians knew Bickel; he had traveled throughout Russia frequently, on his own recognizance (before American recognition of the Soviet government, U.S. passports were not valid for travel in Russia), and he had arranged our exchange-of-news contract with Tass. It was no trouble at all to get everyone's signature on a cheery message to him, and everything went well until I suggested that we conclude it with the word "Tovarioh." At this, a sudden hush fell over the members of Tass who were sitting around the table. And Doletzky, after a moment's hesitation, shook his head and said solemnly, "No, no, Mr. Baillie. 'Tovarich' is only for members of The Party." He glanced apprehensively over his shoulder as he spoke. So we didn't hail Bickel as "Tovarich."

At another of these overwhelming Russian lunches I found myself sitting near Constantine Oumansky, who was at that time chief censor in Moscow. He worked throughout the meal, censoring dispatches, and he was having trouble with his pen. I offered to swap my pen for his, giving him far the better of the deal but getting me a remarkable souvenir: the Russian censor's pen. I told him I would mount it on a red velvet background, and exhibit it on the wall of my office in New York, with his photograph beside it. A few months later, he called on me in New York, and asked whether I had ever put his pen on view. I told him that I hadn't got around to it. He said, "I'm glad you haven't done it, Hugh, and please don't." Then he whispered, "It would not be understood."

That was the phrase everyone used in Moscow, to steer you away from mistakes, or to explain why you couldn't say something: "It would not be understood."

Later, Oumansky became Soviet Ambassador to the United States, and I saw him occasionally in Washington. He was a lively, attractive personality, even though he was undoubtedly a spy. He had cocked eyebrows, which gave him a satanic expression. When I first called on him as Ambassador, I was ushered into a gold-paneled chamber by a footman in the most formal livery. One of the panels slid open in the wall, and the Ambassador entered. We shook hands; and then, through the panel, to my surprise, came a small procession of other functionaries. They were all smiles, and there was much handshaking and introducing. Sherry and caviar were served.

Then, suddenly, Oumansky looked very sore, and announced that the American government had cut him off from his home newspapers, and they were being burned in "Washington, U.S.A.," as propaganda. This, he said, was "very serious." His eyes blazed. He said they had told him he could get *Pravda* only if its editor in Moscow would register in Washington as a propagandist. "This is how we are treated!" he exclaimed. All hands joined in denouncing this insult—some of them in Russian—while we were eating the caviar and drinking the sherry.

Later, we proceeded to a luncheon room, where the familiar fine Russian repast was served and toasts were drunk in vodka. We then sat awhile talking in Oumansky's private office, and he poured brandy made from grapes grown on the slopes of Mount Ararat, where Noah's Ark landed after the Flood. He showed me the bottle. Finally, we proceeded to another chamber, which had been transformed into a movie theater. There we saw Russian propaganda films, including a parade through Red Square. There was a stimulating musical score, in which I detected "Hail, Columbia!" I called Oumansky's attention to the fact that he had swiped an American tune. He said it was of Russian origin. . . .

Oumansky wasn't present at the last reception I attended at the Russian embassy, just before the war. He had been called home "for consultations." His wife was on the receiving line, looking scared. Oumansky never came back to Washington; instead, he was assigned to Mexico, where he died, not long after, in a plane crash.

I always wondered about that plane crash—Russian Ambassador's plane, containing Oumansky, his wife, their secretary and two Mexican aviators. Nobody ever did find out what had caused it, and rumors of sabotage were in the air. From his Mexican embassy, Oumansky was directing Russian espionage work throughout Mexico and Central America, so lots of people might have had a reason to want him dead. My own guess, however, has always been that his own government got him: like so many of his friends and companions in Moscow, he had somehow done something that "would not be understood."

We had been fed so many lavish meals in Moscow that I thought it appropriate for the United Press to tender a farewell dinner just before we went to the train. The invitations were accepted—though only on condition that we would first attend a farewell luncheon which they would give. They had been very enthusiastic about their meals—"You must eat this," they would say, "this is *Russian*"; and then you had to eat it and exclaim about its tastiness, because they were eager for approbation. So we decided we would give them a real American dinner, including Martinis, roast beef and apple pie.

The farewell luncheon lasted so long that we had barely finished our brandies when we had to hurry to the United Press bureau, the scene of our party, and start on the Martinis. After the dinner, we were escorted to the train by all our guests, most of whom were somewhat the worse for wear. The other Americans in the party were singing "Anchors Aweigh." We said farewell to Moscow at the door of a compartment so stuffed with flowers we could hardly get into it to get to bed.

That was a long and tiring night, on hard bunks in a compartment that was apparently airtight. The Russian trains were pre-Czar, and as full of creaks and groans as a ship in a heavy sea. We never made much speed, but as we rounded some of the curves I thought we were in danger of shucking the superstructure into the adjacent fields.

The next day we pulled into the border station between Russia and Poland. There was a brass band playing deafeningly in the station, one spirited march after another. The leader of the band was a happy-looking Russian who carried two pistols hanging in holsters from his belt, as he flourished his baton. Several members of the band were also armed—as though they feared that their music might incite an audience to violence.

Our baggage was immune from customs inspection, because we were under diplomatic courtesy, so we had plenty of time to watch what was happening to the others. One man who was carrying toilet paper with him (a wise precaution, in Eastern Europe) fell under suspicion; the Russian guards unwrapped the entire roll, in a search for hidden documents, and left their victim sitting disconsolately on a bench, enmeshed in toilet paper. A girl who had a book of crossword puzzles really stopped traffic for a while, because the inspectors thought it must be a code of some sort. She made the mistake of laughing at them, whereupon they ripped her book apart.

Our most distinguished passenger was the novelist Kathleen Norris, en route West on a trip around the world. She was especially worried about her cat, Piper, which spent most of his time curled up in a hat and made the whole trip with her. The cat had insufficient papers (you need a lot of documentation, attesting to the animal's health, if you want to take a pet across national boundaries), and Mrs. Norris was afraid he might be seized at the frontier. But she got him past both Russian and Polish inspectors by waving an old vaccination certificate in their faces—holding it upside down.

She was less fortunate with her luggage during the exit search. When I saw one of the inspectors remove the battery and bulb from her flashlight, and peer through it like a telescope, looking for a concealed message, I told our young Russian escort (who was still standing with us) that his people seemed to be giving a quite unnecessary workout to one of the best-known authors in the United States. I suggested that he pass the word. He was a very polite and charming young man who spoke perfect American (which he said he had learned without ever leaving the Soviet Union), so he stepped over and conveyed this tip to the searchers—who thereupon redoubled their attack on Mrs. Norris' luggage.

Finally, reluctantly, they let her pass to the train which would carry us away from the Soviet Union. She marched over to the German Mitropa cars with a suitcase in each hand and her hat over one eye, singing "My Country 'Tis of Thee." Though we hadn't shared her experiences, we definitely shared her sentiments.

Chapter 9

THE KING AND MRS. SIMPSON

"HELLO," SAID the voice on my cabin telephone on the *Queen Elizabeth* in mid-Atlantic. "This is the Duke of Windsor speaking. Would you and Mrs. Baillie like to drop in for a drink with the Duchess and me this afternoon?"

It was a simple invitation: the voice had no peremptory quality whatever. The former King Edward VIII was now a private citizen. In the daytime, a tweedy sort; at night, very correct, in evening dress or black tie. If there was any single attitude that seemed to hang over him, it was not a royal habit of command, but a hapless boredom, relieved only by the presence of the woman he loved.

As we entered the large cabin occupied by the Duke and Duchess, the former King and Emperor was lounging in the big window seat of his suite, in sports clothes, smoking a pipe. His wife was sitting in a deep chair beside him, reading. She was informally dressed, in olive-green cardigan and sweater, a russet skirt, alligator pumps and handbag. Her only jewels were gold-and-ruby earrings. They both got up and came forward to shake hands, and made us feel most welcome.

The Duchess mixed Martinis. I took a highball. The Duke, however, never had a drink before 7 P.M. On the wall was a typical ship's clock, which should in theory have been synchronized with all the other clocks on the *Elizabeth*. But it was fifteen minutes slow: it was Windsor's "whiskey clock." After he had seen that his guests were served, the Duke began to glance impatiently at the clock. When it registered five minutes before the hour, he chucked aside his pipe and said, "The devil with the whiskey clock! I'm going to have a Scotch and splash." Which he did.

We discussed books and politics, in a detached sort of way, though this was just before the war, when not many people felt detached from the political situation. The Duke turned out to be a voracious reader; he knew exactly what was inside every book we mentioned. He was returning from a visit to London, and he spoke with pride of "the King, my brother." Meanwhile, the Duchess chattered along, speaking of the differences between running a household in France and in America.

Both of them were small. In fact, when I first had occasion to stand talking to the Duke, he impressed me as almost a miniature man—perfectly proportioned, but surprisingly small. The Duchess matches him here, as she does in so many other ways. They seemed content, relaxed and easy; suffering, no doubt, from lack of occupation, but used to it by now. Looking at them, it was hard to remember and realize the trials and sneers they had endured in the not-far-distant past.

A couple of days later, at 6 A.M., we docked in New York. These 6 A.M. dockings are terrible headaches. The press swarms on board, the baggage is hustled out of the staterooms, and you find yourself unhoused. The Duke and Duchess were, inevitably, summoned to meet the press, which was massed in the Garden Room of the great liner—reporters, photographers, newsreel cameramen. Preceded by a plain-clothes man, the Windsors came casually down the corridor, heading for their ordeal-by-interview. The Duke saw us, took his pipe out of his mouth, smiled and bowed. And the Duchess widened her expressive eyes and said brightly, "Here I go to have my appendix out!"

They are nice people. Human. Very. And, apparently, they have never blamed the King's forced abdication on "the gangsters and hooligans of the American press"—as the London *Daily Mirror* had done in the final days of the great constitutional crisis a few years before.

What the *Daily Mirror* meant by this piece of editorializing was that in America Edward's love affair with Mrs. Simpson and clash with his ministers had been played out on center stage, in that white spotlight which surrounds the activities of a king. In Britain, however, only a handful of people knew anything about it until the crisis had got out of hand and the King's brief reign (his father had died less than eleven months before) was at its end. The newspapers were dark. The radio was silent. There was no gossip among the citizenry —and in those circles which knew the story, talking about Edward and his lady was simply "not done."

Shortly before leaving New York for Britain, in 1936, I had gone to the theater and heard Ethel Merman sing that it was foolish for her to get the vapors when she heard in the papers that Mrs. Simpson dined behind the throne, because Ethel had a cute king of her own. Miss Merman put this out with her customary whambo-zambo and the engulfing laughter showed that the whole audience knew what she was singing about. Everywhere outside the British Isles, this was the Romance of the Century. Readers of newspapers waited for Mrs. Simpson to get her divorce, and wondered what would happen thereafter.

But in Britain—nothing. I arrived in London on November 12, 1936. The days were short, the weather murky. It was rainy and foggy, and the air smelled smoky. But the gloom was no thicker than the British public's ignorance of the King's romance with Mrs. Simpson.

The great majority of Britishers had never even heard the name of Wallis Simpson. When you spoke about the King's romance on Fleet Street, you were answered with a hesitancy and delicacy suggesting that the subject itself bordered on bad taste. There was no conceivable way of finding out what people thought about the situation, because people didn't know about the situation. Our reporters, covering the story, felt themselves immersed in a vast quilt of silence. Our men were never "pack" reporters. They went with the pack to press conferences and the like, because they wanted to be sure they didn't miss anything, but they relied more on their own sources— which were sometimes so confidential only the top executives knew who the sources were. But in the abdication crisis most sources ran dry. Those on the inside of the situation wouldn't talk, and people who weren't very much on the inside didn't even know a situation existed.

In the windows of Dorothy Wilding's fashionable photography studio on Bond Street, right at eye level where pedestrians could scarcely miss it, there hung a portrait of Mrs. Simpson holding a little dog on her shoulder. Nobody stopped to look at it: nobody knew who the woman was. When Mrs. Simpson was divorced from Commander Ernest Simpson in Ipswich, the event was covered by the American press with direct wires and crack reporters—and the good people of Ipswich wondered what all the excitement was about.

Shortly after my arrival, I began taking steps to intensify our coverage of the story, and some of our friends in Fleet Street suggested that we go easy. We were sending tons of material—pictures of Mrs. Simpson, and stories about the gifts he gave her, and think pieces about "could it be done?" I had lunch with Sir Roderick Jones, chairman of Reuter's, and General Anderson, head of Exchange Telegraph —the two big British news agencies. They were reticent, but I came away with the impression that Edward would have to give up Mrs. Simpson or abdicate. Also that the news reports we were sending to the American press and on the American radio weren't helping the situation. The position was, as the British say, "delicate." It was hoped that if publicity were avoided, the whole affair could still be "tidied up," without any incidents that might reflect on the dignity and sanctity of the throne.

Yet it may have been the very absence of publicity which made Edward's position hopeless. His Prime Minister, Baldwin, was after his scalp. The Archbishop of Canterbury unquestionably regarded him as unsuited for the role of Defender of the Faith (one of the King's titles). With such enemies working against him under cover of press secrecy, the King's position was little better than that of some of his distinguished ancestors, languishing in the Tower at the command of ambitious rivals, while the unlettered loons and varlets of the day remained ignorant of the proceedings against their sovereign.

Toward the end of November, the King involved himself in a serious tactical mistake. Esmond Harmsworth of the London *Daily Mail* had suggested to Mrs. Simpson at a lunch in Claridge's that a mor-

ganatic marriage might be the way out of the impasse. Edward made
this suggestion a matter of policy, presenting it to Baldwin as a formal request. Baldwin sent the request out to the Dominions, phrasing
it in such a way as to indicate his own disapproval, and the rejection
was unanimous. Meanwhile, Mrs. Simpson, speaking at a private
party to a woman she thought was a personal friend, had let slip
word of her hopes that she might become Edward's wife even though
not, in title, Queen of Britain. The next day, to Mrs. Simpson's hurt
amazement, a story about her proposal for a morganatic marriage
was on the news wires all over the world—except in the British Isles.

By the end of November, the news blackout in Britain was beginning to fray at the edges, and it seemed likely that the British public
would soon see the light. On December 1, the Right Reverend A. W.
F. Blunt, Bishop of Bradford, gave the publishers their excuse for
breaking the silence. In a speech at a parochial meeting on the subject of Edward's approaching coronation, he commented that in his
opinion "the King stood in need of God's grace." Exactly what he
meant by this, nobody knew. He may have intended nothing more
than a criticism of the King's failure to attend church services. It is
still considered possible that the Bishop did not, in fact, know about
the King's romance with an American divorcée. But his statement
was printed in the provincial newspapers. On December 2, returning
from a brief trip to France and Holland (where the King's romance
was a prime topic of conversation), I found a small crowd gathered
on the sidewalk outside No. 10 Downing Street, watching government ministers arrive and depart. Always the sign of a crisis in Britain.

The next day the full story broke in London—announced first with
placards reading, sedately, "The King and His Ministers." The *Daily
Mirror*, later to condemn the American press for its handling of the
crisis, was the first to throw off discretion, printing a picture of the
King's intended and posting red-letter bills which screamed "The
King and Mrs. Simpson." People read the news in open-mouthed
astonishment. Webb Miller, then our head man in Europe, said that
the air in London had not been so electric with shock and apprehen-
sion since the German breakthrough in 1918.

On December 4 Baldwin announced in Parliament that the government would not introduce legislation authorizing a morganatic marriage for Edward. Mrs. Simpson left England and went to France. Rumors and speculations on abdication filled the news columns. The King was in seclusion in Fort Belvedere, his favorite among the royal houses, accepting visits only from the Prime Minister and from two or three very close friends—who were not, however, men of great influence in the nation.

For several days King and country marked time, a situation formalized on December 7 by Baldwin's statement in Commons that everything would have to wait until the King made up his mind. In Cannes, Mrs. Simpson said that she would withdraw from the picture rather than cause any trouble.

The next evening my wife and I went to the theater, and noted that at the conclusion of the show the audience simply departed. This was against all custom. Almost invariably, when a stage presentation ended, "God Save the King" was played by the orchestra (or a phonograph record, if there was no orchestra in attendance), while the audience stood. The omission of the national anthem struck us as an ominous sign.

On Wednesday, December 9, the United Press carried a dispatch saying it seemed certain that the King would abdicate. I had previously turned back two similar stories, one from Webb Miller with Beaverbrook as source, the other from Fred Kuh with members of the diplomatic corps as source. I knew the sources were good, but I couldn't be absolutely certain-sure the King wasn't going to change his mind. The story we finally carried came from Tosti Russell, one of our principal reporters in England, who had accompanied Queen Ena of Spain on her flight from her homeland some years before. Russell was a hawklike man with a black mustache, who worked out of his home and showed up at the office only once every two weeks or so. He still saw Ena from time to time, and she saw considerable of the Royal Family. She had given Russell several previous scoops from inside the court, and all of them had stood up.

At 2 A.M. December 9, our office called Harry Flory, who was in charge of the crisis coverage, and told him Russell had just submitted a story that the King had irrevocably decided to abdicate. Flory called Russell at his home to ask the source of his information, and

Russell told him in confidence that it was, once again, Queen Ena. Ena's record of dependability was good enough for Flory, and acting on his own authority he told the bureau to shoot. This took guts. The result was a worldwide beat.

Flory and I did not have long to sweat. Later that day confirmation of the news began pouring in from all quarters, and we passed it on over the facilities of the Commercial Cable Company. On December 10 the abdication statement was read in Commons by Speaker FitzRoy, and Baldwin made a speech about his efforts to patch up the King's problems. To handle this traffic, we had two transatlantic telephone lines. Commons was unemotional, receiving the news with traditional stoicism, and the public seemed equally calm. The general feeling seemed to be one of regret that Edward had "let us down." At that moment he appeared to have very few friends in Britain.

On December 11 the Abdication Bill passed both houses, becoming law at 1:52 P.M. Edward (now Prince Edward) broadcast to the English-speaking world his statement that he could not go on as King without "the woman I love." He called on all to be loyal, and concluded with:

"God bless you all. God save the King!"

It was very Churchillian. Churchill (who was a "King's Man") probably wrote it. But people were not moved—or, at least, they seemed not to be moved. I saw a large crowd standing before 145 Piccadilly, the new King's residence before he moved into Buckingham Palace across the way. There were a couple of bobbies before the building, but there was nothing for them to do. (Strangely enough, this rather narrow building at 145 Piccadilly was the only one in its row demolished by a German bomb in 1940. The bomb extracted this one house as neatly as a dentist extracts one bicuspid.)

On December 12 the new King was proclaimed with the customary brave show, and Edward left for France, en route to Switzerland, abroad the destroyer *Fury*. On the day of the proclamation I heard the Guards bands march down Birdcage Walk, all of them playing "The Stars and Stripes Forever." Regiment after regiment, the whole Guards brigade swung along, and the strains of Sousa's stirring air floated across St. James's Park. It seemed incongruous, considering that an American woman had just caused an abdication. But I don't suppose anyone else realized the curious connotation of the march. I did, and phoned the story.

During the days of tension leading to the abdication, much of our most reliable information was obtained from Lord Beaverbrook, who liked and trusted Webb Miller. To protect his identity, we referred to Beaverbrook only as "The Source," and only two or three of us knew who "The Source" might be. All communication with Beaverbrook was by telephone, from pay stations outside the office. No names were ever mentioned on the phone. If an indiscreet question was asked, Beaverbrook hung up in your ear. This close connection with so reliable a friend kept us on the track without wobbling through days when an error would have been easy.

Shortly after the abdication, Beaverbrook and I were fellow passengers on the German liner *Bremen* en route to New York. I remember him coming along the corridor, hunched up in a tuxedo and wearing an air even more impish than usual. He invited me into his cabin to meet the playwright Frederick Lonsdale. We all had a drink, and then I asked Lord Beaverbrook to tell me the story, the inside story, of the abdication and of the press blackout which had preceded it.

There was a fierce sea outside, and the ship rolled, pitched and creaked. Occasionally we all had to grab the furniture to keep from being dumped onto the heaving floor. Lonsdale impassively sipped his drink, his face a blank. Beaverbrook sat crouched in his tux, looking like a gnome, and talked.

The question of newspaper publicity became urgent, he told us, in October, 1936, when Mrs. Simpson's petition for divorce was due to be heard. The King feared that the divorce proceedings would occasion an outbreak of sensationalism in the British press, and on October 16 he asked Beaverbrook, who was one of his Privy Councillors, to come to Buckingham Palace. He told Beaverbrook that Mrs. Simpson, seeking a divorce, should in his opinion be treated like any other American citizen. The divorce would occasion no more than an announcement on an inside page, if the lady were not an intimate in court circles. It would be unjust to pillory her on that account, the King suggested, and exceedingly embarrassing to the King himself. Beaverbrook replied that the King's contention was reasonable and that he would try to do what was asked.

That same night, Beaverbrook said, he was visited by Sir Samuel Hoare, who had been sent by Baldwin to say that the government was unanimous with the Prime Minister in opposing the romance between the King and Mrs. Simpson. Hoare tried to persuade Beaverbrook that there should be a press campaign against the divorce and against any possibility of a marriage. But Beaverbrook answered that he had "taken the shilling"—an old army term from the days when each new recruit was given a shilling to bind his enlistment in the King's service.

Beaverbrook spoke with Harmsworth of the *Daily Mail*, (now Lord Rothermere), and they called a meeting of the London and provincial press at Warwick House, Harmsworth's residence. The meeting responded sympathetically to the suggestion that the King's friendship with Mrs. Simpson was strictly a part of his private life. Beaverbrook and Harmsworth received unanimous promises of co-operation. Papers in Dublin and Belfast, Beaverbrook told me, were then invited by telephone to concur in the decision, and did so.

In November, Beaverbrook's doctors advised him that his asthma made it urgent for him to spend the winter in Arizona, and he sailed for America on the *Bremen*. While he was on ship, the King began to feel the need for a sympathetic adviser; by cable and by telephone he asked Beaverbrook to return. As a Privy Councillor, Beaverbrook was bound in duty to honor the request.

There was no transatlantic passenger air service in 1936; the best Beaverbrook could do was turn around with the *Bremen*. He arrived in Southampton on November 26 and went directly to the King at Fort Belvedere. There he learned of the King's audience with Baldwin at which Edward authorized the Prime Minister to submit to the Cabinet the idea of a morganatic marriage. Beaverbrook was appalled. He said that such a solution would not be acceptable to the Cabinet or to the people. He urged delay, and told the King that the proposal of a morganatic marriage should be pulled back promptly, to prevent an unfavorable reaction before the King's friends could submit his case to the public.

On his return to London, Beaverbrook learned that the morganatic marriage idea had already been dispatched to the Dominion governments. He told me how he urged the King to move immediately to cancel the messages. But the King felt it was too late for him to take such a step: he had made his mistake, and he would have to live with it.

On December 1, Beaverbrook telephoned Edward and read him a news-agency report on the speech by the Bishop of Bradford. He told the King that the news silence could not be maintained. Edward then asked Beaverbrook whether the *Daily Express* would editorialize on the situation. Beaverbrook advised the King that the first public reaction was bound to be negative—and that the criticism could not be halted unless the King allowed his friends among the publishers to counterattack strongly and promptly. Edward disagreed. He said he didn't want a newspaper controversy that might divide the country. Beaverbrook could not sway him from this position.

Later the King telephoned Beaverbrook again and told him that he'd had another session with Baldwin and that retirement seemed to be the only way out. Edward was still hoping that some favorable development would make such drastic action unnecessary—but he was determined to marry, even if it cost him the throne.

After the abdication, the British press was severely criticized for its long and unanimous silence—a silence that could have been caused, it was said, only by government censorship or by collusion among the publishers. Beaverbrook told me he felt that the criticism was unjustified. There had never, he said, been any official or unofficial censorship of the British press or of any Dominion or foreign correspondent. The government, had, in fact, sought publicity against the King. The sovereign had argued that his privacy should be respected by the press. The precedents for privacy went back to Victorian times, and the press in following the King's wishes had merely "come down on the side of tradition."

The royal family, Beaverbrook pointed out, are compelled to live their lives in the glare of publicity and to undertake public engagements of a fatiguing and tedious kind. In return, they have a right to expect every assistance from the press in preserving their dignity. They have no means of defending themselves from public criticism.

Responsible proprietors and editors, therefore, were united in considering that the King's friendship with Mrs. Simpson did not offer a suitable topic for newspaper comment or gossip—as long as it was only a part of his private life.

The King's marriage was another question, raising constitutional issues of great importance. Such issues could not have been debated in the press, however, until the King's intentions were established. When it became clear that the marriage was a subject of complete disagreement between the King and his ministers, Beaverbrook added, journalists were no longer pledged to silence.

So the press blackout ended in a withering blast of publicity—to which the King would not allow any reply by his friends.

An extremely resourceful man, and a powerful personality in the kingdom, Beaverbrook was clearly the best campaign manager Edward could have chosen. But events moved too fast for him. Certainly, he would never have left the country if he had known how imminent the crisis was. He seemed somewhat impatient at some of the things the King had done while he was away. Once in our conversation, he alluded to his former sovereign as "Edward the Departed," indicating, I felt, an irritation at the King's mistakes. By pushing too hard while Beaverbrook's back was turned, he implied, Edward had fallen into a trap laid for him by his Prime Minister and the Archbishop of Canterbury.

Beaverbrook seemed to feel that Edward, by handling himself better in November, might have retained his throne without giving up Mrs. Simpson—although I don't think Beaverbrook ever saw her as Queen. Beaverbrook's strategy had been to stay quiet and, as an American would put it, play for the breaks. But the King, it seemed, wanted action. And Edward of all people should have known better than to expect success from the strategy he followed. He was familiar with the Constitution, with the traditions and *verbotens* that surround the British royal family. As Prince of Wales, he had carried the flag all over the world, to the enhancement of Britain's prestige and the enrichment of her trade. Gay, debonair, magnetic, he had fulfilled his duty everywhere, in many lands. Some said he was fed up with being King.

Personally, on reviewing my time in England, I felt that Edward's position had always been impossible—with good or bad advice, with or without neatly laid traps. The King could never have married Mrs. Simpson, whether she was called "Queen" or "Royal Duchess" or anything else. The resentment against such a marriage came not only from the so-called upper classes, but also in very large measure from the middle and what in another time would have been called the lower classes. It came from the people who went to the pub of an evening to get their pint of bitter, and to look at the gaudy lithograph of the monarch over the bar. The King is a symbol of Britain itself; and such symbols cannot marry divorcées.

The attitude was vividly expressed by our room waiter at the Park Lane Hotel a few days after the abdication story broke. My wife asked him, as he was fetching our breakfast, what all the excitement was about; she asked whether the opposition to Mrs. Simpson was based on the fact that she was an American. The waiter hotly denied any such idea. "That's not it at all!" he protested. "She has two husbands living, madam! How can we have a Queen with two other husbands living?"

Chapter 10

PEACE IN OUR TIME

I MADE four trips to Berlin in that ominous fourth decade of this century.

In 1930 the Germans were *gemütlich* and peaceable, done with war forever. Veterans apologized for their military service, and made fun of the Kaiser.

In 1932 the policemen walking their beats under Von Papen's "state of siege" were soldiers disguised, and militarism was rising once again. The political parties had organized paramilitary formations, and were fighting in the streets, little armies ready to be joined into a big army.

In 1935 the Germans once again had a real army. It was a small army, only a few hundred thousand men (still small enough so that Hitler could speak of it as a defensive force without smiling), but the Germans loved it as only Germans can. When the band came up Unter den Linden for the daily changing of the guard at the Tomb of the Unknown Soldier, a happy crowd followed the martial music, like the children following the Pied Piper. At the tomb, the ceremonial detachment, smart and polished, wheeled before the shrine, goose-stepping with a high kick, and all the people raised their right arms in the Nazi salute. Brownshirts passed through the crowd, thrusting tin cans arrogantly under everybody's chin and demanding money for some Nazi charity. When I failed to raise my right arm in the Hitler salute, I became the subject of some ugly looks.

But in 1935 the significance of Germany's military resurgence was a more or less debatable matter. Many leaders in the democratic countries thought Hitler was bluffing: the Germans might like an army, but they would never risk another war.

By 1938, when I next came to Berlin, the democracies were no longer strong enough to want to find out whether Hitler was bluffing or not. Germany had annexed Austria, and was now preparing to seize the Sudeten area of Czechoslovakia. There was war talk in parliaments and in newspapers, which was why I went to Europe. When big events were in the making, I always tried to be as close as possible to the source of the news.

Our first stop was London, where we spent ten days, and then flew on to Germany. On our way to the airport we passed Buckingham Palace, just as the Scots Guards slow-marched out, playing "The Garb of Old Gaul." That evening we were on Unter den Linden, where the march was a quick-step—and inescapable. Germany appeared to be, literally, a nation on the march. It seemed that whenever three or four men went out together they had to march instead of walk. I saw labor battalions marching, and labor battalion sentries swinging along with shovels instead of rifles on their shoulders. Again, I heard the clanging, cocky music of the guard coming up to the tomb. "A fine spectacle of goose-stepping," says my diary, "with the drum major kicking high, and the man with the bass horn on the outside of the file striding astonishingly high as they wheeled in the middle of the broad avenue. He seemed to kick as high as the Rockettes." The people were hypnotized by the sight of their soldiers, and gazed at the marching men as if at something sacred, something which was bathing them in benevolence. Hitler was giving them what they wanted.

There was a great deal of construction going on in Berlin in 1938, but practically all of it seemed to be office buildings, to house the rapidly expanding government bureaus. Official cars rushed around the streets honking musical horns. Government intrusion into private affairs was noticeable even in our office. To remain as president of United Press Deutschland, GMBH, our German subsidiary, I had to prove that my ancestry and my wife's were non-Jewish back to the year 1800. (We hired the W. J. Burns Detective Agency to search old parish records in Scotland and inspect old tombstones in the United States until the Germans were satisfied.) The office boy in our bureau proclaimed that he had become the official representative of the Labor Front; and he pasted up a notice on the wall, stating that henceforth the official greeting would be "Heil Hitler." Our executives took down the poster, and undertook to discourage the budding Gauleiter, who then announced that one of his duties was to report to the Labor Front everything that went on in our shop, and we had all better mind our words carefully. Going Nazi had caught the fancy of the young hoodlums, and they were eager to get into uniform and start shoving their elders around.

During this visit to Berlin we gave a formal luncheon at the Hotel Adlon for German and American diplomats and officials. A great deal of protocol was involved, not only in the seating arrangements but also in the number of toasts proposed and in the order they were offered. I had to rehearse the whole act in advance. The first time I lifted my glass, it was to Hans Dieckhoff, the German ambassador to the United States, called home by Hitler "for conferences." He sat on my right. After a lapse of thirty seconds or so, I lifted my glass to Hugh Wilson, the United States ambassador to Germany, who sat on my left. Then Fred Oechsner, our manager for Germany, who was opposite me, toasted the German official on *his* right and the American official on his left. We then lifted drinks to one another across the table. After that, it was ad lib.

I took turns listening to the two ambassadors. Into my right ear, Dieckhoff poured the German line. We were moving among big events, he said, many things going on, who knows what will happen? He said he thought it foolish that peace should be jeopardized for the Czechs—who had been part of another country, anyway, only a few years before. It wasn't reasonable, he argued, that Germany's natural expansion should be restricted by the intransigency of the Czechs. War, he assured me, was out of date. Great issues were now settled by civilized negotiations. . . .

Meanwhile, Wilson was murmuring into my left ear a series of well-reasoned observations. He said he believed that Hitler's strategy was to keep the pressure on Britain and France until they persuaded the Czechs to knuckle under. He was dead right about that. And he quoted Colonel Lindbergh as saying that Germany was building war planes faster than the United States, Britain, and France combined.

That luncheon began at one and ended at five, with the last guest still drinking Pilsener. As host, I had to remain until that functionary had clicked his heels, jerked his bow, and said Auf Wiedersehen. A few minutes before he departed, he made a personal comment to me about one of the younger American attachés. "We should have that young man in one of our labor camps for a while," he said. "He and millions more of your young Americans would be the better for it."

We dropped into Haus Vaterland that evening for a late supper, and followed the usual custom of sending beer to the Bavarian band. When the refreshments came from Americans, the band always responded by playing "The Star-Spangled Banner" and "The Stars and Stripes Forever." This took quite a while, and everybody stood up throughout both renditions. As the tension of the crisis increased, however, more and more Germans refused to rise for what was regarded as our twin national anthem. On my first visit to Haus Vaterland, some years before, everybody had stood up when the band played for us; in 1938, a number of Berliners resolutely kept their seats. You could measure the hostility by counting noses.

On July 24, I left Berlin to tour the Sudetenland, meet the UP correspondents on the spot and survey transmission facilities. It was a brilliant Sunday morning. The streets were full of bicyclists and families out for a holiday, all looking happy and well fed. The driver of our Mercedes-Benz, displaying a misguided enthusiasm, had festooned the car with the Stars and Stripes—and the Swastika. I had to let the flags stay on while we drove through Berlin, because a large crowd had gathered around the car at the marquee of the Adlon, and there might have been repercussions if I had ordered the decorations stripped off then and there. So we got a lot of Hitler salutes in Berlin. As soon as we left town, however, I had the driver remove the bunting.

All the way from Berlin to the Czechoslovakian border we drove through military concentrations—infantry on foot, soldiers in camions, artillery, field kitchens, six-wheeled tractor automobiles and occasional small tanks. You would have thought the war had already started, by the numbers of troops to be seen. The soldiers seemed very young, boyish faces peering out from under grim helmets. When we got into a traffic jam, the kids reached out for American cigarettes.

Against this background of a modern war machine, I was impressed by the primitive harvesting methods still in use on the farms beside the road. Peasants were out in the field, men and women alike, reaping grain with scythes and hand sickles. It resembled a painting by Millet. On the Czechoslovakian side, they wore traditional costumes which had not changed for centuries, and women cou'd be seen doing the week's washing at the central trough in some of the old towns. I was told that the haystacks on both sides of the frontier were camouflage for artillery and pillboxes.

The Sudetenland, where the Germans were in the majority, was full of Hitler salutes and shouted "Heils." More than in Germany itself. Once the Slovakian area was reached, all this disappeared. The language, the alphabet and the people changed. In fact, our German automobile was enough to make the natives resentful, and as we entered Prague, with darkness falling, we were stopped by the police. Our German chauffeur was ordered to produce his papers—and narrowly escaped getting a ticket for too-bright headlights. (This was just a day's drive from Berlin.)

Prague seemed a medieval city, a pile of spires, towers and battlements, with narrow cobbled streets, all the stonework covered by a patina of age. I called on the U.S. minister, Wilbur Carr, who showed me around the ministry. The building was several hundred years old and surrounded by beautiful gardens. I asked Carr where he would go in the event of an air raid, and he thought he would stay put— no bombs would be dropped in that area, he said, because all the embassies were there, huddled close together. Later, however, as war seemed more and more likely, he made arrangements for shelter in Zraslac Castle on the outskirts of the city.

Our great war-reporting team of Reynolds and Eleanor Packard were in Prague, ready for anything. The city was a place of tension. The correspondents were all waiting for the first shot. We sent out a number of test messages and telephone calls, via Warsaw, Bucharest and Budapest, experimenting to find the quickest way of "moving the traffic" if war came. No correspondent is better than his communications.

The Czechs took a surprising view of my visit to Prague. Many of

them were convinced that we were there as part of the effort to save
them from the Germans, that we were somehow associated with Lord
Runciman's British mission which was attempting to patch over the
German-Czech dispute. The desk clerk at the Alcron asked me, as
we registered, "Have you come to help us?" Realizing as I did that
nobody was likely to come to help them, I found his inquiry pathetic
indeed.

From Prague we drove on to Vienna, to look at Hitler's new satrapy.
We were greeted by Robert H. Best, the manager of our Vienna
bureau. He had a South Carolina accent and wore Texas hats. When
the war came, Best went over to the enemy and broadcast for Hitler.
He died in jail, serving a life sentence for treason.

Best was a crackpot, an intellectual gone wrong. He had come to
Europe from Columbia on a Pulitzer traveling scholarship in the days
when such grants were far less common than they are today. In
Vienna, he swallowed the Nazi line, every inch of it. One night at dinner he gave us the full treatment, enthusiastically explaining the Nazi
idea of brotherhood. From others we heard about his liaison with a
Polish countess and his close personal connections with the most
extreme local Nazis. Sometimes I wondered what they made of him
and his fancy costumes. The ten-gallon hat was standard wear, and
he had other getups for other occasions. He came one evening to
the Hotel Bristol to pick us up for dinner, dressed in the regalia of an
Alpine guide, complete to spiked climbing shoes. I can still hear
the sound of his spikes clattering on the Bristol's marble floors. We
could never find him when we wanted him—at the office or at his
home—but somehow he always knew where we were, and would
show up suddenly to join us at places way the hell-and-gone out from
the center of Vienna.

Of course we watched his copy closely for any signs that he was
slanting it pro-Nazi, but he never did. He was too foxy for that. He
never made the mistake of coloring his dispatches, which would have
ended his career with us. And his news sources were excellent. So we
kept him on . . . under surveillance, you might say.

He stayed in Vienna for us until he was gathered up with the rest
of the American correspondents at the outbreak of the war, and put
into a camp to await repatriation in exchange for German corre-

spondents who had been caught in the United States. Then, one day, he was no longer present in the camp; and shortly thereafter he was to be heard broadcasting the most violent sort of Nazi propaganda— "Jew Roosevelt" and so forth—over the short-wave radio. Many years later, from his jail in Boston, after he had been convicted and sentenced, he smuggled out a letter to me, asking me to help him regain his freedom. I ignored the letter.

Vienna after the Anschluss was even more German than Germany, full of Nazi spirit. My diary reads: "It's all new stuff to the Austrians. You cannot turn around in Vienna without having someone give you a Hitler salute. Even the barber does it, with his clippers in his hand, as he accepts a tip. In the Prater I saw miles of park benches labeled 'For Aryans Only.' The Jewish district of Vienna still bears marks of the disturbances there after the annexation. Many of the Jewish shops are boarded up. Others have their show windows smeared with creosote, which is daubed so thickly over the sign that you can't read it. Creosote has also been used to daub in large letters the word 'Jud,' also 'Schwein Juden' or 'Nach Dachau'—the latter being a concentration camp which is spoken of with horror. The district is dead—silent. There are signs at the entrances to parks and museums, 'Jews Forbidden'; large signboards decorate the corners at several busy intersections, with caricatures of Jews, and the words 'Jews are Criminals.' . . .

"People who, a few months ago, were anti-Nazi now go around flipping up their right hands and parroting 'Heil Hitler!' Waiters, parking attendants, hairdressers. Of course all the papers are censored, so the people don't know what's happening. The former Chancellor, Schuschnigg, is said to be confined in the Metropole Hotel, now a secret-police prison. The atmosphere is ominous, medieval, grim, incredible. . . ."

Against this somber background, there still seemed to be plenty of life and gaiety in public places. The beer gardens were crowded, with dance bands and brass playing. In one establishment the lawns were so extensive that jazz was being heard and danced to in one area while Strauss was being heard and waltzed to in another—both floors outdoors on the same broad expanse of turf, but not within earshot of each other.

The sidewalk cafés, while not so spacious as those in Paris, had room for plenty of people and were full from noontime on. Some of the big restaurants were so crowded it was impossible to get in without reservations. Men in various Nazi uniforms were conspicuous in all these places, wearing their costumes self-consciously, like little boys dressed up. But there was nothing little-boyish about the way the Hitler terror gripped the city, behind its lights and its music.

In the middle of our first night in Vienna there was a mobilization of Nazis, who came roaring through the streets in huge trucks, thundering songs and chanting "Sieg Heil!" Soon the people in the Bristol Hotel were looking out their windows at the spectacle, but nobody ventured forth to see what it was all about. It sounded very ferocious and aggressive. Inquiries however, produced the reply that it was merely a routine night exercise.

Even Munich, the birthplace of Nazism, seemed less hopped-up than Vienna. Except, perhaps, in the beer halls. Munich was the place where I was disillusioned about beer, and I have never since been able to regard it as just a pleasant, song-singing beverage. I saw Bavarians by the score fighting drunk on beer. The Munich Hofbrau was a hive of people swilling, yelling, singing and fighting. And it had the biggest and toughest bouncers I ever beheld.

Munich had been the scene of Hitler's abortive "Beer Hall Putsch," which sent him to prison in the 1920's and killed sixteen of his premature followers. He had done a good job of making those sixteen men into national heroes in just a few short years. Their impressive iron coffins lay in a colonnaded open tomb in the middle of town, and sentries stood motionless over them with bowed heads. When the guard changed, six infantrymen marched up and six marched away, without music—but they made their own cadence in the whack-whack-whack of their goose-step. They moved like perfect automatons. Once they assumed their mourning posture, they became rigid; I'm sure not one of them would have blinked at a fly strolling over his eyeball. Hundreds of people visited this tomb daily, giving the Nazi salute and then standing in an attitude of grief, heads bared and gaze downcast.

In another place there was a plaque on a wall to mark a place where Hitler had once escaped assassination by throwing himself on the sidewalk to dodge machine-gun bullets. Passers-by gave the Nazi salute or took off their hats at this point.

We visited the Western democracies, too, in 1938, and found them feeling a vague fear of war, but unprepared to do anything about it. The French thought Hitler was overrated; they simply wanted peace for its own sake. Premier Léon Blum had put the position to me in a formal interview in 1936. "Many in France and abroad," he said, "seem to fear that our efforts in behalf of peace come from weakness. I protest energetically against this situation of weakness. France still boasts the second most powerful military force in continental Europe, second only to Russia. France's naval strength increases every year, and her aviation is at least equal to that of any other air force in Europe." Wrong, of course, on every count.

In Paris in 1938, William Bullitt, now ambassador to France and happier than he had been in Moscow, told me that recent speeches by American officials from President Roosevelt down (including Bullitt himself) had infuriated the Germans but given them pause. He had made an uncannily accurate prediction of the course the Sudeten crisis would follow: "We are going to have a few more serious war scares during September," he said, "but I do not believe any war will actually get going." On the other hand, he also said that he had a great deal of confidence in the ability and willingness of the French to fight if necessary to keep their ancient foes the Boches from overrunning the Continent. Bullitt spoke French with as much ease and fluency as he spoke English, and he was completely at home in the great *salons*. He was faithful to his friends. Once I thought he was spoofing me because he knew I didn't understand the language. He was complaining to me about a UP story he said was inaccurate (though, in fact, we had got it from an Embassy official—which I couldn't tell him). Every few minutes his phone rang, and he launched into a conversation in French. After each call he would turn to me and say, with a straight face, "That was somebody else calling to object to your story."

The British were on the surface the least concerned of all. Life in London was on a "business as usual" basis. Shops and theaters were crowded. The country was beginning to emerge from the depression.

Juan Perón: "I am in favor of freedom of the press," he said to the author, while his hoodlums were trying to muzzle *La Prensa*.

Marshal von Mannerheim of Finland: "The Russians will never provoke
a war with the United States. They creep."

Pope Pius XII, carried on his throne in St. Peter's. "The world is weary,"
His Holiness told the author, "and needs rest."

Douglas MacArthur leans from the podium at the Republican National Convention to call greetings to the author (blurred head, bottom).

Hitler was an ugly and evil threat on the horizon, but the British much preferred to be left alone. There was some talk about shelters and gas masks, but it all seemed a matter of conversation pieces, goblins-under-the-bed stuff. "Oh, yes, there may be a war, but meanwhile—tennis anyone?"

My own impression, however, was that the leaders of Britain had some notion, at least, of what they were doing. After traveling from London to Berlin to Prague to Vienna to Munich to Paris, and talking with correspondents and diplomats all along the way, I felt that it was deliberate British strategy to stall as long as possible, saving face while arranging for the partition of Czechoslovakia in order to appease Hitler, keeping the brakes on his momentum, but yielding a little at a time.

At the end, when the crisis finally reached a yes-or-no stage, they played the show to the hilt. On September 28, 1938, at the height of the crisis, they gave all the appearance of going to war. Gas masks were distributed in London, trenches were dug in parks, sandbag parapets were built in the streets. Chamberlain made a speech in Commons in which he said that the situation was like that of 1914.

At the end of his speech, however, Chamberlain was handed a note saying that Hitler had invited him, Mussolini and Daladier to a four-power parley in Munich on the next day, and would hold off his mobilization twenty-four hours. The scene in Commons as he read the note was most unusual—cheers, and papers waving.

For September 29, my diary reads, "The Four Powers at Munich agreed on partition of Czechoslovakia. Hitler got everything he wanted, except that the occupation will be extended over ten days, the army moving in easy stages, with no steel helmets."

On September 30 Chamberlain returned to Britain, and was greeted by a cheering crowd at London airport. Waving his papers in the air, he took a phrase from the Prayer Book—"Give peace in our time, O Lord." And told his countrymen that he had achieved "peace in our time."

Chamberlain on that day had less than twenty-six months to live. But the peace he had achieved at Munich did not endure even in his time.

Chapter 11

THE WAR ARRIVES

A MONTH before the war finally broke, I was on my way to Europe again, aboard the German liner *Europa* (later turned over to the French as war reparations, and now the *Liberté*). The forward deck was crowded with young men whose hair was cropped so short they looked bald. Husky boys, with a military appearance. Reservists, heading home.

As we entered Southampton water we had to slow down and go cautiously through the submarine net. An affable German steward standing beside me at the rail noted these precautions and remarked humorously, "Looks like these people expect war, *ja?*"

It was evident when we got ashore that the British were in a much more warlike temper than they had been the previous year. The accent was on defense against air raids. Gasproofing materials for homes were selling well in the stores. Traffic stanchions had been painted a yellow which—we were told—would turn pink if there was gas in the air. Shelters were being reinforced and identified. There were signs such as "Incendiary Bombs—Clean Trash from Attics"; and "Enroll to Defend your Liberty." Along the approaches to London the first of the barrage balloons were already pegged to the ground, held under tentlike coverings.

It was hard to understand why the Polish crisis was so different from the Czechoslovakian crisis. Sir Roderick Jones of Reuters enlightened me. Over a lunch at the Garrick Club, I learned from him that the question was a legalistic one. Britain had a treaty with the

Poles which provided that if Poland were attacked, and resisted, and asked for British help, the British would go to their rescue— even though they couldn't conceivably get there in time to do any good, if in fact they could get to the scene of the hostilities at all. But the situation was not really so academic as all that. Poland was the chip on Britain's shoulder. If Germany knocked it off, there would be war. And war seemed so likely that Sir Roderick was annoyed at me for coming over on a German ship.

Business came to standstill in London and throughout England as people waited out the crisis. The barrage balloons went up. From my window at the Park Lane I could count twenty-one of them, silvery against the azure sky. Many who had country houses left London. Every morning I looked across the Green Park to see if the Royal Standard still flew from Buckingham Palace, indicating the presence of the King. Every morning the flag was there: the King was standing by, as he did throughout the war.

On August 22 the Russians loosed the war. My diary reads, "The office phoned, shortly after midnight, with the Berlin communique that Russia and Germany would sign a non-aggression pact Wednesday. Bombshell! The Cabinet met and issued a statement that Britain would stand by Poland anyway. Parliament was called into special session for Thursday. Ambassador Kennedy flew up from Southern France. We are dispatching men to various fronts."

Ed Murrow asked me about the UP's preparation for a possible war in an interview from London on the C.B.S. network. "We have about five hundred correspondents throughout Europe," I said, "and now we are bringing in more staff members to take care of the emergency. Webb Miller arrived here last Monday night by Clipper. He told me he slept all the way from Newfoundland to Ireland. That's probably the best night's sleep he's going to have for some time. Harold Peters, one of our veteran war correspondents, arrived last night on the S.S. *President Roosevelt*. He left the ship here and took an airplane to Berlin, to get there quicker. He left his bride on the boat. Another veteran correspondent who is now on the way over is Henry Gorrell. He served during the Spanish Civil War, where he was captured by the Moors. Ed Beattie is arriving in Warsaw within the hour. He was on vacation up in Sweden, practically on the

Arctic Circle, when we got word to him. He has been traveling ever since. Richard Hottelet is on the Silesian frontier. George Kidd is up in Danzig. I am mentioning the names of only a few, in prominent spots." H. V. Kaltenborn came on the program with Murrow and me, and, in his matter-of-fact way, broadcast bulletins of the mounting crisis.

The men in charge of our coverage were Ed L. Keen, our vice-president in Europe, and Webb Miller. Both had gone through the first war, and had plenty of experience. They worked with Harry Flory, our European news manager; Cliff Day, assistant news manager; Wallace Carroll, manager of the London Bureau; Ralph Heinzen, manager in France; Fred Oechsner, still in Berlin; and Reynolds Packard, manager in Rome. As time went on, we hired new men to help them, pulling some Americans out of Oxford (among them, Howard K. Smith and Charles Collingwood), others out of the British offices of the Lockheed Company, which had a substantial mission in Ireland. It was more difficult, of course, to find new men in places like Berlin and Vienna; and it was impossible in Moscow.

London was the center of the operation in that week before the war. I sat in our newsroom in London and took telephone calls from our men in Moscow, Brussels, Paris, Berlin, Amsterdam and elsewhere. In the last days, however, censorship shut off all calls, and each bureau had to get to New York on its own. While I was in London we set up a communication center in Amsterdam, and made arrangements with the British government whereby messages from Germany were relayed from Amsterdam through London to New York without passing through censorship. This "Amtrans" operation was the focus of our transmission system until the German invasion of Holland.

On the day Ribbentrop and Molotov signed their nonaggression pact (Ribbentrop receiving a welcome complete with Nazi flags at the Moscow airport), I ran into Ambassador Joseph Kennedy lunching at the Savoy Grill. "You better take your wife and get the hell out!" he exclaimed when he saw me, and rose hurriedly to his feet, upsetting an empty coffee cup and spilling forks and spoons onto the floor. I looked around the grill. It was crowded. Obsequious waiters served the food with the swoop and grace of experienced footmen.

Little boys with soiled aprons down to their shoes waited on the waiters, fetching food and staggering out with piles of dirty dishes. Beautiful ladies smiled at handsome and well-scrubbed escorts. Through the huge plate-glass window I could see one taxicab after another entering the darkish dead-end street which leads to the Savoy's front door; depositing more men and women, all set for a gay London lunch. "I'm going to warn all Americans to leave, tomorrow," Kennedy added, giving me a nice news beat, though he didn't know it.

Certainly he was in a position to judge the seriousness of the situation. A bluff, popular extrovert, he was on the best of terms with everyone in the British government. He spoke with the Prime Minister every day, and with Roosevelt every time anything new developed. He said he was encouraging the British to resist Hitler, but he was making no promises. "I'm telling these people," he said, "that we're with them until war breaks out, but if there's a war, that's the end." This was the end: war was coming.

Then began the exodus of Americans, all Americans who could buy or bribe their way aboard any kind of ship sailing across the Atlantic. The queues at the American Express and outside the steamship offices were blocks long, Americans on the lam, filing by the equestrian statue of King George III which stands at the foot of Haymarket. All they wanted was mattress space. Choice sleeping spaces in empty swimming pools or in sheltered spots on deck went for fancy prices.

While the Americans were scrambling out informally, the British government staged the greatest formal evacuation in history—school children, pregnant women, the blind and the aged, all sent from London to the country. They were all tagged and ticketed, and knew where they were going when they marched to the railway stations. (Or, at least, they knew the *name* of where they were going. Many of them had never been outside London in their lives. Hundreds were excavated from the hidden slums and cellars of the city. Some of the "fighting aunties" who were dragged out of their dark cells fought the police with socks filled with broken glass and old razor blades, before they could be subdued and sent to safety.) Medical supplies, water, food and shelter had all been arranged in advance. There was none of the panicky hysteria we have had here in the United States when people talk about evacuating the cities just by chasing everybody out into the country. Evacuees boarded the trains in the morning, and that night they were at their prearranged country billets.

The crisis mounted. Nevile Henderson, the British ambassador to Germany, alternated conferences with the cabinet and conferences with Hitler. Roosevelt sent a peace appeal. On Saturday, August 26, I saw Kennedy again, this time at the embassy, and he seemed almost optimistic. On Monday, the 28th, I sent the following advisory message to all United Press clients:

OUR SOURCES INDICATE STILL HOPE FOR PEACE THROUGH HITLER AGREEING FURTHER DISCUSSION, WHICH MIGHT DECELERATE PRESENT WAR MOMENTUM, AND RESULT IN CONFERENCES LEADING TO COMPLETE AVOIDANCE WAR: OR BY POLES AGREEING SURRENDER; OR THROUGH SOME UNFORESEEN DEVELOPMENT. HOWEVER, THOSE OF OUR INFORMANTS IN CLOSEST TOUCH INSIDE INFORMATION ARE EXTREMELY PESSIMISTIC. THEY ADVISE US PROCEED IN MAKING ARRANGEMENTS ON BASIS WAR NOW MORE PROBABLE THAN ANY TIME SINCE CRISIS OF 1914. MEANWHILE WE ORGANIZING EUROPEAN NEWSGATHERING SYSTEM READINESS COVER MAJOR WAR STARTING ANY HOUR.

ALL COMMUNICATIONS CHANNELS NOW THOROUGHLY OVERHAULED, ALTERNATE ROUTES ARRANGED EVENT BREAKDOWNS OR CONGESTION. DETAILED PLANS WHICH NOT PERMITTED DISCLOSE BEEN MADE FOR MOVING STAFFS OUTSIDE TOWNS, CONTINUING COVERAGE EVENT LONDON PARIS EVACUATED. EVERY AVAILABLE TRANSMISSION ROUTE BOTH CABLE WIRELESS BE EMPLOYABLE CONVEYING NEWS CLIENTS WORLD-WIDELY.

NATURALLY EVERY EFFORT BEING MADE ACHIEVE COMPLETE ACCURACY AVOID CIRCULATING RUMORS OR PROPAGANDA AS FACTS. PRECARIOUS BALANCE BETWEEN PEACE WAR MAKES SUCH RESPONSIBILITY PARAMOUNT CONSIDERATION.

BAILLIE LONDON 6:15 PM AUGUST 27, 1939

This was the last Sunday of peace.

Antiaircraft batteries were established all over town, some in the most unlikely places. Guns were emplaced at Marble Arch; another one was across the street right opposite my hotel windows. Trenches were dug in the parks. Sandbags were stacked in front of the entrances of shops and restaurants, to cut off bomb blast. A test blackout darkened the city. The guards at Buckingham Palace doffed their red coats and busbies, and marched their tours in battle dress. Gas masks were distributed (including one for infants, an envelope large enough to hold the entire baby). Elizabeth Arden did a rushing business in plush vanity bags designed to carry the ugly gas masks. In addition to the place for the mask, Miss Arden's handsome cases had little receptacles for lipstick, rouge, and so forth. The streets were crowded with people, merely standing out of doors and waiting; they packed the streets around all the government offices.

On Thursday, August 31, Hitler announced his sixteen demands on Poland; they were obviously unacceptable. Britain ordered general mobilization. At seven o'clock censorship was imposed and all private telephoning to and from the Continent was stopped. One of the last calls I received was from Fred Oechsner in Berlin. He had to speak guardedly, but he told me, "The balloon may go up tonight." That evening the German radio announced that the Poles had refused the demands, that Polish irregulars had crossed the German border, and that British mobilization had aggravated the situation.

On Friday, September 1, the Germans knocked the chip off John Bull's shoulder. They invaded Poland at 5:45 A.M., and at 10, Hitler told the Reichstag, "Danzig and the Corridor are ours." Chamberlain addressed Parliament, announcing that unless the Germans withdrew from Poland, Nevile Henderson, the British ambassador to Germany, would ask for his passports. That night London was totally blacked out.

At home, millions of Americans left for the long Labor Day weekend, just as if nothing was happening, and they were in their bathing trunks and with their golf clubs in their hands when the first shots of World War II were fired. I was astonished when I got in touch with New York and found that my business office executive brass had scattered to the beaches and mountains. But the news department was, of course, on the job.

Saturday was a day of tension in London. We were under the gun, waiting for the enemy to pull the trigger, expecting at any minute we would be blown to hell. Warsaw suffered nine air raids. Chamberlain kept Commons waiting until seven in the evening, and then announced that the Cabinet was delaying action in hopes that Hitler might yet respond to a peace appeal from Mussolini. The House thought he was delaying unduly, and there was a stormy debate. The Cabinet met again at 11:30, while a thunderstorm roared over London—green lightning in the thick blackout.

At 9 o'clock Sunday morning Henderson handed the German government an ultimatum to clear out of Poland within two hours. At 11, with no response from the Germans, the state of war came into being. Chamberlain announced it on the radio.

Webb Miller called me at my hotel early in the morning to tell me of the British ultimatum, and I hurried to the bureau. I stopped off by the news ticker in the lobby of my hotel and read the latest reports. A hotel clerk was at my shoulder. I said, "Looks like we're for it."

The room clerk loyally replied, "You mean, he is. . . ."

Almost immediately after Chamberlain finished his speech, the London air-raid sirens commenced their portentous banshee wailing. Police bicycled through the streets, blowing whistles and carrying signs: "Take Cover." They looked like relics from a Keystone comedy. This was the way air-raid alarms had been spread during the first war!

Our office was equipped with first-aid kits, food reserves, camp beds and other emergency paraphernalia, including auxiliary lanterns plainly marked "Made in Germany." In addition, each man in our bureau had a badge, like a paddock pass, reading, "Admit One to the News-of-the-World Air Raid Shelter." But nobody budged from his desk. I asked the boys whether this alert was merely a test. They all shook their heads and said, no, it was the real thing—and went on working. We all thought there were a thousand planes coming to annihilate London. I tried to put in a telephone call to my wife at the hotel, but there was no Central. All the girls had gone to the shelters. I sat by the window of our London bureau, thinking of all the interesting things I might have done with my life, instead of becoming a sitting duck for Hitler's bombardment, unable even to make a telephone call to my wife. I issued just one order: shoot the works, and disregard the budget. We were riding an avalanche; the UP would spend whatever might be necessary to stay in the saddle.

In those early days an air-raid alarm really shut down the city. The police stopped all traffic and shoved everybody into a shelter, whether he wanted to go or not. Later on, after people had learned what a bombing was like, the authorities stopped forcing them into shelters. But during this first alert nothing was moving—except Harry Flory, our European news manager, who came driving up during the middle of it. We asked him whether he knew there was an air-raid alarm in progress, and he called back cheerily, "All clear out where I come from."

There were many other false alarms that month, especially during the small hours of the morning. To get out of my room in a hurry during those night "air raids," I put my clothes together like a fireman before I went to sleep—socks in the shoes, pants and suspenders ready to jump into, shirt ditto, the entire layout on a chair beside my bed. I was one of the few people dressed for these trips down to the unused ballrooms, which were classified as shelters. Most of the ladies were in kimonos with their hair in curlers, and the gentlemen were in bathrobes, all acting much put-upon. The scene was like a shipwreck, with everybody very stoical about it: nothing was ever said. It seemed to me on more than one occasion that the actual sound of a bomb exploding would have been a welcome relief from the boredom. At eight-thirty one morning, during an alert which had pulled us down to the ballroom a few minutes before seven, I stepped out into Piccadilly. It was a beautiful clear day, and London was as still as a country town. There was no traffic, the streets were absolutely bare—except for one man strolling the empty sidewalk in his pajamas and bathrobe, smoking a cigarette and scanning the azure skies.

One of the air-raid shelters was the Ladies' Turkish Bath at the Dorchester. What might have occurred, had there been an alarm in the early afternoon when the ladies were getting their massages, would have been one of the outstanding stories of the early war....

During the day, London was quiet. There were no bands, parades or flags. No soldiers marching off to war. I saw only one small group of troops, disappearing into the tube in Trafalgar Square with their rifles and duffel. Window-shopping was out: no windows, except for peepholes through the boards, like those cut around construction projects in New York for "sidewalk superintendents." The museums and zoos were closed. "We have to close, to clean up; so everybody will please leave," said the attendant in the National Portrait Gallery. The doors didn't reopen for five years. You entered hotel lobbies and restaurants through labyrinths of sandbagged passages, and you had the feeling of going through the trenches. Auxiliary water tanks, large pools with rubber walls and three or four feet of water, stood at strategic intersections and in the squares, available in case of fire. Half the taxis in town dragged baby fire engines behind them. Ambulances were parked in rows in the squares.

At night, the city was black. Even flashlights were prohibited, and you had to feel your way, as though you were blind. Among the few who violated the ban on flashlights were the streetwalkers, who shined little pocket lights onto their faces as they solicited business. You could tell when you were on a main thoroughfare, by the shuffle of many feet, even though you couldn't see anybody. Sometimes your sense of smell gave a hint of where you were—vegetables, for example, when you neared Covent Garden market. The bus drivers developed cats' eyes, and kept going without headlights, as did the few taximen who ventured forth in the blackout. When you left your hotel, the doorman steered you through the blackout curtains into a waiting taxi, and you might emerge—if you could afford the price—into the glitter of a restaurant or night club, from the blackout into dazzling lights, from the silence into the clatter of a jazz band, with chorus girls prancing out on the stage. The Café de Paris in Leicester Square was a favorite night spot, and was also rated an air-raid shelter, according to the posters outside, because it was several levels below the ground. During the blitz, the café was hit by a bomb, and almost everyone in it was killed.

I stayed in London long enough to see people get used to the wartime city during the days of what people in America liked to call "the phony war." Before I left, grass was growing out of the sandbags. But the war didn't seem "phony" in London. There was bad news from Poland over the BBC (including the Russian invasion on September 17, the Red Terror loosed on the Polish countryside by the new allies of the man who had proclaimed himself Europe's "bulwark against Communism"). The liner *Athenia* was sunk—an event on which the UP scored a notable beat, because the survivors were picked up by the *Southern Cross,* a yacht owned by a good

friend of ours, Axel Wenner-Gren, who wirelessed the news direct
to our office in New York. The aircraft carrier *Courageous* was sunk
in the English Channel, with a loss of 580 lives. British planes were
dropping leaflets on Germany, and not all of them were coming back.

I had two reasons for remaining—to do something about the incredible British censorship and, if possible, to swing an exclusive
interview with Neville Chamberlain. As originally constituted, British
censorship was an instrument for bottling up news, whether or not
that news might be of value to the enemy. British troops were pouring
into France, something which was to be expected and which was
quite visible all around the French ports of entry. But no news of
their dispatch was printed in the London papers or could be sent out
from England; the British had to learn about it via the French and
American radio broadcasts. When the censorship grudgingly conceded that there were British soldiers in France, it proposed to channel all news about them via official anonymous correspondents, whose
stuff would be signed "Eye Witness," and distributed to all newspapers and press associations. No reporter was to be allowed to have
his own news sources. Fortunately, the first material to come back
from the Ministry of Information's reportorial lackeys was so bad that
it was unusable. One dispatch, for example, described the camp life
of the British troops in France, including a perfectly straight-faced
account, possibly intended to be idyllic, of a batman washing his
officer's socks in the quiet of the evening.

Lord Perth, who was briefly head of this program, agreed to attend
a protest meeting of American and British correspondents in London,
and showed me the place where he expected to hold it—a board of
directors' meeting room, with twelve or fifteen chairs around a conference table. I told him that there were at least a hundred Americans
who wanted to come and register their complaints. He was amazed.

Lord Macmillan and Lord Camrose, in charge of the ministry itself,
attended a meeting and heard a correspondent of the *Daily Herald*
argue that the censorship was so bad it was a positive asset for the
Germans; it could not be more helpful to the enemy if it were conducted by German agents. He said public morale was threatened.
Roy Howard sent a cable to Lord Beaverbrook, telling him that the
censorship was harming the British cause in America. I met with

Beaverbrook, who had been Minister of Information in the first war, at Stornoway House, and he bestirred himself immediately. Shortly thereafter I had a private huddle with Lords Macmillan and Camrose, who listened attentively while making no commitments. But matters soon improved.

One of the first UP men to go out with the British army in France, after the ban was lifted, was Webb Miller, our general manager for Europe and a man who had seen much war. On the day before he was to start, Lord and Lady Astor invited Webb and me to have dinner with them at the Ritz Hotel. Lady Astor had been one of those who argued most strongly for conciliation with the Germans. Now that war had arrived she felt Britain was in great danger, and that America must come immediately to her aid. She wanted to make a broadcast to the United States. As an American, she thought, she could persuade her former fellow-countrymen of the need for immediate intervention.

Lady Astor dominated the conversation. Occasionally she would turn to Lord Astor for confirmation of something she had said.

"Don't you think so, Waldorf?" she would demand.

Whereto he would reply, "Yes, my dear," or, "I hope so, my dear."

Webb had just written a book about the horrors of the Spanish Civil War, and Lady Astor quizzed him as to why he was always going to battlefronts. "Why," she cried, "you're nothing but a buzzard!"

After dinner, Lord and Lady Astor and I got into a taxi to drive to their house in St. James's Square, and Webb walked off to his hotel to complete his preparations for departure. As he strode away into the blackout, Lady Astor leaned far out the window and called after him, "Good night, BUZZARD!"

This was, of course, offered and taken as good-natured pleasantry. But few people hated war as Webb Miller did. He had seen more of it than most generals. He had been with Pershing in pursuit of Villa, and with the Allied troops in the first war. He had covered the Black and Tans in Ireland, the salt riots in India, the guerilla warfare of Jew and Arab in Palestine. He had watched Mussolini's armies march into Ethiopia, he had seen the pigs eating the dead after the massacres of the Spanish Civil War.

Webb rarely talked about war; indeed, he rarely talked about anything. He was a very gloomy man, introspective by nature, and a listener by choice. You could be with Webb Miller in a group and forget he was there, because he made no contribution to the conversation: he just sat in the corner and listened. He had a stony, handsome face with a pallid complexion and a pencil-thin mustache, and I don't think I ever heard him laugh. But he knew people all over the world. When you came to his flat you found people in turbans, men with square beards, cosmopolitan types from the world capitals. His contacts were endless. He had an ability to make people feel he was their friend: even Mussolini had thought Webb Miller was a friend of his.

From this tour of the British army in France, Webb went on to Helsinki, to cover the Russo-Finnish War. Somebody took a wonderful picture of Webb watching the Russian planes coming over to bomb the Finnish capital: not angry, not frightened, stonily surveying the scene. He came back to London in the spring of 1940, and I asked him to head out again for France, because we could smell the German invasion approaching. He was on his way to his flat that night to pick up his credentials when he stepped off or was flung from the train at the high curve near Clapham Junction. They found his body the next morning, when daylight put an end to that night's blackout. For me, that was one of the worst mornings of the war.

My interview with Chamberlain came through, though it never got on the wire. He refused to approve the dispatch I wrote and I refused to sign the substitute prepared by his assistants. But it was an educational experience without equal.

The interview was scheduled, after much negotiation involving the assistance of Ambassador Kennedy, for six P.M. of a gloomy evening when the war was three weeks old. My taxi deposited me at the front stoop of No. 10 Downing Street, the door opened immediately and I was bowed in. All was warmth and coziness. Without any delay, I was shown into the Cabinet Room. The introduction was brief— "Mr. Baillie," said the factotum, "the Prime Minister."

Chamberlain greeted me with a genial smile and a brisk handshake. No others were present. He and I sat at the long Cabinet table. He lounged in his accustomed place, his gavel, blotter, inkstand and papers before him. The room was unchanged since the days of Pitt, and seemed emblematic of British solidity. The table at which the Prime Minister and I sat was the one at which ministers had for generations made decisions that were to steer the course of the world. Opposite Chamberlain hung a large map of Europe, on which Czechoslovakia and Austria still appeared as separate states.

There was a nice open fire in the grate, generating just enough warmth. The paneled walls, the paintings, the heavy portieres served to make us feel shut off from the rest of the world. The war boss of Britain seemed easy and relaxed, and in the best of health and spirits. He showed no evidence of strain or fatigue. His eye was bright.

Chamberlain was a Tory gentleman, the scion of a distinguished family, a reserved and dignified statesman. He was lean and slightly stooped, and he had a scholarly mien, a hawkish face with a penetrating and intense gaze. But his features—and in fact his general ensemble—were smaller than I had expected. Hair and mustache were graying, teeth prominent, and he looked the perfect picture of a Pall-Mall-Club-type Englishman imbued with the sense of order and decency. He was a brilliant talker, like many other British politicians carefully schooled in logic and debate. But ruthlessness left him rather fussed.

When I interviewed him, Chamberlain was still courteously surprised that Hitler couldn't be trusted . . . that his word was mendacious, his "agreements" cynical frauds, his pretended respect for Britain a hypocritical smoke screen behind which he had advanced stealthily until he got ready to shoot. Hitler's insolent violation of pacts, his gasconading oratorical eruptions, his arrogant atrocities —all struck Chamberlain as not only wicked, but also *vulgar*. Hitler was to him a nasty parvenu. As such, of course, he could not be a really serious threat to Britain. . . .

I remarked on all the air-raid precautions I had seen in London. "Yes," he replied, "all these things are quite necessary, Mr. Baillie. But of course there will never be a successful air raid on London. We have an impenetrable barrage all along the east coast of this island, through which no hostile aircraft can penetrate."

I was aghast at this calm proclamation. After I had gulped a couple of times I asked the Prime Minister when he expected an assault by the German armies in the field—or whether the British were going to take the initiative and attack.

"No," he said, "we are employing Fabian tactics, and we are going to continue to do so. If there is any attacking to be done, let the Germans try it. They will be confronted by the Maginot Line and by the British army in strong positions of defense.

"My information is that Hitler will have a mutiny on his hands if he attempts to go through this coming winter without using his ground forces. He cannot keep such a big army idle all through the winter months. The morale of the German troops is already impaired by reading our pamphlets which we drop on them from airplanes."

When I asked Chamberlain if he thought the Italians were likely to change sides, and help the Allies as they had in the last war, he said spaciously, "I would not bar that possibility. And meanwhile I believe the Italians will remain neutral. The Germans cannot count on any help from them."

I asked the Prime Minister whether there was any chance of peace negotiations with Hitler, on the basis of the *status quo ante bellum*, or on any other basis.

He replied, "As long as Herr Hitler and his associates head the government of Germany, there can be no peace and order in Europe, because the commitments which the German government may make from time to time cannot be depended on. Any of the other present German leaders, including Goering, probably would not be able to hold the Nazi system together. The British are prepared to send men and munitions to the front in as large a number and for as long a period as may be required to effectuate the overthrow of Hitler."

I went from the Cabinet Room into the blackout more than somewhat bewildered. How could the Prime Minister of Great Britain have made such ridiculous statements, leaning back in his chair with the casual assurance of a clubman dawdling over his port? I was sure he believed what he was saying, and I knew that it was nonsense.

Chamberlain's ability to utter such nonsense in that upper-class manner had already made him a figure of fun in London—the appeaser with the umbrella. One of the last shows my wife and I attended before the war was an intimate revue in a small theater back of the Savoy Hotel. (A couple of years later I went around back of the

Savoy again, and found the theater a ruin, with a few small trees growing out of the rubble.) The Australian comedian Cyril Ritchard was featured in one of the skits as "Chamberlain's Ghost," and appeared on stage in white derby and gown, carrying a white umbrella, while dozens of pigeons fluttered through the auditorium and settled on him. This was a very big laugh.

But nobody in those days knew how hard the Germans could hit, or how heavy air raids could be. Chamberlain merely underestimated them more than most. And I have come to the conclusion, comparing the London of 1939 with the London of 1938, that Chamberlain's policy saved the British neck. He gave his country a year to rush war-plane production, build ack-ack guns and construct other anti-aircraft defenses, condition the civilian population, plan the massive evacuations from the big cities, train new armies, refit fighting ships, and in every way prepare for the many long months when Britain stood alone and defended herself against the full might of Hitler's onslaught. He gave America, too, another year to get ready. Though he never realized how close the margin was, his strategy saved Britain from quick destruction. History will rewrite the story of Neville Chamberlain.

A few days after this interview, my wife and I left England, and zigzagged across the Irish Channel on the packet *Hibernia*, ducking submarines. We stayed overnight in Dublin, then boarded a train for the Pan American Clipper port at Foynes. It was a real Alice-in-Wonderland train, so slow I thought the engineer was talking to the people in the fields as we went by. At Foynes, as we were about to board our plane, I met Lord Castlerosse, who was working as a columnist and commentator for Lord Beaverbrook on the London *Daily Express*.

During the year between the Sudeten dispute and the Polish crisis the *Daily Express* had printed frequently on page one in big black type the headline "There Will Be No War This Year or Next Year Either." Lord Castlerosse, a month after the war had started, thought peace was still possible . . . but he was a great spoofer, so maybe he was merely pulling my leg.

Chapter 12

ROOSEVELT II

THIS IS not an evaluation of Roosevelt's place in history, but an account of my personal experiences with him.

The first time I met Franklin Roosevelt I was acting as a businessman, not as a reporter. It was 1919, and I was manager of the UP Washington bureau. He was Assistant Secretary of the Navy, and the business I was to discuss with him concerned naval wireless transmission facilities in the Pacific. In those days the UP did not have the elaborate transpacific transmitting facilities it has today. We wanted to lease Navy facilities part time for the use of the news service, and I was in Roosevelt's office to talk terms with him.

He was a slim, elegant young man with a condescending air. He was too busy to give me all his attention: he had checks to sign. He used an elaborate check-writing frame, twenty or so pens writing his signature simultaneously on twenty or so checks. Naturally, he never looked at a check to see who was getting the money. A colored servant stood at his shoulder, removing the sheaves of checks, blotting them, and placing new checks on the frame while Roosevelt told me in a high-nosed manner about his policy toward the United Press and its use of Navy wireless.

I resented his airs, of course, but I was conscious of the fact that I was in the presence of an authentic American hereditary aristocrat. Had he been born in Britain, Roosevelt would have been at least a baronet and probably something higher in Debrett's. Later people would say that he was a "traitor to his class," but I never thought so.

Roosevelt's class was that small number of born millionaires who had never had to work for a living, and he liked *them* well enough. It was the people who had done something to make their fortunes who annoyed Franklin Roosevelt, and against whom he directed his cannonading. Perhaps he felt that the self-made man looked down on him as a Lord Fauntleroy who had never had to push his own way forward in the world—while it was Roosevelt's pose to look down on everybody else. He seemed to consider himself not merely superior, but positively infallible—and I could never figure out whether these were his true feelings or whether it was all an act. Certainly, that day in the Navy Department, I couldn't take Roosevelt's pretensions very seriously. I was a few years younger than he was, but I fancied I had already seen much more of the world than he had—and I had met a number of men who were always trying to convince you that they had something on the ball an ordinary mortal didn't possess. I'd learned not to believe it of them, and I didn't believe it of Roosevelt.

I headed the UP delegation to the 1920 Democratic convention in San Francisco, where Roosevelt was nominated for Vice-President on a ticket with Cox. Neither Roosevelt nor Cox was present, of course—in those days delegates left the convention and went to inform the candidates at their homes, where acceptance speeches were made for the benefit of the newspapers and a small local audience. And all the interest was in the Presidential nomination, in this case a long-drawn-out affair to the tune of "O-hi-O, we're here to do or die, we'll nominate Cox or know the reason why." The Vice-Presidential nomination was quick and unimportant, something you sort of slung over your shoulder on your way to the exits. Nor was the Vice-Presidential nominee prominent—or even noticeable—in the campaign which led to Cox's defeat.

The next time I saw Roosevelt was after his polio attack, when he was governor of New York. His appearance had changed greatly. He had already grown those huge shoulders and the big arms which now flanked a barrel torso. His manner had mellowed, too, though at bottom it was the same old fleering stuff. He was jovial and hearty, and oozed confidence; and he had picked up a tendency to clown when opportunity arose. He had just disposed of Jimmy Walker, mayor of New York, who couldn't hope to stand up to Roosevelt's probing, thrusting cross-examination on the quality and honesty of his administration of the city. Roosevelt had an unusually fast mind (though he could rein it in to any pace required by the situation). When he had a man at his mercy, he reveled in the role, planting his barbs with all the precision and grace of a banderillero working over a tormented bull.

I called on Roosevelt at the White House for the first time on April 18, 1935. He had been in power about two years, and he had expanded greatly in gusto and range. He could and did talk with authority on any subject. He said that the country had recovered about 80 per cent from the depression—and he thought the British had done about equally well. But, he said, there would always be around seven million unemployed, which would be "normal." He brushed aside what he called "the crackpot element," as represented by Huey Long and Father Coughlin; he said their gyrations were merely amusing and had no real impact on the people. And he said he was already looking forward to his second term. The Republicans, he announced confidently, had started about a year too soon on their campaign . . . their issues were dying on the vine . . . they had no alternative program to offer. . . .

A visit to Roosevelt's office was never all work and no play. Unlike Eisenhower, who holds his visitors to the business of their appointment—and takes his relaxation out of the office—Roosevelt liked to devote part of each working hour to storytelling and storylistening. On this April morning he and I went over details of the recent Gridiron Dinner, that annual affair at which the Washington press corps takes off on the political events and political personalities of the preceding months, performing satirical skits that are rarely kind but usually funny. Roosevelt loved these affairs—though he preferred to dish it out, he could take it, too. At that time, he was still fighting his battle to be like everyone else physically, though he had lost the use of his legs, and he would pull himself painfully the length of the dais to his seat. In later years the ballroom doors would be kept shut until after he had arrived and been wheeled to his place for the show. But he seldom missed a Gridiron Dinner.

And at this one there had been an episode which he knew would gladden the heart of a president of the United Press. It was the year of the Lindbergh kidnaping trial, at which the AP had pulled a memorable howler, transmitting a story that Hauptmann was to receive a life sentence. (Actually, of course, he was executed.) As part of the Gridiron festivities, Lyle Wilson of our Washington bureau, who was being initiated, came out on stage dressed in the usual comedy costume of the tough reporter, trench coat with bottle of gin in side pocket, shouting, "Flash—Flemington—Bruno Richard Hauptmann escapes the chair." The heads of the three press services had stood at their seats, in a baby spotlight through the skit. "Did you see old Noyes' face when that happened?" Roosevelt asked, referring to the distinguished and august president of the Associated Press. "It was a red as a ripe tomahto!" He also told me the inside story about how one of our rivals had been beat on the death of Justice Holmes. Because they'd put a new man on the job, the office had failed to identify him when he telephoned the flash, and he'd had to run all the way to the shop with the news. Roosevelt interspersed his story with gusts of laughter, referring to the late Supreme Court Justice as "Old Holmes"—much in the manner of Calvin Coolidge.

Either he had been briefed before my visit or he had kept himself remarkably well informed about the United Press, because he asked me a number of up-to-the-minute questions about the organization. His debonair demeanor was obviously calculated to take me into his confidence, as though I were his closest friend. But—it was a kind of curse—he was signing something during this conversation, too. Only this time it was baseballs, which had been sent up for his autograph. . . .

I went to Washington to talk with Roosevelt after every one of my trips to Europe, to report on the situation as I had seen it and try to pick up angles on where the next international stories were going to break. The President listened carefully to my reports in those years before the war, and asked my opinions of Hitler and Mussolini, Blum and Laval, the heads of state whom I had met and he had not. When I came back from England in 1939, with the war a month old, I found him less curious about what I had seen, more inclined to tell me what he thought was happening. He was deeply worried about the war; he did not, like so many others, think it was a "phony war."

He said that the most important matter before him—transcending even his next election—was keeping the United States out, while guaranteeing the defeat of Hitler Germany. Pursuing these goals, he managed to scuttle the neutrality act with its embargoes on arms shipments, and to squeeze the lend-lease idea through a difficult Congress. His puckishness was gone; he was still ready to give anybody a flick of the tongue, but the gusts of laughter had receded. Still, in telling me about the lend-lease program, he reveled in the cunning he and his lieutenants had displayed to secure its passage through Congress.

Later, when I returned from other trips to Europe, Roosevelt was not in the least interested in what I had seen. Like so many other men in power, he had become entirely a "sender." An audience with Roosevelt became more and more an invitation to a monologue. He listened with routine politeness but visible impatience to the opening remarks I made to him about what I had observed abroad; then he took the ball and the floor, and it was impossible to get a word in edgewise for the rest of the conversation. Obviously he knew it all, and wanted me to be fully aware of it. He didn't need any information from me. . . . It was about this time, too, that he developed the habit of never being ready for you when you entered. He would be reading a paper on his desk, from which he would tear himself away with some difficulty before flashing you the big, cordial smile.

I was often in Washington in the twenty-seven months between the outbreak of the war in Europe and the attack on Pearl Harbor. The place was a maelstrom of people, ideas and information, true and false. But the excitement was not that of impending battle, such as I had seen in London in 1939. Instead, it was the proximity to an oil strike, to Big Money. The teeming hordes of the original New Deal were being joined by still greater mobs of defense personnel. All bureaucracy was expanding, and inside each agency there grew up an intelligence service and a counterintelligence service, to keep track of what the other bureaus were doing and to discourage snooping by the competition.

Roosevelt's press conferences, previously small enough to fit easily into the President's office, now expanded uncomfortably, with 150 to 200 reporters in the crowd, including all the representatives of the Axis powers. There were fewer off-the-cuff answers to questions. Roosevelt was flanked now by six or seven aides, with Lowell Mellett the nearest to him, and he often consulted with his staff before replying. Unlike Eisenhower, who has made it a policy to answer every question (even if only to say that he doesn't know the answer and will have to look it up), Roosevelt had frequent recourse to double-talk and storytelling of the kind that puts a questioner off the track.

His press conferences were in a way a kind of game, a trial of wits between Roosevelt and the reporters, in which the President was backed by a claque, working press who were only too willing to laugh at one of their colleagues when the President told him to go stand with his face in the corner because he had written something the President didn't like. Roosevelt delighted in clowning and doing the unexpected. He would sometimes titter at the most unexpected times, or get off a pun or a wisecrack which seemed entirely out of character with the serious matters under discussion. At other times, his hearty humor and roaring laughter carried all before him.

Some years later, I attended a press conference shortly after the news had reached Washington that Admiral Yamamoto (the Japanese who had said he would dictate peace terms from the White House) had been shot down and killed in the operations around Truk. Roosevelt was asked if he had any comment to make on Yamamoto's death.

"Is he *dead?!* Gosh!" exclaimed Roosevelt in mock surprise, tossing his hands over his head as he spoke Yamamoto's requiem in the room from which the presumptious Japanese had said he would dictate the terms of peace. There was a roar of laughter, and the reporters moved on to other questions.

In the downtown section of Washington, everybody appeared to be well fed and gay. The famous restaurants were swamped nightly. The peak dining hour in Washington at that time was around nine or ten o'clock at night, Continental style, and the night I dined at Harvey's all three floors were mobbed at ten. Wine waiters were kept constantly on the run and there was a shoal of people waiting in the doorway for tables.

It was seen that a good time was being had by all. Prosperity was back.

The British were overrunning the city. At the massive embassy, which was already in the Buckingham Palace class for size, they were building an eighteen-room addition on the front, having completed a thirty-room addition to the rear. There were now three high-ranking British representatives in Washington, Ambassador Lord Halifax and his two ministers, each with an extensive entourage. I had a talk with Halifax after the Germans swept through France. He was affable and relaxed, and we sat in deep chairs in front of the fire in his office, chatting languidly. He thought the immediate prospects were tough, but betrayed no doubt of the outcome.

Most people who were in close touch with the situation thought the British were licked. I had a talk with Ambassador Kennedy at the end of October, 1940, when he was in New York. Kennedy thought that only their well-known obstinacy was keeping the British from recognizing the inevitable. Air raids were closing one seaport after another, and the British merchant marine was sustaining frightful losses from German submarines. The members of the British government, he said, understood that by all standards of previous experience they were beaten; Churchill was just playing for a break, hoping blindly that if resistance were continued something would turn the tide.

Kennedy told me stories of land mines descending by parachute to hang on church steeples, explode, and knock down whole blocks of houses. He had seen people going into air-raid shelters at 9:15 in the morning, having quitted them only two hours before, carrying their soggy bedding and odds and ends, ready to remain in the subways throughout that day and the next night.

"The Germans can come over, any night they want to," he said, "and set the town on fire." Kennedy believed there was a chance that London would suffer a terrible epidemic when the weather worsened, which would be the end of the war. Meanwhile, he thought, the United States should do everything possible to keep the British going, in the hope that we would be decently armed before Britain went under, and thus in a position to stave off the consequences of a

"Hitler peace." Kennedy was in a nervous state personally as well as officially. His country house was not far from the Slough reservoirs which supplied much of London's water and were thus logical targets for the German bombers. And he said that every night he heard them come over, heard the bombs exploding in his neighborhood, and could do nothing but pray.

The feeling that the Germans were about to win was so general that when the *Bismarck* escaped to sea I received messages from many clients asking me whether I did not think this was the end. The *Bismarck* would raid commerce lanes, and that would be the finish of Britain. Knowing something of the British temper and strategic disposition, I felt able to assure them that the German super-battleship would never get back to port: the British Navy was already, by wireless, calling up all the units of the fleet to hunt down the German raider and sink her—as, presently, they did.

Among those most confident that the Germans had won was Henri-Haye, the Vichy French ambassador to the United States. I met Henri-Haye in my office in New York soon after he had arrived to present his credentials, and I found him indignant at the way he had been received. "You might think I was wearing a brown shirt!" he said. He felt the United States had let France down by not coming to her assistance against the Germans, and under the circumstances had no right to object to Pétain's enforced willingness to accommodate Hitler. As far as could be seen, Henri-Haye was a real Frenchman, with no love for the Germans, and he assured me that Pétain was the same.

Later, in Washington, Henri-Haye talked to me about French food shortages. He himself, he said, was more comfortable than before, since he was no longer treated as a German agent, but he feared that his countrymen would starve if the United States refused to send food to France. He suggested that our manager for France, Ralph Heinzen, should visit Lyon, Marseilles and Toulouse and write stories about the people starving in those cities. He would never get any news about people starving in Vichy, Henri-Haye said: "There is always plenty of heat near the sun."

Henri-Haye was a brisk, businessman type who talked American, not English, and he could easily have been mistaken for one of the tycoons who were in town to hustle orders. I felt that he tried to represent the historic France—a severely damaged France, with, as he liked to point out, 1,700,000 young men in German prison camps —and not just the Vichy government. But when the war ended Henri-Haye found it expedient not to go home. Last I saw him, he was a resident of Cape Town, South Africa.

At the German embassy everyone exuded an elegant confidence about the war, together with mild annoyance at the American attitude toward emissaries of the Reich. Dr. Hans Thomsen, the chargé, and his press aide Dr. Heribert von Strempel (saber-scarred) complained that they had no privacy because American agents constantly peered through binoculars into the windows of the embassy building. They said they had no doubt that my entry into the embassy had been recorded on film. Whether or not U.S. agents had made a movie of my passage through German doors, I was pretty sure the Germans themselves were recording my conversation so I watched what I said.

Thomsen and Von Strempel both quizzed me about Lyle Wilson, our Washington manager, who was in Germany visiting Hamburg, Bremen and other cities—and being bombed by the British. We had sent Wilson to Germany and Joe Alex Morris of our New York staff to England at the same time, to form a reporting team which would cover both sides with fresh eyes. Neither was to write anything until his return to America, so there would be no censorship of their dispatches.

Thomsen emphasized that it was he who had made Wilson's trip possible, expedited his visa and travel arrangements. He implied that it would be most discourteous to him if Lyle wrote anything derogatory to Germany as the result of his trip. This sort of indirect censorship was commonplace at that time. It is today, too.

These Germans seemed to have marvelous memories. Von Strempel, in casual conversation, said to me, "The last time you visited Berlin, Mr. Baillie, was in 1938. You stayed at the Adlon. You also went by motorcar to Prague, Vienna, and Munich on that occasion. You stayed overnight at Wolfgang-am-See. You had to buy a toothbrush there, and it was difficult because you could not find the drug-store until it was explained to you that you should look for an 'Apo-theke.'

"You made moving pictures of the guard relief at the Tomb of the Unknown Soldier; and you also took an auto, and through back streets drove to the Brandenburger Tor to arrive ahead of the col-umn which was marching down Unter den Linden from the Tomb . . . so that you were able to take movies of them parading through the Arch—did your pictures come out well?"

Then he added with a smile, "I am happy to remind you that I had a part in arranging your interview with Hitler in 1935."

But the next month the Germans were less courteous, less eager to help. One of our correspondents in Berlin, Richard C. Hottelet, had been seized by the Gestapo and was being held incommunicado. I went to see Roosevelt and Secretary of State Cordell Hull, and Fred Oechsner screamed murder in Berlin, but we couldn't find out where Hottelet was. Meanwhile, every morning, Hottelet's father, who lived in Queens, came to see me—and there was nothing I could tell him. He knew about the Gestapo, and I couldn't tell him not to be scared.

Chargé Thomsen told me that perhaps our man Hottelet had been—with a quirk of the eyebrow—"indiscreet." We raised a major hubbub in Washington circles about Hottelet's arrest, and Thomsen never turned one of his aristocratic hairs. A statement came from Roosevelt himself that everything possible would be done by the United States government to assure Hottelet's freedom and safety. Thomsen seemed amused, and said languidly, "No doubt nothing more will be done to your man than to expel him."

The Germans' purpose in imprisoning Hottelet was, of course, to demonstrate to the entire press corps in Berlin that they were at the mercy of the Nazi government, and that their home offices could do nothing for them if they displeased the Nazi government. It is also possible that the Germans had Lyle Wilson in mind, for he was due to arrive in New York three days after Hottelet's arrest, and Hottelet may have seemed to them a satisfying hostage to hold against the publication of Wilson's stories.

They held Hottelet for weeks, shifting him from jail to jail, while they conducted a war of nerves against our Berlin office. Fred Oech-sner, inquiring after him at one of the prisons where he might have been, was asked, "Was your man the kind who might smash his eye-glasses and cut his wrists?" In fact, Hottelet was not mistreated. They took his bed away when day dawned, and didn't bring it back until nightfall; and when it got dark outside, it got dark inside, since there were no lights in his cell. Also, they gave him nothing to read. But otherwise he was left alone. Being in the hands of the Gestapo, they figured, was in itself sufficient mental torture. Finally, Hottelet was simply taken from his cell, put into an automobile, and then put out on the street and he was "at liberty." No explanation.

With the growing tension in the Far East, the Japanese embassy became a prime port of call for a newsman in Washington, and I had a session with Ambassador Admiral Nomura in his luxurious private office, a veritable museum of Japanese screens and scrolls. He re-ceived me with the usual apparent candor, while soft-footed servants fetched tea and cakes, and he asked me almost as many questions as I asked him.

"What are you Americans going to do with your big army?" he in-quired. "A fleet, an air force, yes—but a big army? Why, the Germans can't even cross the Straits of Dover. Who can molest you here? And surely *you* are not getting ready to attack anyone—are you?"

He asked me whether I thought it was going to be a long war, and when I said I did he looked surprised. He told me that he thought the Germans could not be beaten—they were far from starving, he said, and they were used to frugal fare; like the Japanese, they could exist on little. There was no way of knowing whether he was think-ing of his own country's war plans at the time. He was a giant of a man, a real wrestler in his appearance—polite, of course—contem-plative. "We strong powers should work out some way to get along together," he said in a low voice toward the end of our talk. Then he murmured: "This war should never have started."

Some months later, doubtless with the same grave, thoughtful man-ner, he held Cordell Hull in negotiations while his country's planes roared over the Pacific to sink the American fleet at anchor in Pearl Harbor.

I saw Hull himself, who was distinctly not optimistic. When I thanked him for the State Department's help in protecting correspondents assigned to the belligerent powers, he told me he expected that incidents like the Hottelet affair would become more common as tension increased—which he felt was inevitable. Hull seemed to me the very type of the old-style statesman of integrity and honor, who believed that international agreements and pledges were to be respected; he was outraged at the roughhouse in which he found himself. He didn't think too much of the roughhouse aspects of journalism, either, especially as represented by the columnists. He referred to one member of the United Features stable as a "revolving liar" and a "spherical son of a bitch."

In this estimate Roosevelt certainly concurred with his Secretary of State. The subject came up, I remember, during one of my few wartime interviews with the President. I had come to his office with Dr. Gainza Paz, the director of *La Prensa*, Buenos Aires, one of the great newspapers of the world (and, incidentally, the largest single newspaper client of the United Press, in terms of the extent of the service supplied and the size of the rate paid). During the course of the conversation Dr. Gainza told the President that *La Prensa* used no columnists, and Roosevelt said, "Great! Great!" throwing up his hands in a gesture of delight. He then offered us cigarettes and discoursed on the columnists. He said people read them only to be entertained and amused, not to get the news, and the columnists gave their readers a perverted idea of what was going on. They have no means of knowing what is happening, he said—and neither, he added, do most Congressmen, whose speeches were as misleading as the columns. As an example, he cited Senator Chandler's campaign to have America bear down on Japan. He asked Dr. Gainza whether he knew "Happy"—and he pronounced the name like the crack of a blacksnake whip.

Roosevelt talked to us about the war effort on the home front, and told Dr. Gainza that on his trips through America he would be particularly impressed with the number of women in industry—adding that this posed an economic problem for the future, because three-quarters of the women would not want to go back to domesticity after the war. The heaviest equipment, he said, was now operated merely by the push of a button, so no muscles were required. At the

Ford plant in Willow Run, he said, he had seen a very small girl operate a crane "twice as high as this room," and "Old Ford" had explained that it was all done by electricity.

At the end of the conversation, Roosevelt blew his nose loudly—possibly as a signal to General "Pa" Watson, who was hovering in the vicinity and studying a map of the world. Watson cleared his throat and approached the desk in an aggressive manner, so we rose. As we left, the Pacific War Council entered; Roosevelt had kept them waiting about ten minutes while he relaxed with Dr. Gainza and me. At the door we met President Quezon of the Philippines, and I introduced him to Dr. Gainza. They had no chance to talk, however, as General Watson immediately shouted at Mr. Quezon, "Mr. President, the President is waiting!" So Quezon with another handshake disappeared into Roosevelt's office.

As an aristocrat, Roosevelt naturally and without any conscious decision about it looked down—a long way down—on "the masses." Eisenhower has been criticized for the upper-crust nature of the guest list to his "black-tie dinners," but Roosevelt surely spent even less time with "little people" than Eisenhower does. He was for the masses because, as he said to me several times, he felt that unless something was done to redistribute the wealth in America there might be a serious social upheaval—and also because he was a politician, and the masses had the votes.

He was a great poseur, and loved to tell you that he was President only because the people wanted him, not at all because he wanted the job. "I want to go home," he told Gainza Paz during our talk with him in 1943. "I'm tired of all this. I would like to return to my business. Do you know what my business is?—It's raising Christmas trees." At which self-given cue he went into a considerable dissertation on the art of Christmas-tree farming, announced that he had just put out thirty thousand new trees about one foot high, and that he would have no trouble selling them at maturity through the New York department stores. "Macy's is one of the biggest dealers in my Christmas trees," he said. "In fact, I am one of the biggest Christmas-tree shippers in the world. Talk about Santa Claus!"

I always felt he was a mama's boy; and that his arrogant airs were those of a spoiled kid, grown up. I thought that if enough people

stood up to him he would drop the act. But there were few who dared
face him—not only because of his tongue and his cutting rapierlike
wit, but also because he was capable of studied vengeance on those
who, he felt, had not been entirely loyal to him or had deviated from
the path he had laid out. He could be brutal, too. Once, I remember,
he hauled up our Washington manager Lyle Wilson, put him on the
carpet and gave him a severe scolding—and then handed out a statement about it to the other newspapers and press associations, which
was unheard-of behavior for a President.

And, I think, he prolonged the war for an indefinite period of time
when he foreclosed any chance of any sort of peace with Germany
by appropriating General Grant's doctrine of "unconditional surrender," first uttered at the little battle of Fort Donelson. "Unconditional surrender" forced the destruction of Germany, which we are
still trying to put together again, and loosed the Mongolian forces of
the Russians on the people of Berlin. Roosevelt let the Russians out
of their cage, and they have been out ever since.

But part of Roosevelt's great sense of power was a wonderful ability
to radiate confidence, both in the words he spoke and in the sound
of that mellifluous voice. He came to office at a time when the people needed confidence more than any other quality; when he said
"There is nothing to fear but fear itself" he pulled the country out of
a tailspin that might have gone far deeper without his presence.
Later he became an inspiration to the millions in Europe and elsewhere whose lives and property were threatened by the degenerate
aggression of Germany and her allies. Toward the close of his career,
his voice lacked the resonance and timbre of the earlier days, but for
most people all over the world the aura remained.

If he hadn't died, he'd probably be President yet.

Chapter 13

ENGLAND, AFRICA AND SICILY: 1943

NEWS IS very elastic. What is the big story on page one today might not even have been printed fifteen years ago. In wartime there is only one story—the war. And all but a handful of newspapers rely exclusively on the wire services for their war news. The wire service is at all times the backbone of the modern newspaper; in wartime it becomes the flesh, blood and muscle, too.

At the UP in the early 1940's we had to build a staff and a communications network capable of covering and transmitting—swiftly, accurately and in detail—the greatest number of the biggest stories the world had ever seen. Then we had to find some way of paying the bills for this great expansion in our services. As president of the UP, I was busy.

From a command post at 220 East Forty-second Street I directed our coverage of the war, assigned men, tried to foretell the location of the next big stories, puzzled over the mysterious items of news (dead horses floating in the North Sea) that might turn into to-morrow's headlines (the invasion of Norway). My Order of the Day to our correspondents was always the same—I wanted dispatches that would put on paper the sights, smells and sounds of the war. I wanted our men to be "walking newsreel cameras." Nobody was ever ordered to a fighting front: those who covered the war for the UP were men who wanted to go out and see, who would gladly take the full measure of the risk of being a war correspondent. Many of them were wounded; many died. And I sat at a desk in New York, waiting impatiently for the day when I could get out from under the paper work and see how they were faring, see the war for myself. In the late spring of 1943, the great day arrived.

I traveled by clipper, which was far safer transport than a ship in those days of U-boat wolfpacks and sinking convoys. My companions on the plane were mostly government officials and army officers in mufti, their uniforms in their Valpacks. We had to pass through Ireland, a neutral country which could intern military personnel from a belligerent power; somehow, the Irish customs people never saw a uniform when they went through passengers' luggage. From Ireland we flew on to Poole, which had been all blown up, and the British locked us away in a dining room while they looked us over. I decided to call the UP London office, and found I had forgotten the number, so I asked Wallace Carroll. When I came out of the phone booth, I found Carroll in the capable hands of a policewoman disguised as a waitress who wanted to know what I had said to Carroll, whom I'd been calling, what I'd said to them and what they'd said to me. On the dock I saw somebody I knew and stepped forward to say hello, and a cop promptly came between us: "No communication..." The world was full of spies, and the British wanted to be certain sure that we weren't.

Finally we were summoned one by one into a briefing room and into the presence of three interrogators. One of them pushed forward cigarettes and asked you questions in the most affable manner: Why are you here? Where are you going to live? How did you manage to arrange that—in wartime conditions and all? The second man interpolated a question once in a while, in a less friendly tone; the third just sat there and watched you with a steely stare. After you were dismissed, they talked you over among themselves and decided whether or not to give you the chance of getting killed in the air raids on Britain. . . .

The war was evident everywhere on the train ride from Poole to London. There were no station signs nor highway markers: nothing to help a possible German invader find his way. Pillboxes guarded bridges and crossroads. Around London itself hung the barrier of barrage balloons, and the glass roof of the huge railway depot was shattered; the rain poured in. Harrison Salisbury, then our London manager, met me in uniform, the standard dress for war reporters on duty. London was still a battlefield.

The city was horribly devastated, and its population had obviously thinned out. There were gaping holes where buildings had been, churches were gutted, pillboxes stood in front of banks and at street corners, a huge bunker at the Admiralty for a last stand, cannon and rocket guns in Hyde Park. The parks had been allowed to go back to nature; long, tangled grass and scrub bushes. There was little traffic in the streets, and the people you saw looked tired and pinched. Many of them had been unroofed and were sleeping in subway stations.

All food was rationed (though there were basement "eating clubs" where bootleg meat and fresh fruit could be procured at a price far beyond the reach of the average Londoner).

The cafés were open. I dropped into the Carlton Hotel bar for a drink and remarked that the place seemed to be intact; the barman pointed to the ceiling and said, "Nothing but wreckage upstairs." At Simpson's in the Strand I got a meal of hare soup and shepherd's pie twice in one day, and also a delicacy known as cow's heel. Beshawled women stood in long queues at grocers' and butchers' to get what might be available for their rations. If a butcher put out a sign reading "Offal Today" he was sure of a very long line of customers until it had all been sold. As a visitor I ate far better than the residents, and I was hungry almost all day long. It was easy to reduce.

But the theaters and shops were open, and people were still expected to get to their work on time. London was like a tomb, the mystic charm of the place was gone—forever, I thought then—but Britain was still in business. People stayed put now during the air raids; the shelter at the Savoy, so crowded in 1940, was little used.

Grosvener Square was loaded with Americans—information people, army, spies.

At night, the streets were aswarm with drunks and whores, maneuvering easily through the now familiar blackout.

I spent a few days in England, visiting the air bases from which the American bombers took off to pound Germany—and to take a pounding themselves, because these were the days before the long-range fighters arrived, and we were losing as many as a fifth of the planes we sent out on a raid. Walter Cronkite, who had flown one of the first raids on Wilhelmshaven and written a classic story about it, was then in charge of our coverage of the air war; he took me around. Then Virgil Pinkley, our general European manager and one of the best correspondents the war produced, came up from Africa and pulled me down with him to Algiers. General Eisenhower was organizing the onslaught on Sicily. The correspondents were gathering to cover the invasion.

Over the Mediterranean, we saw the convoys moving toward Eisenhower's mighty rendezvous, and stayed away from them—not wishing to draw the fire of our own marksmen. As we were passing over Algiers, at five o'clock, a tower of flame suddenly shot out of the city, up higher than our altitude, and we circled until our pilot was sure the town was not undergoing an air raid. (Later we learned that a munitions dump had exploded while a train full of Italian prisoners was passing it, killing three hundred persons and incidentally sending up the sheet of flame we had seen. There was nothing about it in the newspapers.) We landed at Maison Blanche, the huge military airdrome near Algiers, and drove into the city in a truck, past crowds of indescribably dirty Arabs, veiled women, fantastically ragged beggars, miserable prisoners of war.

In Algiers, the natives were ignored or shoved aside. To me they looked unimportant and ridiculous. The women's face veils seemed like dirty handkerchiefs; the men's droopy drawers, with crotch hanging down to the knees, were like a clown's get-up. North Africa had been fought over by the Americans, British, Germans, and Italians, and under the weight of these massive forces the locals forgot about any nationalistic aspirations. If there were any Nassers around, they were lying low. Tunisia, Libya, and Algeria were all one battleground, and all Arab—you weren't aware of any boundaries between them. So far as the troops knew, the Algiers Casbah consisted of smelly little shops and bordellos—the latter "off limits" to Americans but not to the British. This led to some resentment. One correspondent I knew was so outraged he borrowed a British uniform, so he could stroll unquestioned past the American M.P.'s.

The French part of Algiers was like a miniature Paris. The city's harbor was packed with ships, and soldiers by the truckload were going aboard. It was the custom to speak in whispers of anything that might involve security, glancing furtively over the shoulder for the spies who were, it was said, dropped into the city every night by parachute. Whatever the number of spies, war correspondents were present in plenty, and there were memorable parties at a French outdoor restaurant high in the hills, where it was cooler, and where the telephone number was—appropriately—"Boozeria Deux." Many of the correspondents now were going off, once again, to war. I helped H. R. Knickerbocker roll his duffel, and had a farewell drink with him in harsh Algerian wine. He would live through this landing and campaign, to be killed later in an airplane crash in India.

I was billeted in one of the United Press rooms at the Hotel Aletti, and later shared the room with John Hersey, then with Fred Painton, who was to die on Guam. Discarded uniforms, boots, carbons of dispatches, letters littered the place. I picked up a telegram at random. It was from one of our men who was going in on the Sicily landing, addressed to our Algiers manager, Reynolds Packard. The message read: "WHAT'S BAILLIE HERE FOR ANYHOW? TO GET THE AFRICA STAR OR WHAT?"

Well, well.

On July 10 we were all aroused at 4 a.m. and summoned to press headquarters at the Maison Agricole. I walked through the black streets with Charley Daly (John Charles Daly), who swung along with his usual aplomb, carrying under his arm a swagger stick with a short-bladed sword, just in case. We were careful to stay in the middle of the road, as the Algerians had a habit of throwing their slops from the windows and balconies. At press headquarters we all sat at little desks, like schoolboys, and heard Colonel John Victor MacCormack of the British army—"Little Mac"—announce that the Sicilian attack had been launched. Pinkley and Packard wrote our story, and I rushed the copy for them, elbowing my way to the censor's window.

Little Mac was a born soldier—in fact, he was born on an army post and had been a drummer boy when there were such things. He was only about five feet tall, but strongly built, a man of great tenacity and Irish wit. He was a favorite with the reporters at Eisenhower headquarters. He conducted briefings with the use of a black-board, maps and a pointer—and an occasional stutter that gave him time to collect his thoughts when the correspondents, most of them combat veterans of Dunkirk and the desert, were pressing him hard.

The news poured in and out by cable and wireless. On July 12, Syracuse (Sire-a-kews-ah) was captured, so we knew progress was being made. But there was no announcement of the twenty-four American planes shot down by mistake by our own guns, the para-troopers who were blown out to sea and dropped in the water and drowned, the gliders carried off by the wind and smashed. (I saw the wreckage later, a neat little graveyard at each.) One morning during a press briefing a munitions ship blew up in the harbor, kill-ing a thousand people and causing the correspondents to duck under their desks in the belief that an air raid was in progress. Only one correspondent stayed above the floor, and that one the only lady in the room—Helen Kirkpatrick. Merrill (Red) Mueller of NBC was at his microphone talking to New York while the dust and smoke were still rising from the demolished buildings by the harbor, but the cen-sors would not allow him to mention the explosion. Nor were we per-mitted to write of the casualties suffered on the beaches, or of the battle fought with the Hermann Goering Panzer Division, which had come up in support at the beachhead. Such things were incidents of a successful campaign: a great victory.

On July 26 I started off for Sicily without papers, strictly on the thumb. I had found that I couldn't get myself accredited to the front without withdrawing one of our correspondents already there, which I was not willing to do. So I hooked onto MacCormack, who had got himself assigned to make an inspection of communications at the front. I knew that Little Mac's red hatband, showing him to be a member of Ike's staff, would crash most barriers.

We flew first to Tripoli over the recent Tunisian battlefields, Kas-serine Pass, Mareth Line, Wadi Zigzau, desolate places now given over to the scars of battle, slit trenches and decaying airstrips. At Tripoli that night we encountered dust, flies, mosquitoes and stink. Little Mac presented himself at the tent of the billeting officer—a harassed individual who sat at a little table, working by the light of a guttering candle, with a staff of Italian prisoners—and demanded accommodations for "two British colonels." He put us up in the luxury hotel of the Castel Benito airport, once Mussolini's pride, now just another ruin. There was no plumbing, no running water. The desert sand had blown in and covered the floors. When you flashed your "torch" into an empty room, you heard the scuttling of cockroaches—and then you saw them. They were of the two-story variety. We dined with the officers, and were waited on by Italian prisoners, who seemed the happiest people in the room. The food was plain, and the water had that good old Lister-bag flavor. A Scotch highball made with Lister water, incidentally, is a taste sensation, and must be drunk to be appreciated. And a sleeping pill washed down with Scotch and Lister water is a medication with a wallop.

Before dawn the following morning Mac and I were awakened by a sentry flashing his light in our eyes, and we went out onto the airfield to thumb a ride to Malta. The pilot of a Hudson agreed to take us. The Hudson had acquired the reputation of a "flaming coffin." There were no seats. The pilot gave us brief instructions, to wit: "If I yell, 'Skip ship,' sit on the deck with your backs against that bulkhead. Then get out as soon as the plane hits the water. This ship stays afloat thirty seconds, and I'm the last man out and I'm not going to wait."

But we had a pleasant, uneventful lift to Malta, landing at an airfield near devastated Valletta, monument to the tremendous and victorious stand made by the British against masses of German and Italian bombers. In Malta we got away from stink-and-cockroach leagues. Here we were the guests of the governor of the island, Field Marshal Lord Gort, who had commanded the British troops at Dunkirk and was an old friend of Colonel MacCormack's. Lord Gort was living in a palace which had been built by Verdala, a Knight of Malta, in 1586, two years before the Spanish Armada. I was put up in a big room I now recognize, from descriptions in people's memoirs and Harry Butcher's book on Eisenhower, as the VIP guest room. It was on the second floor, a very easy climb because the lifts on the stairs were low, to permit the Knights of Malta to ride their horses up and down the steps. Adjoining my room, a few steps below it, was a cell with chains still hanging on the walls. Evidently it had been the custom in times past to keep a prisoner nearby at night, so if you had insomnia you could go down and torture somebody until you felt tired. A batman unpacked my duffel and expressed a willingness to lay out my brass buttons for the evening meal—which was formal dress. He was nonplused when he found I had no dress uniform, and his duties would consist of shaking the dust out of my khaki shirt. The rest of the company at dinner was brilliantly adorned in posh uniforms complete with rows of ribbons. But there were no women: this was the front.

Lord Gort was a gracious host. After dinner he showed me his Field Marshal's baton and his boxes of medals, and pointed out the features of the castle—especially a mural all around the walls of the huge central hall, depicting the life story of Verdala, from galley slave to Christian warrior, Papal audience, triumphal retirement. Lord Gort's personal staff were all Grenadiers, more than six feet tall.

The next morning at 7 my door banged open and the batman brought tea. Breakfast was at 7:30 precisely. Lord Gort had a lectern set up in front of his porridge, and read the *Times* of Malta aloud to the assemblage, stopping occasionally to ask for comments. His English accent was so severe I often couldn't understand a word he was saying. After breakfast we all went for a fast walk about the palace grounds, sweaty work in that climate, then returned to hear the 10 a.m. BBC news. As governor of the island Lord Gort was also chief magistrate; after the news broadcast he held court and dispensed justice to Maltese litigants.

Later that morning, after a formal farewell, we were back at the airport, where one of Lord Gort's aides saw us through the security check and put us on a C-47 (DC-3 to American civilians; Dakota to the British) bound for Sicily. The plane was full of South African troops. We made the flight low, right down "on the deck," to keep off the German radar screens, then swooped up at the shoreline and down again to land at Lentini West, the most forward airfield held by the allied forces. The Germans had the next one. At Lentini West, for the first time, I heard the sound of war, the grumble-mumble-rumble of a battle just over the next hill. And I saw the wounded, lying in rows on the ground in the shade of airplane wings, waiting to be evacuated. They were all in neat bandages and casts;

they said nothing, nor moved. Many of them seemed to be asleep, and probably were—a heavily drugged sleep.

We bivouacked on the ground with British headquarters at Lentini, and I slept for the first time on a "lie-low," a pneumatic blanket. Mine had a leak and always let me down onto a sharp rock at around three in the morning. The press camp was in a lemon grove and was under Major Nigel Dugdale, a hero of the tank fights in Africa and a man with a glamorous reputation. It was said of him that he occasionally opened the hatch of his tank and sounded "Gone Away" on his hunting horn... as the Germans fled. Among the correspondents at the camp was John Gunther, and also Christopher Buckley of the London *Daily Telegraph*. In addition to his great talent as a reporter, Buckley was a memory marvel, and could recite verbatim large portions of the Church of England prayer book. He was much in demand to reel off the marriage service or the burial of the dead— just to demonstrate to skeptics that he could do it. Seven years later he would be dead, killed by a land mine in Korea.

The Battle of Catania was in full blast on the plains below us, and we could see Catania itself on the opposite hillside, shimmering in the heat haze, a whitish town terracing down the lower bastions of Mount Etna, from which rose a thin thread of smoke. Between us and the town lay the Catania Plain, a brown landscape dotted with green trees, looking to me much like California. Down there on that plain were the British and German armies.

During the next few days I was to see the war as it was fought by Montgomery's Eighth Army, the smell of the African campaign still in their nostrils and the sounds of it on their lips; and by Patton's spit-and-polish Americans, many of them going to war for the first time, not gloomy about it, but not cheering or singing, either. I was to stop in at the command post of the 51st Highland Division, decimated at Dunkirk, reconstituted for Monty's Eighth, and speak with an officer wearing a Glengarry scrounged over his eyes. "What part of Scotland are you from?" asked I. "As a matter of fact," quoth he coldly, "I am an Englishman." I was to walk patrols through the mud, and talk quietly with Ernie Pyle while German aerial reconnaissance took our pictures by the light of photoflares in the Sicilian night, and get shot at by Germans on the ground. One early morning they strafed our bivouac. Col. MacCormack, always jovial, raised himself on his elbow as bombs burst around and called: "Am I treating you all right, Prez? Showing you everything?"

I left Sicily on a hospital plane, signing on for the flight as an orderly (fortunately, none of the wounded needed help); and returned via Malta, Tunis, Algeria and Gibraltar. At Gibraltar our Fort picked up a group of "evaders"—flyers who had come down on German-occupied territory and evaded capture. They didn't think much of the name. They wore plain khaki shirts and pants, no signs of rank, and they were still "under cover," which meant that Intelligence officers had told them to keep their mouths shut. Some of them had been months in enemy-held country, after parachuting out of their falling and flaming B-17's.

The lads with whom we journeyed back to England had been hidden in Paris, where the underground gave them civilian clothes and taught them how to look like Frenchmen—even though many of them could speak no French. Some were bold enough to attend the opera, and sit among the German officers, while the resistance girls who were with them did all the talking. They took frightful chances. Capture in civilian clothes meant death as spies—and torture, to force them to betray the French who were hiding them. These men in our plane had been smuggled from family to family, from farm to farm, from Paris to the Spanish frontier. Once across the Pyrenees they were pretty much on their own; and in small groups, or singly, they managed to elude the Spanish police and make their way on foot clear across Spain to Gibraltar. Many of those who made it to Gibraltar had been given up as dead. Many never made it.

They were wary, tough, half-starved and terribly alert from weeks of constant peril... sleeping with one eye open, ready to kill or be killed. Their attitude toward us in the plane was cagey and almost hostile, and they didn't warm up until two JU-88's appeared on our tail over the Bay of Biscay. An engine had conked on us half an hour out of Gibraltar, and we were making slow going toward Britain. Our guns bared like fangs, and the evaders grabbed onto them, fired trial bursts, and waited for a chance to shoot back at Germans. But the JU-88's had too much respect for the B-17 to attack unless the odds were overwhelmingly in their favor. They hung around, waiting for reinforcements that never came. Our evaders, however, warmed up a little, because they'd had a trigger under their fingers, with freedom to pull it. That was what cheered men up in 1943, after a few years of war: the chance to shoot at Germans.

Chapter 14

THE GENERALS

Eisenhower in Algiers . . .

HE WAS still something of a mystery in July, 1943, in those days before the Sicilian invasion. He had been a major for sixteen years (1920–1936), and only a lieutenant colonel on March 10, 1941. Less than two years later, he was a full general. Roosevelt and Marshall had jumped him over the heads of dozens of senior officers to be commander of the Allied forces, mostly because he was smart, a man with the gift of strategy. I went to his headquarters in the St. George Hotel, on the hill above Algiers, hoping to arrange with his naval and press aide, Commander Harry Butcher, for an interview with Eisenhower. While Pinkley and I were in Butch's office, and Butch was looking over the General's calendar, Eisenhower himself popped in the door, looking pink and healthy, though somewhat drawn. (I found out later that he'd been keeping in condition by pitching baseballs to air commander Sir Arthur Tedder and Admiral Sir Andrew Cunningham, who, as cricketeers, were somewhat baffled by his curve ball.) He was not wearing his uniform jacket—Algiers was hot—but his shirt was immaculately pressed. He looked inquiringly at Pinkley and me, and Butcher introduced us, explaining that we sought an appointment.

"Come right in!" said Eisenhower with great heartiness.

To get him started, I told the General something I knew he would not like to hear, though it was true—that people back home had already discounted the Sicilian invasion and regarded it as "in the bag." After the tremendous cleanup in Africa, the capture of Sicily didn't seem so very formidable.

Eisenhower was surprised and disturbed, and gave me a display of the high voltage he turned on when things were going badly. He turned red and the veins in his bald scalp stood out like cords. He stood up at his desk and forcibly explained the difficulties of the impending operation:

"This is the biggest amphibious landing ever attempted. And all amphibious landings have tremendous inherent dangers to the attacking force. We are going in with massive bombardment from the air, a sky umbrella of cover, and gliders filled with troops to establish positions behind the enemy on the beach. There is also to be a heavy bombardment from ships lying offshore. The attack is to be at night. We have the hazards of weather. Our weather forecasters are making the best forecasts within reach of their experience and instruments, but no weather forecast is infallible.

"The coast is very strongly held, and the Germans have the Hermann Goering Panzer Division in reserve, ready to go to the support of any part of their front which may be penetrated."

He bit off his words as he gave the conclusion: "For people at home to conclude that this is going to be a walkover is extremely unfortunate. If we score a big success it will be discounted. If we suffer a reverse, the fact that they expected easy victory will make the shock all the more severe on public morale. Something must be done to change this erroneous impression, in the next forty-eight hours."

I smelled an interview. I proposed to the General that he let me quote his words, and tell the censors to pass my dispatch (I would not, of course, mention Sicily as the objective, as this was still a "military secret," though the Germans were in no doubt about our objective). I would get it on the wires that very night, and kill the complacency at home.

It seemed to me that Ike thought very seriously about approving an interview—but then he swung away from an immediate decision and gave me a further description of the difficulties ahead. He was still, obviously, upset about what I had told him. His face remained flushed, and he spoke in short sentences with plenty of punch.

Meanwhile, probably he was sizing me up, trying to decide whether I did, in fact, have a true picture of the situation back home. He spoke to me about the 200,000 men who were shortly to come under enemy fire at his direction, and read aloud to me a message of encouragement which had been sent to him and signed by a number of clergymen. Then he swung around and looked silently out the window, a very grim expression on his face.

Soon, however, he shook off this mood and with a boyish grin sketched for me the details of the Axis foldup in Africa (with a serious interlude for a warning that we shouldn't expect any repetition in Sicily), and then the technical plans for the co-ordinated assault by three armies, American, British and Canadian, on the Sicilian coast. He spoke for an hour, with only occasional interruptions from me (most of them designed to persuade him to let me quote what he had said). At the end of the hour I saw Harry Butcher glancing at his wrist watch and I suggested to the General that if he felt he couldn't give me a direct interview, perhaps he might let me write a story on the hazards of the invasion, based on what he had told me but not quoting him. To this he agreed most heartily, and the next day the censors passed my "situationer"—a poor substitute for an interview, but a story none the less.

I saw Eisenhower again at a press conference two weeks later, after the Sicilian campaign had begun—and had progressed according to schedule. War reporters packed the room, and Ike entered eagerly, with a flourish and engaging grin . . . plenty of bounce. He spoke a few words of private greeting to the men he recognized—British, French, American, Norwegian, Belgian, Dutch—then plunged intently and aggressively into answering the questions. Now that the game was afoot and going well, he radiated confidence, and he already had that gift—later to show so prominently in politics—of galvanizing his audience. He predicted a mop-up of the Sicilian campaign at a date earlier than his staff had dared to hazard (and they looked dubious and glum while he said the words—but he was right). He had a great victory in his hands and he knew it. He said his au revoir with a sweeping gesture and exited vigorously, almost gaily.

What pleased him most about the Sicilian progress, I felt, was the fact that the Germans had elected to stand and fight at several places on the island—where he knew he could beat them. His strategy called not for the capture of towns and places on the map, but for the destruction of the enemy army. The symbol of his headquarters was a crusaders' flaming sword; if he had flown a crusader's banner, too, the device would have read, "KILL THE GERMANS." That was precisely what his armies were proceeding to do.

"Butcher" Harris . . .

The bombing war against Germany in 1943 was run by Air Marshal Sir Arthur Harris of the Royal Air Force and General Fred Anderson of what was then the U.S. Army Air Force. They headquartered at High Wickham, a town which was so secret, as a result, that it didn't publicly exist. You spoke the name in a whisper.

I met Harris in his above-ground offices, where he showed me stereopticon views of the damage done to enemy military targets by the British bombers. He was a red-headed, mustachioed South African, a serious man; he showed photographs of wreckage like a researcher pointing out the results of his experiments. He told me he thought the British had survived the early years partly because of enemy errors. "Thank God for Hitler's mistakes!" he said fervently; "otherwise we wouldn't be here." The Germans feared and hated him, called him "Butcher" Harris. At that time he firmly believed that aerial warfare could beat the Germans into submission with a minimum of Allied casualties. "Germany," he said, "is being destroyed, city by city. It isn't necessary to eliminate their war plants to halt production. Unroof the workers. Put the people out into the streets seeking shelter. Then they won't show up to make munitions."

The Air Marshal escorted me into his underground offices. The entrance looked like that of a coal mine. The two sharp sentries at the gate made sure of my identity, even though I was accompanying the boss himself. Below, I found level after level of complicated transmission centers, control panels, all the paraphernalia that went into the "brain" of the British bombing; and many officers and men working intently over plans and charts. All the statistics on bomb tonnage dropped, ammunition available, petrol consumed and on hand and en route, reconnaissance mapping for future operations, casualties both men and planes, results achieved—all were kept here, in the atmosphere of a business office, underground. Climbing back into the open, you emerged from a strange dream into the grounds of a quiet English manor.

Sir Arthur took me home to lunch. He drove at a high speed, with the concentration of a professional racer. (Later he drove me into London; it was one of my most exciting and dangerous experiences of the war.) At his cottage, he fussed around the kitchen, preparing the meal—a tasty soufflé. The charming Lady Harris presided at the table. Then a fast trip back to underground HQ, and he laid on a raid of 638 planes for that night. . . .

Anderson's strategic center was near by, in what had been a monastery garden. Jeeps rolled over the wide paths on which the monks had strolled, reciting their breviaries. It was all very peaceful and serene. Anderson was a tall, bronzed type, visibly Texan. He, too, showed me stereopticon views, maps, charts and such, and then took me downstairs. Five levels below the ground we came through narrow corridors into a big, spacious, airy chamber with a high ceiling. Along the walls were maps of all the bases in Britain, dotted with colored electric lights which flashed on to show each airdrome's state of readiness—planes, bombs and personnel on hand. Anderson studied the illuminated maps and had himself further briefed by members of his staff, each officer a specialist in one department. He reviewed the results of recent raids, the newest tricks in German camouflage (fake conflagrations, lakes and rivers in the wrong place, cities where no cities existed), the weather forecast, known German fighter and flak concentrations. One possible target after another was rejected—mostly by the weatherman—until finally Anderson ordered up an attack on the railroad yards of Paris.

"Yes," he said definitely, "we'll hit Paris." Then came a stream of orders. Each field was alerted and given its specific target. In a few hours the young pilots would be strolling into the ready-rooms to hear their instructions, the planes would be armed, bombs trundling up on little carts to be hoisted aboard, the long belts of machine-gun and cannon ammunition would be placed in the guns, the hospitals would be put in battle readiness.

As Anderson and I walked casually out of the plotting room I looked at him with great curiosity. Here was a man who had just issued the signal for an attack in which more missiles would be fired than at Waterloo . . . which might be a great success, or a dismal fiasco for which he would be blamed. Yet he appeared utterly unruffled, calm as an oyster.

"General," I said, "don't you ever lie awake nights after you've given the word—thinking it over and visualizing what might be happening as the result of your orders?"

"Why, no," he replied, puzzled. "Why should I? Every factor has been taken into consideration. We know what we are doing, the risks that are being taken, the results to be expected. When the planes start coming back, I'll be on hand to get the reports as soon as the men have been interrogated; I'll review the costs, and study the photo-rekky pictures to see what we accomplished. Then we'll hit them again."

Another scientist . . .

Tooey Spaatz . . .

As warmhearted and genial a guy as you could find. I was stuck in England in September, 1944, without authorization to proceed to the Continent, when he invited me to visit him at his headquarters in Granville, Normandy. He was a lieutenant general then, boss of the heavy bombing operations that were vomiting destruction, fire and death all over Germany. He had been a pilot in the First World War, and had shot down two German planes at St.-Mihiel, and his career was a history of aviation. He was a tough soldier with a benign demeanor, a man who loved his friends and pitied his enemies. The Germans hated him as much as Harris, and a few days after I left they staged a commando raid on Granville, from one of the offshore islands which they still held, hoping to capture him; but Spaatz had already moved on.

Spaatz was living in a trailer just outside a château—usual procedure with American generals. They had picked it up from the British, who had learned the pleasures of trailer life in the desert, where there were no permanent buildings to occupy. Guests were entertained and dinner served in the château itself. Just outside the main building at Granville was a compound containing hundreds of Ger·

man prisoners, who stood or squatted on the ground and took the pouring rain: no shelter. Near the château there was a neat walled vegetable garden which now contained nothing but German graves— thirty-eight in all, neatly packed in, each with a marker made to look like a big Iron Cross, a name, and the year 1939.

Every day, Spaatz received evaluations of the situation inside Germany, in the areas where his fleets of bombers were engulfing cities, factories and populations, man-made holocausts one after another. As he studied these reports, and prepared orders for the next day's assault, he played with his two black cats, Buzz and Doodle, named in England during the buzz-bomb and doodlebug days. They roamed freely through the trailer, over desks and chairs and papers, while he worked; he might give the orders for a massive air strike while a cat peeped out from inside his Air Force jacket.

Few generals trusted reporters the way Spaatz did—at least, the ones he knew. I was in his trailer once during a frank discussion on the subject of dropping supplies to the Poles who had been caught in a premature up-rising in Warsaw—while the advancing Russians sat on the far bank of the Vistula and waited for the Germans to suppress the Polish insurrection. It was Spaatz' opinion that an air drop on Warsaw would waste time and planes that might be better occupied in burning down and blowing up Germany—and that the material and rations would probably fall among the Russians or the Germans, not the Poles. During this conversation two or three other senior officers present gave me the hard eye, but Tooey included me in the huddle. "That's all right about Baillie," he said; "he's okay."

Some nights Spaatz had poker games with distinguished casts of players, the General himself presiding. He decreed the hour at which cards should be dealt, and the hour at which the game would end. The rules were announced during evening mess. Tooey's guests were mostly transient officers and war correspondents, and if anyone had been a conspicuous winner, and departed with his gains, Spaatz had been known to send a plane to fetch him back for the evening—provided he was reasonably near by and his duties did not preclude a few more hours of recreation at Tooey's green baize table. "Kimmell," he said with mock severity to his pilot, "Beattie and Gallagher owe money to the game. Go and find them and bring them in." On this occasion, however, Gallagher of the AP was too busy at the front to join Spaatz' sport, and Beattie of the UP had just been captured by the Germans—though we didn't know it yet. Spaatz was with me a few days later when I received the message telling of his capture, and the group of us decided to autograph the cable as a souvenir for Beattie when he got out. Spaatz wrote, "Hope you were captured, not ruptured"—an allusion to an old desert story about the patrol which announced that it was coming back to base in a message received as "Rommel captured. Returning immediately." When the excited British turned out to receive their distinguished prisoner, however, it developed that the patrol had actually sent a somewhat different message: "Camel ruptured. Returning immediately."

I remember one of these poker games, after Spaatz had moved his headquarters to St. Germain, where I arrived to find General Ira Eaker, a very strong player, and Jock Whitney (then just escaped from the Germans, now our ambassador at the Court of St. James's) already seated around the table. I abstained, feeling that I was not yet ready for such championship class. In fact, Tooey himself might have abstained—he was more often than not a loser. The object of the game was not winnings, but therapeutic relief from planes and bombing, death and destruction....

The Field Commanders . . .

I met Omar Bradley in Sicily, at the American press camp, when he came to give a briefing. He was not then the commanding general of all American armies in the field; in fact, he was under Patton. Eisenhower later told me that Bradley was a man who could take a battle with all its complexities and ramifications, hold it "in the hollow of his hand" and mold it into the shape he desired. But it was not until Normandy that he became commander of the army group.

Bradley was the only general I ever met who actually went out into the field, to the advance press camp, to steer correspondents straight. He shook hands with all of us that morning in Sicily; then his aides laid out the battle maps on the face of a couple of huge boulders, and in his quiet, dry, modest way, like a schoolmaster, using his long steel-tipped walking staff as a pointer, Bradley gave us a lecture on the military position. The thumping and banging of the fight went on just over the next hill, and occasionally you could hear the three sharp rifle cracks of a sentry warning of German planes coming in. Bradley offered us a piece of personal advice—not to go too far forward, and above all to avoid straying into minefields that had not yet been cleared. "Otherwise," he said, "you may cease to be of any further use to your employers."

I didn't notice Bradley taking his own recommendation. He was all over the front, usually close up, seeing things for himself.

I met Bradley again the next year in Verdun, where we dined together at the hotel beside which he had parked his trailer. He was as forthright and informative there as he had been in Sicily, showing me the maps and allowing me to sit in while he discussed the position with his staff officers. There in Bradley's trailer, it all seemed as detached and statistical as peacetime maneuvers... or a study course in the battles of the Civil War. But you could hear the rumble "up forward," and occasionally an explosion shook the trailer to remind us that this war was real and still with us.

In Sicily, too, I saw Major General Guy Simonds, who commanded the Canadian division in Montgomery's army. He was sitting under a tree, drinking tea while he ran the battle—an informal command post for an informal army. Officer after officer came up to him, saluted smartly, described the position and asked for orders. Simonds would then consult his map, do a little figuring, issue the requisite instructions and pour himself another cup of tea. Between visits from his subordinate officers, Simonds found time to tell us about the battle on his front, impersonally, like a young surgeon explaining the details of a rather complicated operation.

In Europe the next year I saw Patton himself, by appointment, in his trailer near the front before Metz. He was wearing a short brass-buttoned jacket with neckerchief, whipcord riding trousers, knee-length boots; and on the table beside him lay his famous belt with his two equally famous revolvers. He greeted me with a surprising question "Mr. Baillie," he said, "do you think I overdress?"

"Why, of course not, General," I said. "I think a general of an army ought to dress up to his position. Why—who says you over-dress?"

He looked at me closely for a minute, to see whether I was just giving him a snow job, and then said, "I have a son in the army who suggests that perhaps my attire is too dressy for the front. I like good clothes and good tailoring."

Then he got back to business. He said, "Don't you think the British are making suckers out of us? They have got my gasoline again. So here I am hung up in front of Metz. We ought to be attacking the place right now with everything we've got. But my tanks are parked out there, waiting for fuel."

He went on to tell me that he intended to take Metz by assault, be-cause this had never been done in modern warfare. Patton had re-searched all the sieges and battles of Metz, throughout history, and he had maps all over his desk, showing the fortified areas around the city. He told me that at one time he had actually had patrols in the town, but had been forced to pull them back because he could not make an assault in strength until he had fuel for his armor. He even had to limit his bombardment of the forts, because ammunition was rationed. The Third Army, which he commanded, had outrun its supplies.

An officer now saluted at the door of the trailer, and announced that General Patton's briefing was ready.

Patton stared at me with his blue eyes for a few seconds, and I thought I was about to be "excused." Then he said, "I will take you to my briefing, Baillie, if you will pledge me your word of honor that you will never reveal to anyone, until after the war, that I did so."

So we walked a hundred yards to a large barn where Patton's numerous staff was assembled. They all rose as he entered. With me at his heels, he mounted the platform. He pointed to me. "Gen-tlemen," said he, "this is the Invisible Man. He is here but he is not here. None of you see him here. Therefore you will say nothing what-ever about his having been here. After he leaves here, he never will have been here. Gentlemen, meet Mr. Hugh Baillie, the president of the United Press."

I looked out over the faces before me, the faces of Patton's officers, who had taken the Third Army on its spectacular whirlwind drive across France and into Germany—and were to take it audaciously over the Autobahns of the Vaterland. They looked back at me, some with quizzical expressions, some as deadpan as Buster Keaton, and then gave their attention to the briefing. Patton lit a big cigar, relaxed in a chair, and concentrated his attention on the charts. He was briefed on every aspect of the battle, the logistics situation, casualties, weather, information elicited from prisoners. The briefing officers lectured at the maps, with pointers, and Patton interrupted with penetrating questions. Occasionally a question came from the floor. When the briefing was over, I moved around among the officers, shaking hands with those I knew and exchanging a few words of greeting. Then I returned to General Patton, who was standing with a group around him, thanked him, and announced the departure of the Invisible Man.

The great, driving General, the awesome disciplinarian, thereupon assumed a sly pose, put his finger to his lips and puckishly went, "Shushhhh . . ."

Monty . . .

We were proceeding toward the front lines in a jeep on the battlefield of Catania when we came upon a hole in the ground which was the post of command of the 51st (Highland) Division. From it emerged a smallish, lanky figure in a faded suntan uniform, sleeves rolled up, wearing shorts and desert boots. There was no mistaking that black beret with the insigne of the Royal Tank Corps, and a general's badge. It was Montgomery. He carried a two-foot pointer with which, evidently, he had been going over the maps and charts in the P.C. His gaze fell on Colonel MacCormack, my guide and escort.

"Ah, MacCormack, isn't it?" he demanded, sticking out his pointer at the little colonel. "I haven't seen you since the King was in Africa. And who is this with you?"

Little Mac had become ramrod-stiff, all five feet of him; he now stepped briskly forward, saluted with a 180-degree swoop, and told the General who I was. Montgomery thereupon proceeded to give me news.

Montgomery was the warrior par excellence of the last war, with neither wife nor home waiting for him: his wife had died before the war, and his house, with all his possessions and memorabilia, had been blitzed by the Germans. He had arrived at his great command as a substitute, when General Gott was killed in a plane crash on his way to Egypt. He had taken the British Eighth Army, battered by Rommel's Afrika Korps, and made it a proud and consistently victorious *corps d'élite*. Those who were members of Montgomery's Eighth still distinguish their ribbons with a very tiny figure 8. They remember; and so does Monty.

He was a merciless driver. He kept himself in excellent physical condition, and expected the same of his officers. He was reputed to be able to fall asleep and wake up at will. He was abstemious, neither smoked nor drank. If he was in a group of Allied officers who were having a drink, he would sit apart from them. Among his own people, cigarettes were not to be lighted until he gave the word. Sometimes he paraded his officers at the double, complete to obstacle run, and then assembled for a talk. At such times he did not care for sneezing and coughing or any similar interruption: those who were afflicted by these paroxysms of nature left the meeting. If they didn't leave immediately, Monty would stop talking and freeze them with a look until they took the hint.

Monty paid no attention to danger. He drove around the Sicilian front in a canary-colored open sports car, the only one of its kind in that country, easily spotted by the spies who were everywhere and by German aerial observers. His black beret made him conspicuous from a distance when he was surrounded by his officers. He was always dropping in on his divisional commanders and conferring with them in their trailers—or in dugouts just behind the front. As he passed other cars of troop columns he would give his characteristic salute, terminating in a comradely wave of the hand. Often he would stop, hand out cigarettes, stand up in his car or his jeep and harangue his troops like a football coach between the halves—or halt a passing car and quiz its occupants as to who they were, where they were going, and what was transpiring in their sector. He was on the go from first light to dark, checking positions, making decisions, keeping morale at flaming heights.

Mathematically inclined (and, like Eisenhower and Gruenther, a ferocious bridge player in his off hours), Monty was capable of the most intense concentration. He preferred oral to written reports, and insisted on brevity. He put a time limit on officers reporting to him—and enforced it. He seemed not to hear unimportant interruptions or observations by the people to whom he was talking. If a subordinate had difficulty comprehending him and carrying out his instructions, Monty simply booted the man out and replaced him, with the air of a mechanic changing a spark plug. Masses of paper irritated him: he wanted to hear the information from the person who had it, and then give his orders on the spot. Later, when he was with SHAPE, he announced that if a paper chase was to be conducted as part of a training program, his office would freely supply the waste paper.

Monty was easily bored, and press conferences were among the things that bored him. I have seen him sit at a conference, balancing a pencil carefully on his fingers, seesawing it back and forth with a faraway look on his face while he answered questions. But occasionally a question would attract his special attention, and then he would address that particular reporter in a very intimate man-to-man fashion, looking fixedly into his eyes. And he liked a gallery. If he had a story to give you he reveled in the giving. But he had a reputation for giving out very little news.

Fortunately, that first time I met him he had three stories to give. "Baillie," he said crisply, "have you seen my Order of the Day to the troops? NO! WHAT! Well, you shall have it at once." He turned to an aide at his elbow, seized the paper and thrust it at me. I was not surprised that this was my first sight of it when I read the date and found it was *tomorrow's* Order of the Day. In it Monty declared: "The enemy is now hemmed in. We have knocked Mussolini off his perch. We will now drive the Germans out of Sicily."

As I read the paper Monty said, "Have you heard about my very successful conference with General Patton in Palermo?" No word of this had been issued; I confessed ignorance here, too. He registered surprise, and proceeded to tell me about it: "The co-operation of our armies in the drive for Messina was agreed upon. The Americans on our left are going wonderfully. It is a race to see whether they get into Messina before we do. But we have got to work together as we are doing. General Patton is an inspired leader—a great soldier. He and I are doing famously together." I wondered whether any two such showmen as Montgomery and Patton ever ran their armies flank to flank charging on a common objective, in any war.

"And by the way," Montgomery snapped, "I nearly killed myself in that Flying Fortress of yours yesterday—the Fort I won from you on a bet." (The bet had been between Monty and General Bedell Smith, Ike's chief of staff, as to whether the British would capture Sfax by April 15. They did, and Montgomery collected.) "The brakes burned out and the pilot had to slew the Fort halfway around to stop it before we did a ground loop. It was a near thing—very."

These were three hot stories, and Montgomery knew it. He peered at me sharply, to see whether or not I was taking it all in. I was. Then he went off to run his war.

As a tactician, Montgomery was often criticized (not to his face) by those who felt that for all his fanticism and flamboyance he was too conservative. At that moment, in fact, there were many who felt that he should be exerting more pressure on Catania while the Americans battled their sanguinary way through the sinister mountains on his flank. But Montgomery was a perfectionist, who mused long over battles won and battles planned. He regarded war as a giant mathematical problem, which you solved—like General Forrest in the Civil War—by "getting there fustest with the mostest." He believed in bunching up the firepower of his guns so that all the missiles from a wide arc would explode in a comparatively small radius. When he went into a tank fight he believed in having more tanks than the enemy, even if he had to wait a few weeks.

I saw Montgomery over and over again during my two weeks in Sicily, visiting the front in his open canary car, often driving on roads in clear view of the enemy with his pennon whipping from the wireless telephone mast. Then, the following year, I met him in his caravan at Eindhoven, in Holland. His trailer consisted of bedroom, living room and office, and next to it was a large tent which shielded his communications center. Another tent held his immediate attachés and the map room. Over the whole was spread a camouflage net. As I sat in the trailer, I heard a loud scrambling overhead.

"That's Hitler up there," said Montgomery, referring to his wirehaired fox terrier, which was scuffling about on the netting. Meanwhile, outside, Rommel, a cocker spaniel, was sniffing the area. In the more northerly climate of Holland, Monty had changed his uniform. He now wore turtle-neck sweater and corduroy trousers, plus, of course, the trade-mark beret. On the wall of his trailer were two large lithographs of Rommel, evidently taken from newspapers. In one the German field marshal looked very feisty, cap over one eye, confident smugness about the mouth. In the other he looked haggard and distraught, eyes weary. "That's Rommel before he met me," said Monty, pointing to the first picture. Then he pointed to the second picture: "And that's Rommel after he met me." It was like a patent-medicine ad: before and after taking. "Do you know, Baillie," Monty said, "I should like to capture Rommel one of these days, and sit him down right there where you are sitting. Then we could spend the day discussing his mistakes."

Monty's favorite campaign was still the one in Africa, and he delighted in talking about it. He took paper and colored pencils, and sketched for me a map of the battle of El Alamein, and another map of the Mareth Line, to show me how it had been done. He was like a coach giving a chalk talk on the plays that won the game, analytical but enthusiastic.

At that time the British were sustaining a very bloody nose in the Arnhem bridgehead, where paratroopers had been dropped and were fighting in isolation, because land troops had been unable to come to their relief. Montgomery seemed oblivious to the problem as he talked to me about Africa. His orders had been given, the fighting was going on, the issue was still in doubt. But he had no doubts about the correctness of his orders, and he was never one to pace the floor and sweat and worry.

"The Germans," he said, "are beaten. It is only a matter of time. Their best soldiers are dead. We are capturing old men who have no business being at the front, and youths who haven't had time to learn to be soldiers. Yes, we have been checked at Arnhem, but it won't be for long. Soon we shall have Arnhem, and Nijmegen, far behind our advance. But we must proceed in such a way as not to waste our men. We have no fresh divisions coming in."

As Montgomery stepped from his trailer after our conversation an officer came forward, saluted and showed him an announcement of a soccer game to be played in Brussels in a couple of days, between Belgian and British teams. The announcement bore a legend, in large type, that the Field Marshal would be there, and the officer wanted assurance that Monty really would show up.

Montgomery stilettoed him with a glance. "Football game!" he snorted. "Absurd! Ridiculous!" He about-faced and re-entered his caravan, showing by the expression on his face that he had affairs of greater moment to worry about.

The last time I saw Field Marshal Lord Montgomery he was riding a horse up Piccadilly in June, 1953, in the Coronation procession of Queen Elizabeth. (The Irish Guards, marching ahead of him, were playing the "United Press March," which Paul Lavalle wrote for me on my promise to have it played before the Queen. I had made the promise and I kept it—but it took some doing.) His companions were a lot of other field marshals and generals and high brass of Britain and the Dominions, in full dress. The crowd hardly recognized him.

Had he rumbled up Piccadilly in a tank, sticking his head and shoulders out of the hatch, and wearing his black beret, he would have stolen the show.

Chapter 15

THE EUROPEAN FRONT: 1944

THEY WERE very open about it. I had already been to the war, in 1943. I wasn't "working press" by their definition: I was head of a wire service. And, they said, they were beseiged with applications from publishers who wanted to "rubberneck" at the front. They couldn't give me authorization to return to Europe.

So I wrote Lord Beaverbrook, who had invited me to visit him in England whenever I wished, and he took care of my papers from the other side. . . . In early September I headed out for Europe.

The skies over Britain were now safe for travelers, and we flew directly into Croydon airport. Driving into London, I passed miles and miles of wreckage, much of it old, but some of it new—wrought by the tiny pilotless planes, the "buzz bombs" with which the Germans had been hitting at the city. Near the UP bureau, at the juncture of the Strand and Fleet Street, there was an astonishing new pile of debris, where a block of buildings had been blown down by one of these almost aimless missiles. The men at the office looked a little grimmer and thinner: like everybody else, they had been through plenty. Some were veterans of the Normandy campaign, back for a "rest." London seemed empty, with little traffic on the streets. Few taxis were still braving the blackout, and if you went out at night you walked back to your hotel, past skeletons of buildings, the night filled with chatter, laughter, noise, footsteps—all heard, but unseen. People when you saw them were shabby and gaunt, but still cheerful.

Especially cheerful now, because—according to official sources—

their ordeal was over. On September 7, a full résumé of the good word was handed down by Duncan Sandys, Winston Churchill's son-in-law, then chairman of the "Flying Bomb Counter-Measures Committee," later Minister of Defense in the Macmillan cabinet. "Except possibly for a few last shots," Sandys said in a press statement, "the Battle of London is over." He then recalled that in April of 1943 Intelligence departments had picked up the first murmurings of a new long-range Nazi bombardment weapon of a novel type, and had confirmed their reports through aerial photography over Peenemunde. This advance warning had helped the government prepare to meet the horrors of the flying bomb—now, presumably, a thing of the past.

"All along," Sandys concluded, "we have known that there was only one completely effective way of putting a final stop to flying-bomb attacks. That is by actually capturing the firing sites. This has been happening in the last few days. . . . This visitation which London has so bravely endured has been painful enough. Had it not been for the vigilance of our Intelligence services, the unrelenting efforts of the British and American Air Forces, and the effectiveness of the defenses, London's ordeal might well have been many times more severe."

Accompanying Sandys' statement was a statistical résumé of the damage done by the 8,000 buzz bombs which had been launched against Britain during the previous 80 days. Some 2,300 of them had hit London, the statement said, and casualties as of a month before had reached 4,735 killed. The implication, clearly, was that all such troubles were now a thing of the past. That night the waiter at the Savoy pranced into my room with a tray of drinks, chirping, "No more fly bombs at any rate, sir! The war will be over by Christmas!"

The crowd that was receiving the drinks included Virgil Pinkley, Ernie Pyle, several other correspondents and some officers. We were discussing the press reshuffling that would be necessary when Eisenhower moved SHAEF from London to Paris. After the waiter left, the conversation shifted to Sandys' statement, and the general gleeful reaction to it. One of the officers said, "Well, if the Germans have anything to throw, tonight's the night. Public psychology here will be perfect. I haven't seen people so cheerful since I arrived."

A few minutes after he spoke, at 6:45, still broad daylight in September, the first supersonic ballistic missile hit London. Made in Germany by Wernher von Braun, who is now making them in America. We heard a heavy explosion and then a prolonged rumbling in the sky, away off in the distance behind the Thames. This rumble was the noise of the missile's approach. We dashed to the windows and looked out (not recommended procedure if an air raid is actually occurring), and saw the usual queues waiting for buses, people homeward bound. Evidently the explosion had not been heard at street level.

It took us most of the evening to locate the explosion, but finally we did—a big hole in the ground in Chiswick, with armaments experts looking for bits and pieces of the weapon, and rescue teams sifting the rubble for human remains. There was no question about what it was: the Germans had a new weapon. I wrote my story, and the next day went round to Admiral Thomson, head of the censorship, to find out why it hadn't been sent. Nothing doing. The British didn't know if the Germans could tell where their new rockets were hitting, or even whether the projectiles were landing in the British Isles or in the sea. So there was an absolute stop on any mention of them. Not until two months later did the censorship permit any report whatever on the V-2. In the meantime, I had returned home, been interviewed, spoken on the radio, written about the war—all, of course, without any mention of the news the British were hiding. I had signed the war correspondent's pledge, and it never occurred to me to break it. Finally, one day in New York, I saw my own story of the first missile come off the wire, released from limbo, and still news.

With the one big story in London firmly tied up by the censorship, I was particularly anxious to get to France. The British, however, having okayed me up to London, felt they had done all they were obliged to do. The Minister of Information, Sir Brendan Bracken— later Lord Bracken—told me that he thought my acceptance of Beaverbrook's invitation had obliged *me* not to ask for authority to go any further. But each general made his own arrangements, and when Tooey Spaatz asked me to come visit him—and asked his chief of staff, Brigadier General Ted Curtis, to fly me in from London—nobody could say anything about it.

During our conversation, incidentally, Bracken gave me the first hint I had that an incredible new weapon was in the works. "Do you know, Baillie," he said, "the great peril today is that the Germans could throw a missile the size of a football, which would blow down a third of London when it struck." He pronounced it "miss-isle." The Allied governments did not know that the Germans had abandoned their work on an atom bomb; what they did know was that such a weapon was feasible, and might be produced at any time.

En route from Spaatz's headquarters to Paris, I learned that the enemy was not the only danger in this war. The drive from St. Germain to Paris was supposed to be as peaceful as a ride through Central Park, but the Maquis, the French guerilla forces, were abroad, and suspicious of everybody. They stopped our car as we neared the city. I pulled off my hat, which was a mistake. One of the Maquis looked at my crew cut and noted my inability to speak French. He said "Ah, les Boches!" and stuck his pistol in the window. Fortunately, my companion in the car was French Air Commodore Blumenthal, and he talked them out of it.

In Paris I found the UP bureau virtually intact. The Germans had removed the teletype machines, but otherwise they had not disturbed anything. Two of our European employees, Jean DeGandt and Emilio Herrera, had maintained the offices, met and answered the questions of inspecting Germans, and by diplomacy and tact prevented the enemy from clearing out the place. No business had been transacted, of course, but our letter files were just as we had left them, the pictures and maps still hung on the wall, and everything was in readiness for us to resume work.

Superficially, the Germans had behaved well in Paris, but while I was there the French showed me a place of horror, a place that made all the atrocity stories of both wars seem credible. It was at Issy-les-Moulineaux, an industrial district just outside the Paris city limits, on the southwest. A big airfield is in the district, and on the edge of the airfield stands a long, low, squat building made of concrete and red brick. At one end the roof slopes sharply upward, and when I was taken there with Joe Grigg, our manager for France, there were three whirling ventilators at the tall end, to clear the fumes from the building. It was a death factory, one of the most efficient the Germans had built.

We were shown in by a French corporal. The first room we entered was a steam-torture chamber with walls of a spongy material. The room was about twenty by thirty feet, and some twelve feet high. The condemned entered the room with the thought that they were going to be given a bath. At the entranceway the Nazis stripped them naked, and pushed them inside. The jets of live steam were turned on, and the victims were scalded to death. On the spongy walls there were thousands of handprints, showing where sufferers had jumped in hopes of escaping their agony. Some of the prints were incredibly high up on the wall, up to the slots of thick glass windows behind which the Gestapo sat to watch the prisoners in the steamroom.

In an adjacent space, under the same roof, there was a shooting gallery in which the targets were human beings. At one end of the range were three wooden stakes, about five feet high, to which the prisoners were fastened. The three stakes were half chewed through with machine-gun bullets which had been fired a distance of about one hundred feet. On one side was a heap of discarded stakes which had been gashed through; on the other side, a neat stack of fresh stakes not yet used. Scattered around the floor were bloody blindfolds, old shoes, bits of clothing. I noticed a woman's high-heeled pump in the litter.

Here the Germans brought those they regarded as traitors, and members of the Resistance who fell into their hands. Executions were carried out on an assembly-line basis. Every day, truckloads of the condemned were brought to this death house, where those who were sentenced to be cooked alive were pushed into the steamroom, and the others were herded to the shooting gallery. Those who managed to live through the steam torture were added to the list of targets for machine-gun practice. The dead were buried in a long corridor with a lumpy sandy floor, which ran the length of the building at one side. The Germans had kept score on the wall—four downward strokes and a cross hatch showing five French interments, each German burial recorded by means of a coffin drawn in chalk with a cross on top and the victim's name—"Franz"—inside the box.

The existence of this death factory had not been discovered until after the liberation of Paris. The population of Issy-les-Moulineaux probably did not know what was going on, because the building stood off by itself, and the screams of the victims were muffled by the thick walls. There might be some argument as to the number of people who died in this horrible box of a building—which still stands, in the grounds of the French Air Ministry. But there could be no arguing with the devilish bas-relief of those thousands of hand-prints on the wall, made by people jumping and clawing in agony as the live steam was turned on them.

As we emerged into the daylight we saw scores of people hanging over the high board fence which surrounded the installation, looking at us. The death factory was closed to the public, and only a few visitors had been allowed. The people on the fence stared at us with-out saying a word.

The armies were now fighting over old battlegrounds, and when you went to the front you found yourself in ghostly places where the two wars blended, where the bones of the First were being blown up by the shells of the Second. I went past Verdun on my way to see Patton, and nearby I recognized landmarks and told the jeep driver to turn left—to Fort Douaumont and Fort Vaux, to the Trench of the Bayonets, where a file of poilus of the First War still stood in their collapsed trench, rusty bayonets sticking out, a mausoleum built over them. And to the gigantic Ossuary, one of the biggest sepulchers in the world, which contained the bones of thousands of Frenchmen, picked up from the fields and stacked in tiny coffins. The memorial was deserted now. There was not a soul to be seen, over that vast desolate stretch where Pétain had said, "They shall not pass," in that old war. From the front lines, a few miles ahead of me, I could hear the rumbling cannonade of the new war.

Again, I found myself in Ypres, never fully rebuilt from the ruins of 1914–1918, where the soldiers of the new war heard ceremonies in memory of the old war. At nine o'clock they sounded Last Post at the Menin Gate to honor the half-million British troops who had be-come casualties after marching up the Menin Road to hold the Ypres salient. On the Menin Gate are the names of more than 25,000 Brit-ish who disappeared during that four-year battle. One plaque on the wall simply states that 2,337 of all ranks, of the New Zealand Expeditionary Force, lay somewhere nearby, without graves.

The bugler's silvery mournful notes sounded out on the night—
interrupted by the roar of the Red Ball Express as truck after truck
went by, heading forward with supplies for the men at the front.

I drove from Verdun to Liége in horizontal rain in an open jeep—
neither top nor windshield was allowed—and then on to an advance
O.P. with Henry Gorrell, one of our top war correspondents. The
observation post was almost too far "advanced." It was in a German
brick farmhouse, two stories and attic, with steep stairs. To get
there, we had to go on hands and knees, one at a time, across an open
field. From the garret window we could see into the enemy lines
through powerful binoculars mounted on tripods. Right in front
was a German factory, belching smoke. Our shells were bursting
in the vicinity, but not hitting the factory; obviously, an attempt was
being made to preserve it. The men who were on watch in the O.P.
were a bit nervous at having us in their midst, afraid the Germans
had seen us crawling up to the building and might decide we were
worth a salvo. We gave them the fidgets, and they were glad when
we said we were leaving. The major in charge escorted us to the
front hall, where I saw a big white flag on a long staff, standing in the
wrought-iron German hat rack.

"Congratulations!" I said to the major. "I see you captured some
of the enemy, and you've got their surrender flag."

"Oh, no," he said. "That's ours."

Leaving the O.P., we found we *had* attracted attention from the
enemy. Shells fell around, and when we got into the woods "shrap-
nel air bursts" whacked overhead. Gorrell had been caught in these
things before—he was a man with an uncanny instinct for when the
enemy was about to return fire; he would sniff the air, and say, "Let's
get out of here, it's time for the return mail"; and he was always
right. A day later the return mail reached me, and the jeep in which
I was traveling left the road too abruptly. We all wound up at a
field dressing station, where I found myself not only "seeing, hearing
and smelling the war"—my instructions to correspondents—but feeling it, too.

That night I compared notes with Jack Frankish, who had been to
another part of the front—a bright-faced, ruddy kid not long out of

the University of Southern California. A few months later, he was killed in the German counterattack which recovered most of the territory I had just traversed, and went into history as the Battle of the Bulge.

This part of the war was being fought by General Courtney Hodges' First Army, and I had dinner with him at his château. We could hear the crash of V-2's dropping in nearby towns throughout our repast, and General Hodges felt obliged to react to the sound. "What a futile waste of time," he said. He was a quiet, studious type. He told me his forces were making "big medicine." So were the Germans, though nobody knew it yet.

Then I was in London again, watching a buzz bomb fly past my bathroom window and listening to the German radio (which had just broadcast a fine rendition of "Home on the Range" by an English-singing male chorus) announce that the Americans had been repulsed once again before Aachen. Virgil Pinkley and I decided to go look at the battle, planning to leave London in the morning and get back in time for dinner. Pinkley arranged with Troop Carrier Command to ferry us and our jeep to an airport within twenty miles of the front, and then take us and jeep back that same evening. It seemed like a good stunt at the time. Actually, we were five days in Belgium and Germany before we got back to London, still wearing the same smelly clothes and carrying a Hotel Savoy towel which had somehow turned black—and *sans* jeep, to the despair of the officer in charge of it, who thought he was going to be court-martialed for its disappearance. But we had witnessed the fall of Aachen, one of the great spectacles of the war: the fire-swept city, the area of the fire gradually contracting as the Americans fought their way in and our artillery and air bombardment was lifted from the captured streets. Then, with a corner of the city still in flames, the bombardment suddenly stopped entirely: Aachen had quit.

On my return—which was much more easily said than done, involving four nights in progressively more disreputable clothes—I went to tell the story to my host in Europe, Lord Beaverbrook, at Gwynder House, his office in Whitehall as Lord Privy Seal.

"Where have you been?" asked Beaverbrook, in his abrupt manner.

"Why, Lord Beaverbrook, I have been at the Battle of Aachen," said I. "I was there when the town surrendered."

"*Aachen?*" said he, frowning. "Never heard of it."

"Look," said I, going to the map on the wall and pointing. "It's right here—the first town in Germany captured by the Americans."

"Oh," said he, "you mean Aix-la-Chapelle. Aachen was the old name. Well, that's all over now."

Going to the telephone on his desk, he called his London *Daily Express*, to be sure they were using the right name of the town—Aix-la-Chapelle, not Aachen.

Chapter 16

JAPAN AND THE EMPEROR

I HEARD the war come in with the banshee sirens of London on September 3, 1939; on August 14, 1945, I heard the war go out with the shrieking, celebrating air-raid sirens of San Francisco. I was on my way to the Orient. On August 28, General MacArthur credentialed me to his command.

The press had gone into Tokyo ahead of the army. Frank Bartholomew, who was later to succeed me as president of the United Press, reopened our Tokyo office before General MacArthur accepted the Japanese surrender on the deck of the battleship *Missouri*. He sent me word that the Japanese were very polite and accommodating, and our men were well quartered in the Imperial Hotel. (We didn't stay there long; the Imperial was soon reserved for officers above the rank of chicken colonel, and we were shunted to the Dai Ichi.)

My arrangements were to fly to Tokyo via Naval Air Transport Service. Tooey Spaatz was in San Francisco, and when he heard I was traveling NATS, he reacted like the proprietor of a rival airline. "You'll never get there," he said jovially. In a more serious vein, he suggested that the travel bottleneck at Manila was slowing everybody down, and that I would get to Tokyo quicker if I left the navy service at Guam and allowed the army to fly me directly to Japan. So I laid over at Guam, where I renewed acquaintances with General Curtis LeMay, whom I had known as a colonel in England two years before, and who had commanded the bombing raids which destroyed

Japan. LeMay gave me a special briefing on how the job was done, using charts and a long pointer. At times he scowled at me quizzically, chewing his cigar, as if wondering how much of all this I was comprehending. Then he took me to the office of General Nathan Twining, who was in command at Guam and is now Chairman of the Joint Chiefs of Staff. LeMay left word with an orderly that I should be taken up that afternoon for a ride in a B-29, the weapon which had done the damage in Japan.

Presently General Twining came breezily into the room, throwing his hat onto the desk. I told him that my orders from General LeMay were to go up with him in a B-29 and see "how it was done."

He replied, "Sure—but would you rather go to the ball game?"

"Naturally," I said. "Let's go to the ball game." So we sat in a bleachers marked "For Colonels Only" and watched big-league players in Army Air Force uniform battle for the championship of Guam. At regular intervals, big black planes marked "P.O.W." flew over us on their way to drop supplies to the recently liberated prisoners of war in the various Pacific islands . . . and China . . . and Japan . . . and Manchuria.

The next morning General Twining was up at four o'clock, in his bathrobe, to have a final cup of coffee with me before I took off for Japan in the two-engine DC-3, a long haul for a two-engine plane. I hadn't slept much, because there was a sentry walking up and down on a gravel path outside my window—alert for prowling Japanese, who were still to be found in some quantity on the island of Guam. The crew of my plane—who were going to Japan for sight-seeing, not for assignments—gave me a wide berth at first, because they had mistaken my war correspondent's insignia for the single star of a brigadier general. Once the error was cleared up, they accepted me as one of the party.

We landed in a typhoon at Atsugi, where I was quartered temporarily in the kamikaze barracks, from which Japanese pilots dressed in ceremonial death robes had gone out to launch themselves and their planes as projectiles to destroy the ships of the U.S. Navy. From what you read about the kamikazes, you would have thought they went forth from a kind of temple. But the barracks was a slum: one-story wood shacks with pools of stagnant green water around them, duck boards running over the mud from the door to door.

Finally a Marine in a jeep showed up, and we drove through miles and miles *and miles* of the ruins of Yokohama. It looked like an overgrown golf course. Then we crossed the little river which divides the two cities and began a long trip through the ruins of Tokyo. (A sign at the river read, "ENTERING TOKYO, Courtesy of the 1st Cavalry Division.") When you got up into one of the surviving buildings and glanced out over the city, Tokyo looked like Pompeii—a ruin, and an old ruin at that; 9,700 acres destroyed.

Everything was smashed to hell. You sensed it even in the nights —which were completely black because there were no facilities for illuminating the city. You would wander through the streets and stumble over the wreckage of an automobile blown up and onto the sidewalk during one of the bombing raids. Once I was out at night with Count Watanabe, who worked for the newspaper *Tokyo Maini-chi,* and commented that we must be in the country because I heard the sound of chirping insects. He corrected me politely: we were standing in the middle of what had been the white-light center of Tokyo, the city's Times Square.

I went to the offices of one of our prewar clients, *Nippon Dempo,* and found its proprietor sitting in a room covered with dust and freezing cold. A gale blew in at us through the holes where the windows had been. He wore a tweed jacket, plus fours and rubber boots —all that was left of a once-extensive wardrobe. And he kept getting up to work on a fire which he was trying to keep ablaze in a little stove near his desk.

But the Japanese were very polite about it. They would tell you apologetically, with an amiable smile, how their grandmother and grandfather were burned to death in the street during one of the fire raids—or simply asphyxiated when the fire storm ate all the oxygen. I sat around with newspapermen at the Hotel Dai Ichi, which was press headquarters, drinking Suntori "Scotch-type Scotch" (MADE IN JAPAN) and debating why the Japanese didn't just up and kill us all—they still had some three million men under arms in the home islands, while the American "occupying army" was little more than a corporal's guard. Driving back from MacArthur's headquarters in a car full of staff officers, I passed a contingent of Japanese soldiers in fine physical shape, marching off to be demobilized, and noticed how they licked their chops at the sight of our car—all that brass they could knock off so easily if only the Mikado would let them.

The Dai Ichi itself was no prize. The roof was partly off, and when it rained you could hear the water slopping down from floor to floor. The pillows were the hardest I had ever put under my head, and I wondered what was in them; I slashed one of them open and found it full of rice husks. Every so often a pest-control squad from the army came around to every room and swashed everybody and everything with DDT. One night the Dai Ichi caught fire, and Japanese fire engines rushed to the scene (the firehouses were among the few structures standing; during the bombings, since they couldn't hope to control the conflagration of the city, the firemen had sensibly concentrated on saving their own equipment). Our sentries were under orders not to admit Japanese to the Dai Ichi, however, so they turned back the little firemen and little engines and put out the flames themselves.

One of the few cheerful-looking places in Tokyo in those days was a block-long Yoshiwara House, ornamented with red-white-and-blue bunting, which decorated the drive from Tokyo to Yokohama. We drove to Yokohama every day, because MacArthur still had his headquarters at the port, and every time we passed we saw long queues of GI's (both officers and enlisted men) lined up from the great gates, clear around the corner into the next block. Signs on the institution told its history: first, "We start the business at 11 A.M."; then, "We start the business at 10 A.M."; then, "We start the business at 2 P.M."; and then, "Closed. We are resting." Finally, an official proclamation from the Provost Marshal General: "Off Limits." That was the end of the Yoshiwara House.

Despite the well-known difference between East and West, GI's seemed to experience little trouble in these intimate areas of experience. Among other advantages, they had phrase books, designed to help them in less dramatic situations, but containing individual words and phrases that could be pieced together to serve any occasion. One of the most popular jobs of piecing together produced the Japanese for "Lie down, madam. The government of the United States will reward you."

Bartholomew and I went to the army hospital in Yokohama to visit Tojo, the former prime minister and leader of the war party in the Japanese government, who had tried to commit suicide with a pistol when the Americans arrived to take him into custody. Tojo was propped up in bed, with a thick bandage around his middle. He was attended by two nurses and a surgeon, and guarded by an MP sergeant who seemed quite prepared to shoot him down if he tried to commit suicide again. We were keeping him alive so he could be tried for his war crimes and duly hanged. Tojo greeted me by raising himself painfully from his pillows and making his best effort at a Japanese deep bow—one for Bartholomew and one for me. He told us he was not sorry his suicide attempt had failed. Honor had been satisfied, anyway. In his code, evidently, a good hearty cut at the ball was just as good as a home run.

Bart had been on the spot for Tojo's attempted suicide, and had described it in one of the great stories of the war. I asked him to tell me about it, and received the following response:

"On September 11, 1945, about 3:00 P.M., I arrived at Hideki Tojo's home in Setagaya-ku.

"I had learned from a reporter on the *Tokyo Mainichi*, Toichiro Takamatsu, that the General had returned to his house in the Tokyo suburb. I wanted to interview him.

"Takamatsu and I found Tojo's home without trouble. We talked our way past Japanese police guards at the driveway entrance to the rather modern residence, which was half Western, half Japanese. I knocked at the front doors. No answer. 'General not at home,' a guard on the walk below told me; 'he take walk.' We waited.

"Soon I heard a side window opened, sliding horizontally in the Japanese manner. Takamatsu and I went around the garden to the south side of the house, and found Tojo peering down at us through horn-rimmed glasses.

"His bald head was very brown. He seemed lean and in good condition physically.

"'I am Tojo,' the man above us said, and repeated: 'Tojo.' He showed his teeth, which gleamed under his mustache.

"Takamatsu was so overcome I had difficulty in getting him to interpret. Through Takamatsu I told the Prime Minister our mission

He seated himself on an interior window seat and thoughtfully considered the two of us on the lawn below.

"We were interrupted by the arrival of an officer of the American Counter-Intelligence Corps, Major Paul Kraus, whom I had known slightly in San Francisco when he was geologist for the Standard Oil Company.

"I looked toward the street outside Tojo's private roadway and saw Kraus' jeep followed by an entire parade of correspondents in other vehicles. The newspapermen were just then spreading over the area and beginning to search for telephones. It was 4 P.M.

" 'Open the door,' Kraus told Tojo. 'I am coming in to present my credentials.'

"Tojo waved his arms and replied in Japanese: 'Unless this is an official order, I do not care to discuss it.'

"A nisei interpreter named Ono interpreted this for Kraus. Takamatsu told me: 'The General says he does not understand English. If the Major's warrant is not in Japanese, he won't understand it.'

" 'Tell him to quit this damned fooling around and let's get going,' Major Kraus said angrily.

" 'Tell him to open the front door so I can present my credentials.

" 'Tell him to prepare himself for a trip to General MacArthur's headquarters in Yokohama.'

"Ono translated to Kraus; Takamatsu to the other correspondents and myself. Tojo slammed his sliding window shut. He seemed as angry as Kraus, but we assumed he was moving to the front door to comply with the Major's orders. We went back across the lawn again to the front of the house.

"Halfway to the door, a flat-sounding 'whack!' came from within the front room we were circling.

" 'What's that?' Kraus asked involuntarily.

" 'Your pigeon just shot himself,' I said.

"Kraus raced for the front double doors. They were locked but he was able to pull them open. We piled into the small entrance hall. The interior door to Tojo's study was also locked. Kraus called upon him to open it. There was no reply. Kraus mounted an interior step for leverage and kicked in the door.

"The man who started the wars of the Orient was seated in an easy chair, his legs crossed. He wore a blood-spattered, white sports shirt, a part of which was burning dully; khaki whipcord military trousers and high boots. Behind him on the easy chair was a cushion which the pistol bullet had pierced; there were blood-stained feathers from the cushion scattered about. His brown bald scalp was spangled with big drops of sweat.

"On the floor beside Tojo was an American Air Force Colt .32. Blood bubbled and frothed from a six-inch wound across his midriff.

"Past the double doorway to an adjoining room in the Oriental part of the house, through which a faint smell of incense was discernible, I had a brief glimpse of a young man in white robes seated cross-legged and sobbing. I learned later this was Tojo's secretary-aide.

"Tojo was breathing heavily and was unconscious. Servants quietly appeared bringing a narrow bed into the sparsely furnished combination office and living room.

"Tojo regained consciousness, and began to talk in Japanese. Ono was not there. I rushed into an adjoining hallway and retrieved Takamatsu, who knelt with us beside Tojo.

"The translations came jerkily, because of Tojo's wavering on the brink of unconsciousness and the excitement of Takamatsu.

" 'I am happy to die—happy to die,' the Prime Minister said.

" 'I wanted to die by the sword . . . but the pistol had to do.'

"Later I wondered why. There was a samurai sword on the wall by the south window.

" 'I assume responsibility for the war.

" 'Banzai! . . .' "

A few days later, Bart and I visited another former premier of Japan—Prince Konoye, who had been head of the peace party and was in far better odor with the American occupying authorities. (Though he later committed suicide by poison when he learned he might be listed as a war criminal.) The purpose of our visit was to arrange for me to interview Emperor Hirohito, through whom MacArthur was governing the defeated nation. Konoye's own house in Tokyo had been demolished, and he was living in a suburban mansion built by a pill king.

We entered through a gate, then followed quite a ramble through
Oriental landscaping and over hump-backed bridges until we
reached the grassy terrace where the prince and I were to talk.
(When I left, an hour later, I stepped through a doorway from the
house immediately into the street: the more elaborate entrance was
a matter of "face.") In the middle of the lawn stood a table, and on it
a bottle of Black Label (real, not Suntori) Scotch whisky. A white-
jacketed servant stood by to pour. There were six in the party—for
the UP, Bart, myself and Frank Tremaine, now general manager of
UPI News Pictures, in New York; for the Japanese, the Prince, plus
Messrs. Shirazu and Ushiba of the Foreign Office. Shirazu spoke with
an English accent, and looked the perfect diplomat—one of the very
few well-dressed men I saw in the devastated Tokyo of 1945.

At first our conversation seemed aimless, but gradually Konoye,
Shirazu and Ushiba began talking animatedly to one another in Japanese. I had the feeling—correct, as it turned out—that Shirazu and
Ushiba were ably presenting our case for an interview to the Prince.
Presently we all took off our shoes and went inside Konoye's temporary residence, where we sat on matting and drew up a list of questions for the Emperor. There was not much give-and-take about the
negotiations. Bart, Tremaine and I made all the suggestions, which
were then discussed by the Japanese in Japanese.

Shirazu apparently showed the questions to the Emperor. The
next time I saw him we had a long conversation about how my interrogations should be phrased and what answers the Mikado would
give me. Two days thereafter, I was summoned to the Prime Minister's residence, where I saw Ushiba. He told me I was to have tea
with the Emperor the following day, and he handed me a long letter
of instructions, describing in meticulous detail how I was to conduct
myself in the Divine Presence.

I was to report shortly before 4 P.M., the letter said, at the Foreign
Office, where I would be taken under the escort of T. Urabe. I was not
to initiate any conversation with the Emperor, nor to ask him any
questions. All this had been taken care of by means of the questionnaire, which would be waiting for me, in a completed form, when I
left the Imperial Palace after the interview. The Emperor was to do

all the talking—if he felt like it. If he didn't feel like talking, there was to be silence. . . . I was to be present when the Emperor entered the room at 4 P.M.; the tea was to last twenty-five minutes; I was to depart when the Emperor rose, pick up my interview, and get into the official car which would carry me from the palace grounds. These were not requests: they were orders.

There was also a postcript, saying it was to be hoped that I had made arrangements to get past the American sentries. Otherwise I wouldn't be able to enter the palace. This caused me first to laugh and then to hustle around to the Provost Marshal's office, where, after I did considerable explaining, a second lieutenant gave me a pass into the imperial grounds.

The pass got me in—but just barely. I made my rendezvous with Urabe, and we drove over a bridge toward the formidable wall around the palace. As we passed a point opposite the main building, I noticed, my escort doffed his hat. At the Saka Shita Mon gate we encountered the American sentries, kids wearing steel helmets and carrying bayonets, who looked very closely at Urabe—one of the tallest Japanese I ever met—and handled my pass as though it were an infectious disease. Finally they called the officer of the day, who told me he was under orders to let no one in. It wasn't until I told him I had just come from MacArthur's headquarters that he changed his mind; the magic name of the general opened the doors.

Once we were inside the compound the atmosphere changed. This was a sacred place, like a church. Obsequious servants bowed low on every side. Urabe and I ascended a flight of heavily carpeted stairs, then walked through many long corridors, past bowing attendants. In an anteroom off the audience chamber I was introduced to the official interpreter, Katsuzo Okymura, who was wearing formal diplomatic dress—morning coat, striped trousers, tall stiff collar, gray cravat. I asked Okymura whether my meeting with the Emperor was to take place in the traditional throne room.

"Oh, no," he replied softly. "Your bombers destroyed that." He said it with a slight air of being sorry for me because our aviators had committed such a gaffe. This was not, he told me, the old imperial palace—that had been bombed out. "The Emperor," he said, "is living in a small cottage. This building used to house the palace offices. We are making it do, for the present." Half the buildings in the extensive imperial grounds, which stretched like a park for blocks in all directions, had been destroyed. The gate through which I had entered was temporary: wreckage within the walls around the former official gateway made the traditional route impassable.

"Now," said Mr. Urabe, "it is time to go in."

I found myself in a large room furnished in a European style, with French furniture and Japanese vases and screens. There was a businesslike electric clock over the door through which the Emperor was to appear. At one end of the room was a slightly elevated section, with two high-backed armchairs vis-à-vis, a tea table at the elbow of each. I went up and stood by my chair.

Promptly at 4 P.M. the double doors swung wide, and His Imperial Majesty entered. He was attired in a frock coat, striped trousers, stiff batwing collar with curved rather than pointed edges, and a four-in-hand tie. He was rather taller than I had expected, and slight. He wore steel-rimmed glasses. His hair was not so closely cropped as pictures had led me to believe.

The Emperor bowed, and we shook hands. We sat down, and Hirohito's entourage sat down, too, a respectful distance away from us—the Minister of the Imperial Household, the Grand Chamberlain of the Imperial Household, and the Grand Master of Ceremonies. They abstained from the conversation, which was entirely between the Emperor and myself, Okymura interpreting so easily you were scarcely conscious he was there. The Emperor and I sipped our tea and ate little cakes which were slid under our noses on silver trays, by footmen so unobtrusive they were practically invisible.

Hirohito's manner was rather scholarly, somewhat like that of the traditional college professor. He was tense, but most courteous and evidently eager to keep a conversation afloat. He wriggled itchily in his clothes. He had a habit of gurgling in his throat and nodding his head as I talked, repeating, "Ach, zo! Ach, zo!" like a German. He laughed frequently, smiled broadly, and kept nodding.

He asked me my impressions of Japan, and when I replied he commented that this was not a very good time to get the best impression of the country. At this he chuckled, and the three gentlemen of his household echoed the sound, starting their pattern of echoing his mood, which they would maintain throughout the interview.

The Emperor asked me about my hobbies, to which I countered by inquiring about his golf. He recalled having played golf with the Duke of Windsor when that romantic figure was still Prince of Wales; and mentioned that he had also played with the British governor of Ceylon. He told me stories of both matches. Next came baseball, and I reminded him that there had been games between Japanese and American teams before the war, and wondered aloud whether they could be resumed, now that the war was over.

"Well," he replied with a slight smile and a quizzical expression, "we haven't had much time to practice lately."

Every once in a while during the interview, American planes buzzed the palace, shaking our insides—the Emperor's and mine—and everybody else's, no doubt; and drowning out the conversation.

Finally the Emperor expressed the wish that my stay in Japan would be enjoyable, and indicated by making a slight movement in his chair, as if to rise, that my audience was finished. We all stood up, the Emperor last of all. He bowed to me, and I bowed to him. With a broad smile, he extended his hand. After the handshake, he turned and bowed to his three courtiers; and the smile left his face as though it had been snapped off, like an electric light. The three men bowed low, and His Imperial Majesty left the room. It was exactly 4:25 P.M.: the tea had been fitted into the time allotted, as neatly as a television program.

About halfway back down the long corridors, I was ushered briefly into a cubicle where the text of the questions and answers was handed to me. Then I stepped into a waiting car and drove down the graveled roadway through the great gates, past saluting Japanese guards and American sentries, into the ruins of Tokyo.

Newspapers all over the world carried the written questions and answers—in which Hirohito said that Japan had been placed on an entirely new footing and would prove herself equal to membership in the family of nations. Japanese censorship, however, kept the story out of the Japanese papers. Whereupon MacArthur abolished the censorship. . . .

Making my farewells to Japan I had lunch with Foreign Minister —later Prime Minister—Yoshida. He warned me that the bloodless

occupation was only "by virtue of the Imperial Will," and that if anything were to happen to the Emperor, it might cause a great change
within Japan, which would be "unfortunate for the invader."

After lunch, Yoshida escorted me to the door with a benign smile.
Outside, it was seething rain. The Foreign Minister helped me into
my trench coat.

"Quite a coat!" he commented, in his perfect American.

"Yes, Mr. Minister," I answered. "I have worn this on several war
fronts."

He pretended to examine it closely. Then, puckishly, as I stepped
out the door: "No bullet holes in it—yet—hah?"

Chapter 17

CHINA AND CHIANG

I WAS probably the only man in the world who wanted to go to Chungking that autumn of 1945; certainly, I was the only American. The big push was in reverse, over the Pacific and home. From Tokyo to Chungking involved two steps—first to Shanghai, which was accomplished via Tex McCrary, who was serving as an Air Force P.R.O.; then from Shanghai to the wartime Chinese capital, which I was able to arrange only through the personal intervention of General Stratemeyer. Only special crews could fly to Chungking, which had a difficult and rather primitive airport—"as muddy as the next paddy," one pilot said. And those special crews were all trying to fly the other way. Meanwhile, I waited in Shanghai.

It was an incredible city, in those first days of "peace." Allied warships, among them the *Nashville,* sat in the Whangpoo bristling with guns, surrounded by picture-book junks. Hawkers huckstered rice on the sidewalks of the Bund, the great street of European buildings fronting on the Whangpoo—the Cathay Hotel, the offices of the great merchants and shippers, the banks. The city swarmed with indescribably filthy and tattered beggars. Waifs died in doorways, and were gathered up every morning.

A seemingly endless inflation had destroyed the value of Chinese currency. At our bureau—a fourth-floor walkup in King Edward VII Street—I was equipped with a roll of thousand-dollar bills (Chinese dollars) as large as a loaf of bread. A ricksha took me back to my hotel. At the first bridge (arched), the ricksha man pretended exhaustion and sank to his knees; whereupon several children rushed forward and shriekingly offered to boost us over. I tipped them $1,000 each. At my hotel, which offered a rather shabby luxury, each guest was assigned a houseboy, whose first duty was to sell the newcomer a roll of toilet paper—for $10,000.

The noise of the city never let up—a constant ululation of human voices. All night long the peddlers beat sticks together in a cadenced clack-clack code which identified their wares; there were cries and firecrackers, and a continuous babble of voices. In Foochow Creek I saw the junks jammed together, and the weird, drab-looking people who lived on these strange boats. Many of them had not been ashore for years. Bearded Sikh cops directed traffic at street corners, looking shopworn. They had worked for the Japs, too. I was shown Bridge House, formerly a Japanese jail, and the ugly Ward Road prison; and my guides told me horror stories about what had occurred therein.

Finally, the Air Force found me a plane and a crew (which did not come with the plane, and didn't know what was in it: after we were aloft, they found out that we had no parachutes and our radio didn't work). Four hours later we were in Peishihyi airport, where a heavy rain was beating down into thick mud. From there we drove twenty-five miles to Chungking, over some of the world's worst roads, past sights that seemed to come from the age of Marco Polo.

Despite the weather, everybody was working on the farms, water buffaloes pulling the plows. Ladies and gentlemen came along in litters carried by coolies—and we passed hogs riding in similar fashion, carried as a guarantee that they wouldn't run off any weight on the trip. (They were also blinded to make sure they wouldn't run away; if they were to be butchered immediately, their eyes were put out; otherwise, their eyes were merely sewn shut temporarily.) I was shown a youth who had a large black hog on a leash, and was told that this was the young man's career—tending the hog. Evidently, values were quite different from those to which I had been accustomed.

We got lost in Chungking trying to find the press hostel and Colonel Raymond's place, where I was billeted. I finally told the driver I was going to stop the first car that came along with Americans in it. The car that appeared carried a bright red plate with a single star on it, indicating that its passenger was a brigadier general. My driver was somewhat upset at the idea of halting such a dignitary, but I did it. While I was parleying with the general, his car slid slowly and sedately sideways off the muddy high-crowned road and into the ditch. So out piled the general and his guest—who turned out to be the distinguished historian Dr. Douglas Southall Freeman of Richmond, Va.—and we all slipped and slithered in the goo, getting the staff car back on the road. Everybody pushed.

Colonel Raymond's place had been built by Americans, and it was concrete, like most of the buildings that were still standing in Chungking—which, of course, had been bombed repeatedly. What was left of the city struck me as rather ramshackle. Breakaway doorknobs. Windows that wouldn't work. Plumbing likewise. And the place was a stink-hole. A miasma arising from the Yangtze covered the stone-block paving with a film of ooze, and you had to watch your step as carefully as though you were walking on ice. I had dinner one night at the Ministry of Information, and a long legged rat ran the length of the dining hall without causing any comment. Like most Chinese cities, Chungking was amazingly overcrowded, and swarming with children.

I had a cozy bed under a mosquito net the size of a Crusader's pavilion. Beside my bedroom was a fine tiled bathroom, with tub and toilet—but you couldn't use either until coolies with buckets had filled the tub, or the tank of the toilet.

My invitation to visit the Generalissimo had come after I sent him a questionnaire, so he knew why I was coming, and all I had to do was inform him of my arrival. Presently, a messenger arrived with an invitation to have dinner with Chiang that night, and receive the answers to my questions. A staff car skidded through the mud with me, up the hill to the spacious compound which overlooked the city and the Yangtze, and contained the mansion occupied by Generalissimo and Madame Chiang Kai-shek.

When I arrived at the compound I was told that one of our war correspondents, Bill MacDougall, was staying at one of the Generalissimo's guest houses. He had been found in a Japanese prison camp in Sumatra and brought to Chungking on his way home, traveling with a party headed by Assistant Secretary of War John McCloy. We had had no word of Bill in three and a half years, and I hurried to see him. He was a skeleton—but his spirit still burned brightly.

"Bill, I thought you were dead," said I.

"So did I, several times," said he. Then he added, "Say, Hugh, how about my pay for the last four years?"

"It's waiting for you in New York," I replied. "You can collect it when you get there, unless you want it sooner."

Bill told me some of his adventures in the few minutes we had together in Chiang Kai-shek's guest house. He spoke in a very matter-of-fact manner. He had been caught when the Japanese overran what was then the Dutch East Indies. He had stayed behind after all the other correspondents departed, to send the last possible word. A lot had happened while he was locked away by the Japanese: he had never heard the name Truman; he didn't know what the OPA was; the words "gin rummy" meant nothing to him.

Bill later got his pay, regained his weight, went to work in our Washington bureau—and afterwards studied for holy orders. It is unfortunate that civilian organizations have no medals for such as he.

Chiang's party presented a glittering array of brass, both Chinese and American, plus such distinguished guests as Secretary McCloy and Dr. Freeman. Chiang himself wore a very plain uniform, contrasting with the brass buttons and the orders of the other officers present. The few women in the room were led, of course, by the beautiful Madame Chiang. Everybody stood around talking and drinking cocktails. It was a gay and animated scene, far removed from the muck and leaden misery outside.

When we were seated at the long banquet table I found I was at the Generalissimo's left hand. Opposite me sat U.S. Minister Robertson, and at his elbow Dr. K. C. Wu, the Minister of Information. Madame Chiang sat at the other end of the table. Our conversation was casual at the beginning, until the Generalissimo, whose manner had been extremely cordial, said something abrupt to me in Chinese. Dr. Wu translated it as, "I thought you were going to interview me!"

I replied, "Yes, Your Excellency, I am. I have the questions right here in the pocket of my field jacket. But is this the time and place?"

"Certainly," he said. "Go ahead! Interview me. . . ."

So the interview proceeded forthwith. Before long, the other diners—diplomats, Chinese and American officials and distinguished guests—became aware of what was taking place at our end of the table, and gave their attention to the questions and answers. The Generalissimo had brought with him to the dinner his written answers to my questions, and as I consulted my notes for the interrogations he consulted his for the replies. This continued while the servants unostentatiously changed plates. Between questions, toasts were offered and drunk to various personages at the table. It is unlikely that such an interview ever was given before such a gallery under such circumstances.

Chiang radiated personal magnetism beneath his friendly manner. His poker face broke easily into a smile, and while his replies were studied and carefully considered, he delivered them rapidly. He looked young and in the best of condition despite the long war through which he had borne so many crushing responsibilities. I noticed that whenever the Generalissimo proposed a toast or responded to one, he took a slight sip of wine. The waiters did not refill his small glass, though they were busily keeping everyone else's glass brimful.

I started by asking him whether the Japanese were being sufficiently punished for their atrocities committed during the war, and he replied: "The first thing to do is to punish the people who were responsible for the war, under due process and with a fair trial. The treatment of the Japanese people should be viewed in the same light as the Germans are treated."

"Should UNRRA or other United Nations organizations offer assistance to Japan?" I asked.

"In this connection we must take a long view," he answered. "I should think that the United States should approach the problem from the humanitarian standpoint. Again I would say, Japan should be treated in the same light as Germany."

"In your judgment, should the Emperor of Japan be permitted to continue to rule?"

Chiang Kai-shek replied, "In Cairo I told President Roosevelt that the question of the continuance of the Emperor of Japan should be decided by the Japanese people themselves. I still hold to that opinion."

"How would the will of the Japanese people be expressed?"

"By freely elected representatives," the Generalissimo answered.

The interview covered the attitude that Chiang had toward the restoration of foreign holdings in China, how the airlines should be operated, his ideas for the development of the country, and other economic matters. From the tenor of his replies, I gathered that he held rather progressive—even advanced—views in this area. Like many others, however, he had no notion of what was coming in the Far East. I asked him, for example, whether he cared to comment on the independence movements in Indo-China and the Dutch East Indies. "Should they be free?" I asked. "Or should they return to their old regimes?"

"They should have a high degree of autonomy, greater than ever before—for a beginning," he replied.

Again, I asked him, "Do you feel more optimistic than ever before with regard to China becoming unified and having an end to internal strife?"

"Yes," he said with unusual enthusiasm. "Much more optimism. It's so much *easier* than ever before!"

As in most of my interviews, I eventually got around to freedom of information. Chiang replied without hesitation: "We have just abolished censorship, except in the recovered areas. We expect to abolish it in those areas as soon as conditions return to normal. We are all for freedom of the press. . . ."

The dinner and the interview ended together. Chiang carefully folded his napkin, and called to Madame Chiang in Chinese, evidently suggesting the guests adjourn to the drawing room.

Madame Chiang clapped her hands. "Stingers, anyone?" she inquired. "All those who know how to make stingers, please come with me, and we'll prepare them."

Then followed an hour of party conversation in the drawing room, Madame Chiang chatting in perfect English and smoking cigarettes in a long holder, the Generalissimo speaking through an interpreter but participating freely in the talk. His rather confident expression never left his face. Obviously, he considered the war won. And while there was a deal of mopping-up to be done, he regarded what was left as far less important than the victory which had been attained—and which, though he didn't know it, was rapidly slipping away from him.

He was, in brief, living in a fool's paradise. The results of the Yalta conference had not yet been brought home to him. In Manchuria, the Russian armies were handing over to the Communist rebels the weapons they had captured from the Japanese. Ahead of Chiang lay the disastrous "Coalition" government, sponsored by American advisers, during which the Communists were to learn at first hand how weak Chiang's position really was and how easily he could be overthrown.

Because he had so little notion of what the future would bring, his answers to my questions seem either obvious or meaningless today. But they were news in 1945, when Chiang was one of the Big Five, and they were worth headlines all over the world.

A month or so later, Chungking got its first inkling of what was actually happening up north. Shortly after my return to New York on November 16, I received a message from Dr. Wu, warning me that the fighting on the Manchurian border might be serious, and hinting that the Russians were backing the Chinese Communist army. Since we were backing the army of Chiang Kai-shek, this situation was, as Dr. Wu put it, "pregnant with peril to American security."

As it still is . . .

Chapter 18

MacARTHUR

THE DAY I met MacArthur in Yokohama, he was perhaps the greatest figure in the world. He was occupying Japan with a handful of men, against an enemy army not yet demobilized and all around him. His authority was everywhere, but you could not see it. There were few American soldiers in the streets: he kept them out of sight. The Emperor was taking MacArthur's orders, and the people of Japan obeyed their Emperor. Only once did he assert his authority over the Mikado: when he had Hirohito call on *him*, instead of going to the Imperial Palace. Hirohito arrived in top hat and formal dress, to find General MacArthur in an open-necked shirt.

Back home, however, there were many who felt that MacArthur was being "too easy" on the Japanese. People wanted revenge on the Japs, rather than the smooth administration of an occupied country. I wanted an interview with MacArthur, and I decided to use this criticism from home as the key to the door. The aim was to make MacArthur mad enough to wish to reply, at which point he was sure to observe that I was on hand to take it all down. So I showed him clippings from editorials in newspapers back home, in which he was accused of being lily-fingered, of setting himself up as a patriarchal, benevolent leader of the Japanese people when he should be acting as a conqueror crushing the Japs under his heel.

MacArthur was first incredulous, then angry at the criticisms. He attributed them to the machinations of personal enemies and political

foes. But he was not accustomed to giving interviews: his pronouncements were usually issued to all the press, and came down like the
tablets of truth out of the cloud on top of the mountain. He had no
desire to sit down and allow himself to be queried by an individual
reporter.

MacArthur greeted me at his offices in Yokohama with the dramatic swoop of a man meeting an old friend after years apart—
though, in fact, he had never laid eyes on me before. He tossed off a
few orders to his aides, then took me by the elbow and steered me to
the dining room. Sentries jerked to attention at his appearance, and
stood rigidly staring into space under their shining helmet liners. He
gave each one a cheerful wave of the hand, which started as a salute
but wound up as a flourish.

His manner was much as I had expected from the accounts of
others: imperial and majestic. He sat at the head of the table in a
swivel chair, and when he started to talk, deep silence fell in the
room. His staff officers lit their cigarettes as quietly as possible, click-
ing their lighters under the table. The General began discoursing on
the military significance of the atom bomb, which, he said, had ren-
dered armies and navies obsolete. (I could well agree with him, having flown over Hiroshima and Nagasaki, once populous and thriving
cities which now looked like unfinished real-estate developments:
streets, but no buildings.) As he spoke, he became oblivious of his
surroundings. He turned around in his swivel chair so that his back
was to us and his remarks went out the window, where a sentry was
walking up and down, boots crunching in the gravel.

He continued in this manner for forty-five minutes, while the rest
of us at the table sat in respectful and absolute silence. Then he
turned his attention to other matters, among them my remark that
Domei, the Japanese news agency, had been carrying stories to the effect that American soldiers had been starting disturbances and mis-
treating peaceful Japanese. I asked MacArthur if the stories were
true, and while assuring me that they were not he scribbled a note on
a piece of paper and handed it to one of his aides.

Other subjects came up and were disposed of, and finally the luncheon broke up and everybody went back to work. It was made very
clear to me that everything MacArthur had said at the luncheon

table was off the record—no publicity—no "interview." I rode back
in a staff car with General L. A. Diller, his chief P.R.O., to whom
MacArthur had handed the scribbled note during our brief conversation about the Japanese news reports. He asked me if I would be
interested in seeing what MacArthur had written, and I said I would.
He took the scrap of paper out of his pocket, unfolded it, and handed
it to me. MacArthur had written two words:

"Close Domei."

The next day, as it happened, Frank Bartholomew and I were to
have tea with Furuno, president of Domei. He knew I had had lunch
with the General, and he certainly knew that his offices had been
padlocked that afternoon. He was extremely polite to Bart and myself, but we drank his tea with some concern. We thought we might
be Mickey Finned.

I kept pressing MacArthur for an interview, but without success.
He moved his headquarters from Yokohama to the American embassy in Tokyo (which had not been harmed in the bombing raids).
It was expected that he would enter in state, with a parade or at least
a show of force. But, instead, he made the trip very quietly, in his
closed car, with no panoply or ceremony whatever.

Word went around that I was in contact with the Supremo, which
led the Japanese to assume I must be a Very Important Person. One
day a delegation came to me with a suggestion for me to lay on Mac-
Arthur's desk. They told me it was obvious the Japanese home islands couldn't accommodate the population. Therefore, in order to
avoid future wars, a deal should be made *now* whereunder Japan
would get New Guinea!

"Most of it is poisonous jungle," said the spokesman. "We will make
it into a smiling paradise."

I told the delegation that they had come to the wrong department.
I was only a reporter (which they did not believe), and I could not
carry their message to anyone in authority. I suggested that they
take the matter up with the Australians.

Meanwhile, American opinion was becoming more and more
critical of MacArthur's management of the hated and defeated
enemy. MacArthur decided that he would have to reply to it, and
told me he thought he would hold a mass press conference. I advised

him—quite accurately, too—that his best way to assure a big play for what he wanted to say was to give me my exclusive interview. And, finally, he came around. Once he decided to go ahead with an interview, he got right into the swing of it—so much so that he called me at my hotel after I left to give me some more questions and answers for my story.

MacArthur held the interview in a paneled room in the Dai Ichi offices, headquarters of a big insurance company and one of the few large buildings that had survived the bombing. Paintings hung on the walls, and the room had an air of luxury; it gave no hint that we were in the middle of an unimaginable destruction. But the ruins of the country were much on MacArthur's mind—and on mine. I had seen cities and industries pulverized and paralyzed. I had seen square miles of land, once teeming business districts or crowded residence areas, reduced to hideous ruins and seemingly endless jungles of weeds and rubble. In 1945 we would have locked away in an institution, for his own good, anyone who predicted that within a decade Japan would be our strongest ally in Asia, and would once again be a commercial nuisance to Western European and American manufacturers. MacArthur's remarks must be understood against this background.

He said, "Japan will never again become a world power. Japan industrially, commercially, militarily and every other way, is in a state of complete collapse. Her food supplies are scarce, and she faces conditions in this emergency that may well become catastrophic. Her punishment for her sins, which is just beginning, will be long and bitter."

MacArthur told me that in his opinion the Japanese people would never again bet on militarism—their favorite horse, which had just run last in the race. He said he planned to keep the Japanese on an austerity basis, particularly in regard to sports, entertainment, luxury of any kind. (These plans were later changed.)

"There seems to be an impression in the United States," I said, "that you are going to tolerate the existence of a standing army of Japanese who will do most of the policing in Japan. Would you care to comment on this?"

"There is no fabric of truth in this statement," MacArthur replied vehemently. "The Japanese army is being completely demobilized by October fifteenth, and absolutely abolished. And the remnants of Japan's navy are doomed to destruction—except for minor specimens which may be retained for scientific or museum purposes."

I asked him whether the presence of the United States troops in Japan should be called an invasion or a pacification.

And he replied, "Neither. It is the occupation of a conquered country by the forces which defeated it."

As he uttered these words, in sonorous cadence, the Supreme Commander needed only a toga to become the picture of a Roman Caesar proclaiming a stupendous victory. His aquiline visage was stern and unrelenting. He rose, and his mien and bearing were majestic. He turned and paced slowly to the window, where he gazed meditatively over the burned and blasted ruins. He stayed on his feet after returning his attention to my questions, striding up and down the room, with a loping or gliding motion, puffing slowly on his corncob pipe with its very long stem. He seemed preoccupied and far away—but, in fact, he was completely alert to what I was saying, and his answers were carefully phrased.

MacArthur's parade up and down the big office varied in speed; sometimes he walked fast, sometimes with slow portentousness. Occasionally he would throw his tall frame into a couch or a deeply upholstered leather chair, sink into the cushions, and stare out as if peering into another dimension. When he was not answering questions point-blank, he followed his own chosen line of discourse. If you interjected a remark that was not precisely in point with what he had been saying, he would listen courteously and then resume his monologue where he had left off, as though nothing had been said and there was nobody in the room but himself. He was never in a hurry to finish a sentence.

I had been raised in an atmosphere where you talked loud and fast and got to the point—otherwise you would find that your audience had departed, and you were left talking to yourself. No such compulsion ever bothered MacArthur. He said what he had to say, and would not be hastened, interrupted or ignored. If you didn't care to listen, that was your hard luck. He even had his own pronunciations, which were not to be corrected by any person—or any dictionary. If the dictionary disagreed, it had better change and get down to date. For instance, the word hara-kiri, which was frequently heard in Tokyo in those days. To MacArthur it was ha-*rick*-iri. And that was that.

The question of war criminals came up in the interview, because the subject was much on everybody's mind. Every morning, we in the pressroom at Radio Tokyo were handed a new list of suspected war criminals to be seized. The list was known as "MacArthur's Hit Parade." It was eagerly grabbed by the correspondents, and scanned for "names." The Japanese did their own arresting. Many turned themselves in when their names appeared on this roster. During this interview, an officer came in with information that General Doihara—commander of the Japanese Sixth Army, which was in charge of disarming the troops—might have been guilty of war crimes himself. MacArthur leaped from his chair, made a sweeping gesture, and cried, "Arrest him!" A few minutes later, Doihara was in custody.

MacArthur told me that the war-criminal trials would begin shortly, and I asked him what would happen to the accused. He looked at me in a startled way and said, "Why, Baillie, you can't ask me that! As the Supreme Commander I am the supreme court in these matters. First they have to be convicted. Then they can appeal to me. And I am the last word. Therefore I cannot possibly tell you now what their fate is going to be!"

Then he jumped to his feet and raised an arm into the air—fist clenched—and exclaimed with the utmost vehemence, "But I'll tell you one thing, Baillie! The guilty ones are not going to escape. They're going to be hung!"

I asked him: "Now that the war is over, have you any political ambitions?"

He replied emphatically, "None whatsoever. I have never entered politics, and never intend to do so. I have stated before, and reiterate now, that I started as a soldier and shall finish as one. I am on my last public assignment, which, when concluded, will mark the definite end of my service."

At the finish, MacArthur ushered me to the door with a casual flourish, and I could almost hear the fanfare of trumpets. I rushed back to our offices at Radio Tokyo to put my notes in shape—to the tune of "Swanee River" and "Old Black Joe" sung in Japanese. This daily broadcast of "American folk music" (mostly Stephen Foster) was deemed to be a part of the re-education of the Japanese people. It was the Japanese themselves who had thought it up, however, not the Americans.

Early the next morning, I submitted the interview to the General, and he okayed it—adding several more questions and answers, and editing the manuscript in his own handwriting. I held my breath as he put these finishing touches on the document—fearing that at any moment somebody might suggest that the interview be given to the entire press corps, to be released simultaneously by everybody.

Just as I was heading for the door, with the papers clutched in my hand, the blow fell. General Diller, who had been very helpful throughout, felt it his duty to speak up—as Chief Press Relations Officer, he would have to deal with the other correspondents after they had read my interview in the papers and had heard from their home offices.

"General," Diller inquired, "what shall I tell the Associated Press, and the others?"

MacArthur thought for a moment and then replied mildly, "Why, neither the Associated Press nor nobody else has *asked* for an exclusive interview."

When I visited MacArthur some weeks later, to say good-by on leaving Japan, I asked him for an autographed photograph, which he inscribed to me as his "old comrade in arms." As he started to write my name on the picture, he hesitated over the spelling, and glanced at me inquiringly.

"Dinna ye ken hoo t'spell the name *Baillie*, Douglas MacArthur?" I inquired dourly, in broad Scots.

He looked at me for a long moment. Then wrote it. And spelled it correctly.

MacArthur was not a man you forgot easily. I had met the most dramatic figures of the war—Patton, Montgomery, and others who were master showmen as well as great soldiers. But I had never encountered anything like the Supremo. For some time after leaving his presence I remained in a sort of hypnosis, and I am sure many others have had the same experience. MacArthur's magnetism was enveloping. His hatreds, when he gave a glimpse of them, were shocking in their spiritual conviction. They were alive; they had drive and impact of their own. His words rumbled like the bass chords of an organ—not the voice so much as the manner of speaking, with syllables launched like missiles: "Treason." "Infamous." "Malevolent." "Horrendous." Such words gave scope for the full power of his expression, and he savored them as he uttered them.

So the MacArthur of five years before was much in my mind when I entered his office again, in the third month of the Korean War. He looked a bit leaner than he had then, and I thought his hands shook a bit more. He was seventy years old. His work in Japan had been successfully completed. Japan had been considerably rebuilt, though many of the structures were flimsy, and the Japanese had come to revere MacArthur as they revered their Emperor. He had been one of the most astonishing proconsuls in all history. And now he was fighting a new war . . . without adequate troops . . . in an area which he had every reason to believe had been written off by Washington. But he was the same MacArthur, striding up and down his room, puffing at his corncob pipe with the long stem, as energetic as I remembered him.

He remembered me, too. "Where have you been, Hugh?" he asked as we shook hands. "I was about to post you A.W.O.L."

MacArthur filled me in on the origins of the Korean War, as seen from his headquarters, and described the hardships of the campaign. We were then pinned into a corner of the peninsula, hanging on by a fingernail, and MacArthur explained the technique of hanging on:

"We have made the enemy delay and deploy," he said with all his gusto and drive. "This was his first big mistake. When confronted by small forces of Americans in the early days of the war, he hesitated, and spread out in a wide front; whereas a column of tanks followed by trucks carrying infantry could in the first days have pierced directly through to Pusan. The small forces we were able to put in so quickly provided the necessary holding action which cost the enemy his plan of swift occupation of South Korea.

"Now he has made another mistake, by massing around the Pusan perimeter and extending his supply lines to their present attenuated length—a situation of which I intend to take full advantage."

This was as close as he came to telling me about the Inchon landings, which were about to be launched, and which would recapture South Korea and demoralize the North Korean enemy. But there was a glint in his eyes. He had completed his plans for this masterstroke, and only a few days later his troops would be going ashore. . . .

When he heard I was bound for the front, he gave me a brief word of advice: "You will find this different from any action you ever saw in Europe. . . . Take care of yourself, Hugh."

I returned to Tokyo in time to ride with MacArthur in his new transport plane, the SCAP, on his first visit to Korea after the success of the Inchon landings. We made an early start, shortly after 5 A.M. The Supremo had a swivel chair situated in the waist of the plane, and there he was left severely alone with his thoughts. He swung around in the big chair, this way and that, looking out the window or down the aisle, where sat tons of brass. As we neared Korea we picked up a fighter escort, which flew alongside, above, and below.

MacArthur was first out of the plane at Kimpo airport, and after the flourish of salutes he and his staff drove off in closed cars, with us reporters pursuing them in jeeps, eating dust. The air around Seoul was tainted with smoke and death. The route of our "triumphal procession" was past smashed and burning buildings, along streets where telephone poles were smoldering like dying torches, over a pontoon bridge. At the Korean capitol building, before an audience of dignitaries, high brass, and haggard, unshaven Marines and GI's, MacArthur ceremoniously handed the government of Korea back to Syngman Rhee. Above him glass shards were tinkling down from the wrecked dome of the building, and in the galleries guards armed to the teeth and festooned with hand grenades kept close watch in all directions, and even peered down the long corridors with binoculars. The enemy was only ten miles away, and had counterattacked that morning. And MacArthur, with full solemnity, interrupted his speech to call on his audience to rise and join him in a recitation of the Lord's Prayer.

The story of this ceremony turned out to be a notable beat—because Ernie Hoberecht, the United Press manager for Asia, had set up relays of correspondents and made perfect arrangements with the Signal Corps. Our story was in newspaper offices all over the world far ahead of any other report on MacArthur's speech—proving once again the importance of securing your communications in advance. When we got back to Tokyo I wrote a "side-bar," a follow-up on the basic story, stressing the emotional charge MacArthur brought to his reading of the Lord's Prayer. This was no leisurely essay, either. I sat at my typewriter calling, "Boy-san! Boy-san!" whenever I finished a line, and a boy would come running, rip out the paper, and take it to the teletype. This follow-up story got even bigger play than the news break—proving once again the value of having something good to communicate.

MacArthur drove at a fast clip from Seoul back to Kimpo, and our jeep had a time keeping up. We took great quantities of the infamous Korean dust. The props of MacArthur's plane were already turning when we arrived and scrambled up the ladder, and MacArthur laughed heartily at my dust-caked face as I entered the cabin.

I was in Europe some months later, when the Chinese volunteers poured over the Yalu River and attacked MacArthur's advancing armies. Since I had always found MacArthur approachable, I thought I might get something from him which would throw light on the situation, and I decided to cable him a questionnaire. By this time, the great commander was being sniffed at as "Uncle Douglas" by junior attachés around Europe, and the drift of affairs was plain to be seen. A. L. Bradford and R. H. Shackford of our Paris staff met me at the restaurant Drouant in Paris, and the three of us together drew up the cable to MacArthur.

The answers came through a few days later, and they told an important story. "MacARTHUR SPEAKS!!" cried the New York *World-Telegram*, in an eight-column banner headline—with a subhead reading, "We Must Win Now or Fight in Europe."

MacArthur's reply to me ran three thousand words. After referring to the "privileged sanctuary" from which the Chinese emerged and from which their supplies were dispatched, the General declared that the North Korean army had been "totally defeated," and that the Chinese had then "initiated an entirely new war to cover the North Korean defeat." He said that an army of two hundred thousand Chinese had been discovered confronting the UN forces when they attacked, November 20, and that the Chinese had been reinforcing and building up ever since. Their purpose, he said, was complete destruction of the United Nations command and conquest of all Korea "in one invincible movement." This had been averted, and the UN forces were fighting on "against military odds without precedent in history."

There was much grousing in Europe about the Korean War, and MacArthur knew it. He replied, "If the fight is not urged with courage and invincible determination to meet the challenge here, it will indeed be fought, and possibly lost, on the battlefields of Europe."

Then I was riding in MacArthur's parade in New York on his first return to the United States since before the Japanese war. He returned as a conquering hero—but as a conquering hero deprived of his command, unceremoniously removed and shoved aside, by order of President Truman. He was a leader without an army. The second lieutenant who stood in the hysterically cheering crowd was in the chain of command; five-star General MacArthur was not.

A few days later I called on him at his offices in the Armed Services Building at 90 Church Street in New York—where, according to the song he had immortalized, he was presumed to be "fading away." He sat in civilian clothes behind a big bare desk. There was nothing going on. The room had a barren look.

MacArthur told me how the war in Korea could have been won. His idea, of course, was heavy bombing along the Yalu—*without* the use of atom bombs. He believed the Russians would never attack the United States unless they had a blueprint of victory, a war they could not possibly lose. Therefore he felt perfectly secure in his plan for heavy bombing to cut off the Chinese soldiers in Korea and prevent their reinforcement. He felt certain that such bombing—coupled with a landing of Chiang Kai-shek's army along the Yalu line—would quickly and victoriously end the war.

He was conscious of the risks involved. "In the next war," he said, "the situation will be the same as if two men were sitting with revolvers pressed against each other's bellies. . . . Each pulls the trigger, and that's the end." But for that very reason, he was certain that the Russians would not have intervened. He said that when he was relieved of his command, we as much as told the Communists that they did not have to worry—that we did not intend to take the steps necessary to win the war. Which was confirmed by the eagerness with which we gobbled the bait of their armistice proposals.

MacArthur . . . architect of so many victories . . . idolized by cheering millions . . . the man who personified American success in arms—and success in governing conquered peoples . . . commander of the Rainbow Division in the First War . . . Chief of Staff of the Army . . . superintendent of West Point . . . told me as he sat in his bare office that he was receiving no "inside" or confidential information from the Pentagon or from anywhere else. The couriers passed him by with their stacks of mimeographed memoranda about what was going on inside the Army, what was still going on in Korea. All he knew was what he was told by old friends, or what he read in the papers. This treatment amounted to a boycott by the Army, of which he was an eternal legend. He was excluded. But he did not complain. Instead, he continued to fight for his plan to win the war in Korea.

He may have been wrong, but he seldom made military mistakes. I thought then that he was right, and I think so today. But I felt no air of anticlimax about this talk with MacArthur. He looked much the same as he had when I had last seen him in the Far East—except that he was not in uniform, and his face was perhaps a trace more haggard. He still seemed supercharged with energy, ready to let it loose where it would do the most good, if anybody in power indicated a need for it. Nobody did.

Many felt, in the aftermath of the roaring reception given to MacArthur by the American people, that his policies would now win out even though he had lost his command. MacArthur may have thought so himself: he did not speak or look like a man fighting in a lost cause. But I knew better. I had seen another great American hero parade through the streets of the cities to shrieking acclaim and deafening applause—and I had witnessed the defeat of Woodrow Wilson.

I had seen it all before.

Chapter 19

INTERNATIONAL KALEIDOSCOPE

Nuremberg . . .

IN THE earliest days of history, the winners of a war killed the losers as a matter of course. Now it was being done again, as a matter of law. The leaders of Hitler's Reich sat in the dock while testimony was heard and law extemporized for the purpose of hanging as many of them as possible. But through the gloomy courtroom, as the testimony unfolded, floated the horrid specters of Dachau and Belsen: they would be killed for good reason.

They sat in two rows, in a box, the rear seats elevated so those at the back could see everything that went on. A stony-faced file of American MP's stood guard.

Goering, lounging impudently in his armchair, seemed to be laughing at the whole affair. He knew where he was keeping a cyanide pill, for use at the proper moment; and meanwhile, he intended to enjoy himself.

Ribbentrop, shrunken in baggy clothes, stared palely, particularly at me. Evidently he remembered our conversations at the time I interviewed Hitler. His arms were folded high on his chest, in his characteristic pose, and his lean visage tilted up.

Hess was going through an act, pretending to be crazy. He laughed, simpered, talked aloud, fell asleep, shook as with cold, had to be covered with army blankets. Here was the Deputy Fuehrer who had flown to Scotland while the last great fire raid fell on London—

now reduced to playing the fool, in hopes of escaping the scaffold.

Von Papen looked as foxy as ever—and evidently was, since he managed to get acquitted.

And there was Schacht, the banker and financial genius. He scowled, and pulled himself physically away from those who sat with him. His story was that he had never been a Nazi, and that he was in the wrong company.

Keitel, the imperious field marshal, had in his days of glory flourished his baton and treated all around him with the utmost hauteur; and he still maintained his proud bearing. But it wasn't helped by his uniform. He had lost a lot of weight, and his decorations were missing. I saw him herded to the toilet—stooped, head outthrust— by a couple of cocky-looking MP's.

Grand Admiral Raeder, who had challenged the sea power of Britain and America, seemed faintly amused. He smiled slightly, and did not seem unpleasant.

Doenitz, the last Fuehrer, the man who had capitulated unconditionally, argued that as the head of a fallen state he didn't belong in the prisoners' dock. He had a long neck and a long face, and stared impassively without focusing on anything or anybody, like a wild animal in a cage.

Seyss-Inquart, the oppressor of the Netherlands, who as Gauleiter had enjoyed the power of life and death over millions, was still quite dandified and correct in his demeanor.

On October 1, the sentences were handed down, and eleven men were condemned to death. Goering beat the gallows with his cyanide capsule. An attempt was made by the Allied Control Council in Germany to keep the executions secret, and to bar the press. I took the lead in fighting this maneuver. I wrote to General Joseph T. McNarney, American representative on the council, recalling the "never-ceasing battle fought by the American press in behalf of the people's right to be adequately informed. . . . Secret executions would be regarded by very many newspapers as a rebuff to this American principle." Furthermore, I added, "secret executions are liable to give rise to rumors of all sorts, such as: that some of the guilty were not killed at all, but were secretly reprieved for various reasons and se-

cretly incarcerated to be of possible use to the Allies in some way or
other at some future date. These rumors would, of course, be highly
imaginative; but secrecy breeds highly imaginative rumors."

Finally, in response to American pressure led by the United Press,
the Allied Control Council reversed its decision.

On October 16, in the small hours of the morning, Goering committed suicide and the rest were hanged. The whole gruesome business was on an assembly-line basis, and it took perhaps two hours
for all ten war criminals to plunge through the trapdoors manipu-
lated by American GI hangmen.

Ribbentrop went first.

Mannerheim . . .

Everywhere I went in 1946, people were baffled by the Russians.
In Paris I talked with Senators Vandenberg and Connally, and with
Secretary of State James F. Byrnes. They wanted to know what the
Russians were up to. Ambassador Jefferson Caffery told me that the
French expected to see Cossacks in the Place de la Concorde within
five years.

Finland was about as close as you could come to Russia without
actually being in the Soviet Union. In Finland, in fact, you were
likely to have Russians on both sides of you, because Soviet troops
were occupying a large enclave which they had "leased" from the
Finns at gun point. And Finland's Baron Carl von Mannerheim knew
the Russians about as well as anybody in Europe. He had fought
them in defense of his country, and he had been an officer in the
Russian army himself, in the days before there was an independent
Finland. I went to visit Mannerheim at his headquarters—or, rather,
his retreat, since he was inactive—near Helsinki.

"The Russians," he said, "will never provoke a war with the United
States. . . . They creep."

He was sitting in the living room of his house, surrounded by the
trophies of his glittering career, which crowded the tables and hung
on the walls. He was dressed in civilian clothes, but his aide wore a
brilliant uniform with bright red trousers. Outside the house were
two uniformed sentries, who acted bored. He looked like a long and

lanky Englishman, and his manner was somewhat austere. But he talked freely about the Russians—though their lines were only a couple of miles from his home, on the other side of town.

"The Russians burrow," he continued. "They are doorknob rattlers. They go from place to place, trying windows, looking for an opportunity to get in. Once in, they are very hard to dislodge. . . . Nobody can tell what they are up to, because what they are after today may be something else tomorrow when the situation has changed to give them an opening elsewhere. They are great extemporizers. But of one thing you can be sure: They will never take on a war unless they are sure of winning, mathematically sure. And they will never put their own troops into action if they are able to arrange to get the people of some other country to do the fighting, to their ultimate advantage.

"They always take the long view," Mannerheim continued. "They aren't in a hurry. They await the favorable moment, then they make their move. I know how they think, how their minds work. It doesn't make any difference who is at the head of their government. Their objective is always the same—to spread their areas of domination. Their tactics may change; their target, never."

He stared for a few moments into the fire which crackled on the hearth, and neither of us said anything. Then he added, "They aspire to be the greatest and most powerful country the world has ever seen."

He hoisted his spare frame out of his deep chair, walked up and down the room, and then went on:

"This is no temporary situation. There are two worlds. They are more separate and hostile to each other than in the days when the English and the Spaniards, and then the English and the French, fought wars with each other for many years. Or it's like the wars with the Moslems when they came up into Spain. Because there is a religious element here. Bolshevism is a religion with them. They want to convert us all to it, by one means or another.

"They will never relax their efforts, except temporarily, as a ruse. They will always be listening and sniffing for the next opportunity. In the years to come you will see their frontiers expand, although those in the forepart of the expansion won't always be Russians. They may be of other races, which have been converted."

Throughout the length of our conversation, Mannerheim never smiled. He seemed to be meditating aloud rather than answering questions. He talked entirely without emotion, and with no effort whatever to sell his viewpoint, or to convince me. But unlike others I have interviewed, whose statements were soon made foolish by the progress of events, Mannerheim was right on the target. What he said is as true today as it was in 1946.

The Russians were all over Finland, extracting reparations from a defeated country. They ran the garages which housed the motor pool, and the towering Hotel Torni was bright with lights from windows where, floor on floor, their accountants were working over the Finnish economy. The mechanics around the motor pool were mostly ruddy and husky. They looked like farm boys, and they weren't bothering with high questions of state—they were just keeping the cars running. They weren't in any particular hurry about it, though: it took them two hours to fix a flat for us. They strolled the streets, always in twos, with overcoats down to their heels.

While in Finland I spent considerable time with Eljas Erkko, publisher of the *Helsingin Sanomat*, who had gone through a hard war. He showed us where bombs had gouged holes in his plant, coming in through the roof and going through all the floors to the basement. Throughout the bombings, he had continued to transact "business as usual"—a resolute man, plenteously endowed with common sense. We dined with the Erkkos at the Savoy, and emerged into a sleet storm, which meant wading in slush to cross the square and get a car. Mrs. Erkko, a distinguished lady who had seen the Bolsheviki close up, on the rampage—but didn't talk about it—removed her shoes and stockings to walk across the square. She didn't mind plowing barefoot in the sleet, but she couldn't spare those shoes. There were no others to be had. Back at the Hotel Kemp, the wind was whistling through chinks around the windows, and there was a nice little snowdrift on the floor. The kindly maids—and big strong girls they were, too—took pity on the soft-living Americans who weren't accustomed to such hardships: they put hot-water jugs in the beds. There was no other heat in the room, nor in the water pipes. I didn't get thawed out until next day, when I took a *sauna*, or Finnish bath—which is fine, if you don't mind being scrubbed by an old woman.

Smuts . . .

By accident of the alphabet—there being no reporter in the group whose name began with "A"—I sat next to Field Marshal Smuts at a luncheon in Cape Town in 1948 for a party of visiting American publishers. He fixed me with his bright blue eyes over his snow-white whiskers, and all through the lunch warned me of a terrible danger overhanging the world. He believed that the Russians were planning to invade the Scandinavian countries, and that the attack might come at any minute.

I was deeply impressed by his vigor and his seeming grasp of the subject, and also by the magnetism he exuded as he hammered home his story. But, of course, it was all useless, professionally. He assured me repeatedly that what he was saying was all "off the record." He considered it unbecoming for the head of the Union of South Africa to utter such sinister warnings about a supposedly friendly state.

Later that day, all the members of the party attended a reception at the Prime Minister's official residence, Groot Schuur. Smuts showed us through the house, which had been built by Cecil Rhodes. We were duly impressed by its burly magnificence, including a bath-tub almost large enough to serve as a swimming pool. Afterward all the publishers, most of them with glasses in hand, assembled around our host while he talked, at first easily and pleasantly, about the state of affairs in his own country and in the world at large. From this, it was but a short transition for him to get back to the subject of Russia. And the next thing I knew, he was telling the whole crowd everything that he had told me at lunch. He was warning that Russia was set to pounce, and that Norway would be Target Number One. This, he feared, would precipitate the Third World War—and in matter of a very short time, unless immediate and wise steps were taken to avert the menace.

Everyone listened with the keenest attention. But none of the Americans took any notes, because the setting was a private party.

Finally Jack Wheeler, head of the Bell Syndicate, took advantage of a brief pause in the remarks to interrupt and ask, "Mr. Prime Minister, we presume this is all 'off the record.' "

To which Smuts replied, "Oh, no! Go ahead and quote me as freely as you wish."

We were all caught off balance. How could anyone go back and pick up statements of such a sensational nature out of the air? The whole thing was pure dynamite. And yet the story was loose. Most of those in the group looked at each other—and then at me. I was the only press-association man there; and the United Press served most of their newspapers. The conclusion was obvious.

Fortunately I had the collaboration of two South African news-papermen, one of whom had made a shorthand transcript of the Prime Minister's remarks. As he said to me afterward, "When Smuts starts talking, you never can tell what he's going to say. And you never can tell when he will suddenly decide to make it all public. So I've grown careful, and I always make notes."

Escorted by these two Cape Town journalists, I went directly to the cable office. There we put together the UP story and sent it on its way. No opposition service got around to doing it for about twelve hours.

The Prime Minister's dire predictions failed to come true.

Stalin . . .

He seldom gave interviews: that was well known. And I had gone to see Hirohito, Chiang and MacArthur—all his enemies—only a year before. So I could not hope to be welcomed into the presence of Joseph Stalin. Furthermore the Moscow press corps, after my Grand Slam of the previous year, would be onto me as soon as I showed up. But there was an outside chance that he might answer a cable. I sent him thirty-one questions, without any great hope of receiving a reply.

A few days later I was at a newsreel theater in London when I felt a sudden urge to leave the show and return to the office, late at night. Just as I entered the bureau, the man in charge was trying to get me on the phone.

"Stalin is answering your questions!" he shouted.

We went to work. We rushed our crew of translators to the bureau in the middle of the night, and soon had the dispatch rolling over our various transmissions to newspapers and radio stations throughout the world. In the midst of this the Russian Embassy monitor telephoned, advising us that he would give us three hours' head start on the story. This was most unusual. It was customary for the Russians to release such things simultaneously to everybody, by means of wireless. I cannot explain why they deviated from their usual practice in this case, unless they were trying a journalistic experiment—to see whether an exclusive interview with Stalin would get a bigger initial play than a "handout." The handout came later, and of course everybody printed it anyway.

I had asked Stalin, "In your opinion, what is at present the worst threat to peace?"

He replied, "The incendiaries of a new war, foremost, Churchill and those who think like him in Great Britain and the United States." In the days of Khrushchev, such pronouncements from the Russians became commonplace—but this was the first time that the head of a Great Power had called a leading statesman of another a "war incendiary," at a time when the two countries enjoyed apparently friendly relations.

I had asked Stalin what should be done to guarantee that Germany never again became a military menace. His reply: "It is necessary to extirpate in practice the remnants of Fascism in Germany and to democratize her most thoroughly."

He went on to say that the German people should be allowed to reconstruct their industry and trade, and become self-supporting.

With regard to the fate of the war criminals, then much in the news, Stalin said he thought all of them should be hunted down and punished.

I had asked him the attitude of the Russian government toward the presence of American warships in the Mediterranean. His reply was one word: "Indifferent."

In reply to my question as to whether Russia possessed the secret of the atom bomb, he replied in the negative. He did not add that his spies were busy on the problem.

The next day I was stormed under with messages of congratulation on the Stalin story. One of the most welcome came from Eddy Gilmore, Moscow manager of the Associated Press. Good sportsmanship, indeed.

The Stalin interview also brought me—almost immediately and not at all pleasantly—my moment of closest contact with Sir Winston Churchill. I had seen Churchill in groups many times, and had admired his eloquence and his masterly personality. But this was the first time he ever gave me his undivided attention, and it was by no means the occasion I would have chosen.

One of Stalin's replies had dealt with the question of Russian troop dispositions in the Balkans, and Churchill, always a strategist, had issued a statement commenting on the military aspects of the interview. Unfortunately, the paragraph he chose to single out was a mistranslation from the Russian. We had already caught the error and sent out a correction when my telephone rang in the London office. It was the former Prime Minister.

"Mr. Baillie," he said, "you have put me in a position of uttering an erroneous statement." He then treated me to his opinion of people who "put out false information," speaking with all his usual force and eloquence, and with controlled fury. I tried to tell him that we had carried a correction, but he was not listening to anything I had to say. Finally I was able to arrange to go to his house and talk to him in person.

Entering, I found myself before a rumpled and angry man chewing irritably on a cigar. He immediately began inveighing against me again, continuing where he had left off, in a portentous, solemn manner. Finally I broke in for a long enough stretch to tell him that we had caught the error, and sent out a correction, before he issued his statement; that it was our bad luck he had seen the original interview but not the correction.

He took the position that the damage had already been done, and that he could not be expected to keep up with our corrections of our errors. He was very one-track about it. He told me he was issuing a statement to the Press Association, a British news agency (not, of course, to us), disclaiming responsibility for the error in his original communiqué and placing the blame where it belonged.

I had addressed Churchill throughout as Mr. Prime Minister, and as our interview came to an end I told him that everybody I knew still thought of him as Prime Minister, though he was out of office. He was not noticeably pleased, and our talk ended on the same irritated note with which it had begun.

Later I had another occasion to try to please Churchill, when we were seated next to each other at a dinner given by Bernard Baruch in New York. I told him the anecdote of the Russian and Turkish generals, negotiating on the battlefield in the nineteenth century, when one of them began to denounce the other in broad Scots. The other promptly responded in kind, and they found they were both from the same Scottish town, Kilmarnock. They paid their mutual respects as countrymen, and then returned to shooting at each other in the Russian and Turkish causes, respectively.

Churchill heard the story out, then turned to the guest at his other hand to start a new conversation. Again, I had failed to get through to him. . . .

Attlee . . .

I met him at Number 10 Downing Street . . . in the same room where Chamberlain had assured me there would never be any German air raids on London. The date was October 27, 1950; the Korean War was what most concerned Attlee—and myself. He turned out to be a short man who sat hunched in his suit, smoking a pipe, bald head thrust somewhat forward. He had a ready grin, was very affable, but didn't much resemble the Captain Attlee who had fought at Gallipoli in the First World War.

I asked him whether he believed a full-scale war with Russia was likely in the near future, and he said that he didn't think so. There might, he said, be other instances like Korea—"since the Russians are very generous with other people's lives." He remarked that one such war was already under way in Indo-China. But he judged that the Russians might be disposed to go slow on secondary wars if they didn't meet with success.

"If the Russians try something and it doesn't work," he said, unconsciously echoing Mannerheim, "they are inclined to switch and try something different. Look at the air lift in Germany."

He said he thought the Russians would in the future devote much of their attention to "the home front." He chewed his pipe and looked out the window at the Horse Guards Parade.

"By that," he added, "I mean subversion and treason."

Attlee felt that the Russians had made a mistake in Korea; they had stirred up the United States and shaken us away from our attachment to disarmament. As a result of the Korean War, he said, the United Nations was stronger than ever—stronger than the old League had ever been.

"The old League," he added, "always ran away—never faced up to anything. The United Nations has demonstrated its potency. It's a great thing for world morale."

Much as he approved the results of the Korean War, however, he didn't think much of the war itself. It was obvious that he had no enthusiasm for wars in Asia, "where the white race could be poured into a bottomless pit. . . . "

Truman . . .

I saw a great deal of President Harry Truman, frequently in connection with Perón's persecution of *La Prensa*, and to cover the news. After my return from Korea and Europe in 1950, I went in to tell him what I had seen and to get his views about it.

He received me with a twinkling eye. He was, in fact, quite a twinkler. His lenses magnified his eyes and made them look bigger than they actually were. In my conversations with him, he struck me as a fatalist—that is, he felt, as the Scotch say, that "what maun be maun be." Massive events, at least, are foreordained, and there is little that mere mortals can do about them. We are all caught in the clutch of circumstance, fell or otherwise. He never appeared to be worried about anything. When decisions had to be made, he made them, without fretting about it. And how many big decisions he had to make! The dropping of the atom bomb, the relief of British forces with American troops in Greece, the air lift to Berlin, the "police action" in Korea—all Truman's. They came easier to him because he regarded them as a part of history rather than as a question of personal judgment.

Truman said he did not know what the outcome would be in Korea, except that we were there to stay, and that he intended to draw a line in Asia beyond which Communism should not advance. He understood, he said, that the Europeans were nervous about our Asian engagements, afraid that we would become so deeply committed in Asia that we would have no time for the defense of Europe. But, he said, events would prove we could handle both situations.

He said that he had been badly fooled by the Russians. When he assumed the Presidency, he said, he had to read a stack of documents "this high" and attempt to absorb all the policies to which he was expected to adhere. One of these policies, he said, was that the Russians were our friends. So he went to Potsdam with the best good will in the world toward the Russians. A grave mistake was made, he said, in pulling the American armies back from the vicinity of Berlin just before the end of the war in 1945.

But now, he said, when the Russians acted ornery, they could take a look at the ruins of Berlin, and remind themselves of what we could do to them. . . .

Pope Pius XII . . .

It has been my observation that when Americans decide to lam out of a country, they really lam. In April, 1948, they were getting the hell out of Italy, almost as fast as they got out of London when the war began in 1939. Elections were scheduled for April 18 and 19, and it was commonly believed that the Communists were going to win it—or, if they didn't win it, would use the occasion for a revolution.

Rome looked as though a revolution were already under way. The Communists made all the noise. We passed streetcars which they had seized and covered with demonstrators like a swarm of bees, on the roofs and clinging everywhere they could get a handhold. Red flags with hammer-and-sickle hung from the overloaded cars. But everybody seemed happy. It was a lark. They were having as much fun as when they used to cheer Mussolini, with their "Doochay!" in the Piazza Venezia. I saw few ferocious faces, or grim ones. Laughter and merry shouting prevailed.

Parades had the right of way. We halted several times on our way in from the airport to let them pass. The people were whooping and hollering, and flaunting their hammer-and-sickle banners with great enthusiasm. They jeered and gesticulated at our American car and at us Americans. Occasionally they ran up and thrust their heads and shoulders inside. If we dared sound the horn to squeeze through, men popped their eyes at us, and grimaced. But it all seemed part of the fiesta.

Our hotel rooms had big balconies with high balustrades, through which wo could view the demonstrations outside our windows. Two or three rival speeches were being made at once, through loud speakers. Each orator had his own crowd, which provided him with well-timed applause. But at the exact hour fixed by the police for curfew, a sudden silence fell. The haranguers shut up. Out went the lights, down came the banners, and everybody went home quietly. The act was over for the day. This, I recalled, was exactly as it had been in the era of Mussolini, when the demonstrations seemed to be switched on and off at will; emotions surged or subsided as if directed from a central control panel. The Romans still had "the discipline."

Next day the employees disappeared in large numbers from all the Rome hotels and restaurants and stores; every citizen, in order to vote, had to go to his birthplace. The tradition descended straight from the Roman Empire—and was the reason Christ was born in Bethlehem, where Joseph and Mary had gone to be "enrolled" by the state. There was a tremendous turnout to vote. Nuns went to the polls. Cripples who hadn't been outdoors for years were carried in wheel chairs or on stretchers. Women went with their infants in arms. The queues waiting to ballot were blocks long. But everything was reasonably quiet: so far as I could see in Rome, or our reporters could ascertain elsewhere in Italy, there was little if any underground Communist activity.

Election day was two days long in Italy, and the rush was still on when we woke the next morning. But the word was out that the Communists had been beaten.

It had been generally understood that the Vatican played an important part in the election—as it was entitled to do under the terms of the Lateran Pact, which was written into the postwar Italian Constitution. The Holy See would have been strangely isolated in a Communist country had the Reds won. On April 20, while throngs of Communists still jammed the street in front of their newspaper, looking at the bulletins which displayed false returns showing the Reds leading, I had a private audience with His Holiness Pope Pius XII. Our small party was taken in by Myron Taylor, then the President's ambassador to the Vatican.

We proceeded through many vast halls, corridors and throne rooms. The magnitude of the establishment was overpowering. All the huge chambers were in use. They might resemble art galleries—and, of course, they do contain some of the great art of mankind—but there was an overlay of drive and business, of purpose and energy. There were couriers bustling around, priests of varying ranks going earnestly about their affairs, waiting rooms full of people with appointments to see dignitaries of the Church. The Vatican was visibly alive and active, a vibrant powerhouse.

We passed a detachment of the Swiss Guard, and they snapped to attention at a word of command, in honor of the American Ambassador. They still wear the uniforms Michelangelo designed for them, which make them look as though they had just stepped out of a medieval painting. But they were as military and spit-and-polish as any outfit I ever saw. They were also tall and husky, with an alert and sharply-trained look.

For a few minutes we tarried in an anteroom to the Pope's office, chatting with several monsignors who spoke American and Irish-accented English. Then the door swung open, and we moved inside.

The first effect was one of surprise, as you looked around the large room for the Pope, expecting to find him in a commanding position. What caught your eye, however, was an altar with a painting of the Virgin above it. And it was not until you had searched the room that you realized the Pope himself was at your elbow, seated at a desk to the immediate right of the door through which you entered. He was wearing white robes and skullcap, and looking us over benignly, with a kindly smile.

Ambassador Taylor presented us, one by one, and the Pope clasped hands with all. His greetings to Ambassador Taylor might almost be described as jovial. His Holiness took charge of the conversation, in flawless English, identified each member of the small party, and asked questions about what was going on in the places we had recently visited. He alluded to his own trip to the United States when he was Cardinal Pacelli, and to his early experiences flying in airplanes.

His appearance was tranquil and serene. He had a mobile and expressive face, and while he occasionally looked grave, he frequently smiled and sometimes laughed. It was a happy face, despite all he had undergone during the Nazi occupation . . . the recent near thing with the Communists . . . the persecutions of the princes and faithful of the Roman Catholic Church in various areas of the world, all of which came to his attention, to his desk. Two telephones sat on the desk, one white, one black. He was not in the least withdrawn or set apart, but in his presence one felt separated from him by an emanation of sanctity, an invisible curtain around him. He radiated confidence, and of all men I ever met, he seemed to take the most genuinely long view, looking ahead for literally a thousand years.

The Pope made a statement regarding the election results (which, we were informed, had kept him up until one o'clock that morning). He thanked God for the rout of the Communists. And he added, with head bowed, "The world is weary, and needs rest."

Clare Boothe Luce . . .

It was not in the least unusual for me to run into Mrs. Clare Boothe Luce, because we lived in the same apartment house in New York. But now in 1953 I was seeing her for the first time in her role as ambassador to the government of Italy. She was still new to the job, and thinking hard about it.

"I am no Lady Bountiful," she said. "In fact, ever since coming here I've had to tell people on all sides that American funds are going to be either discontinued entirely or greatly reduced."

She received me in her office—a standard United States Embassy installation with heavy furniture, paneled walls, and an American flag on an upright staff. In that businesslike setting, the beauty of the lady made a striking contrast.

She did not like the idea of calling in important personages to explain that in the future there would have to be less aid to Italy. "I am always the bearer of bad tidings," she said. And she was concerned that the reduced aid program might undermine the prestige of NATO

—make the organization "lose its oomph," as she put it. "You can't expect these people to get out of the holes in which they live, with insufficient food in their bellies, then put them in uniform, and arm them and tell them to fight the Russians. Everybody keeps saying the Italians won't fight; the reason is, they have nothing to fight for. If an army travels on its stomach, the Italian army couldn't get very far."

She had a number of remedies to suggest. She thought the United States should build houses in Italy for the people who were still living in caves, and arrange a plan whereby we would rent the homes at a reasonable return—"no usury, but a fair profit." She thought such a housing project would do more to strengthen the Italians against Communism than the organization of two divisions of troops for NATO.

Mrs. Luce thought it should be possible to appeal to American business instinct to help the Italians. "I'm not talking about handouts," she said. "I'm talking about investments. The Brazilian ambassador was just in here to see me, and he is waiting outside now. He would like to take into Brazil hundreds of thousands of Italians. He says Brazil needs population. But the Brazilians haven't the money to get immigrants established, once they arrive. And you can't just dump them off the boat, give them a pack on their back, and let them fend for themselves."

She went on to suggest that we should invest money in Brazil to help establish Italian immigrants in that country—the investment to be repaid out of the increased prosperity the Brazilians would enjoy. "The same goes for Australia, Canada, and many other countries," she said. "And we should be taking many more Italian immigrants into the United States. You can take an Italian Communist into Connecticut, and after he has been there a short time he will be shouting, 'Down with Communism!' and 'Up with the Pope!'—just like all the other Italians in Connecticut."

As I was leaving, I remarked on her rather frail appearance. She nodded, but said, "I am going to stick it out." Then she added, "You know, continually telling people 'No, there isn't any more money' doesn't enhance your popularity. And while in a recent poll the three most popular individuals in Italy were said to be the Pope, De Gasperi and me, in a few short months I can easily become the most *un*popular person."

But she didn't. Not all her ideas for improving the condition of the Italians were put into practice—by any means. But during her time as ambassador she exerted an influence which was definitely felt. When she arrived in 1953, United States prestige was declining seriously. Before she left, it was well on the upswing once again.

Adenauer . . .

I went to visit him during the Korean War period, when the world's attention was more on Asia than on Europe, and he was disturbed about it. As it happened, I was lunching with him when the replies to my questionnaire to General MacArthur began coming in over the wire. The message was delivered to me in short "takes" at the lunch table, and translated for the German Chancellor. Adenauer's stone face became more grim as he heard MacArthur's words. This tough old Rhinelander was doing his job and did not want any interruptions from the Far East. And the Korean situation made a background for every moment of our conversation.

Adenauer gave a great impression of strength, despite his advanced age. He had the stature of a Prussian general—though he was no Prussian—and he carried himself with great dignity and force. He was mentally tough. He said what he had to say. And he meant it.

He was impatient with the Korean War, and therefore with MacArthur. What he deemed of highest importance was a strong American army, with strong European allies, confronting the Russians along their western border. The Germans should be equal partners, he said, in any such armed force. "Only then," he added, his chiseled face looking grave indeed, "will America be able, in concert with the free West, to launch a peace offensive against Russia with a real chance of success."

As for Korea, he said he thought it was Russia's plan to bleed the United States into a permanently weakened condition by prolonged wars in Asia, so America would never be able to confront Russia in Europe with a military force which the Russians would consider truly dangerous.

De Gaulle . . .

I saw him first when the role of Conquering Hero was fresh upon him, shortly after his entry into Paris in 1944. I was received by him in his presidential palace. He was a very commanding figure, in full uniform, looking down on you from a great height—and looking down his long nose, disapprovingly. He gave me a reception as hostile as any I have ever experienced. He didn't even ask me to sit down.

I remember telling him that we had found our Paris bureau intact, with nothing disturbed, and had been able to get right back to work. He sneered and said, "Pictures of Laval and Hitler still on the walls, no doubt." We had sent Ralph Heinzen, our manager for France, down to Vichy after the fall of the Third Republic, to cover the news from Pétain's capital. This was the place for him to be, at the source of the news. But to De Gaulle, any contact whatever with Pétain and Laval was treason to France and the allied cause, and he was not going to forgive us for it.

In those days Americans were not accustomed to such frosty receptions from the French. We were the saviors, and your American uniform was open sesame to everything—including free rides on the Métro. But to the strong man of the French, we were suspect: we had dealt with his enemies.

Nine years later I saw De Gaulle again, and found he had mellowed—somewhat. He was almost a forgotten man in 1953. His offices were in an underheated stone building on the left bank of the Seine, and he was trying to run a political party—the RPF. He wasn't getting very far with it. He wore rumpled civilian clothes. Around him was a dedicated gang of young men—husky, most of them—wearing crosses of Lorraine in their buttonholes. We talked about the plight of France, and he denounced the politicians of the Fourth Republic.

In 1958 he didn't even have a political party, he seemed to have disappeared. But the reports from France in the spring gave me the feeling that he was about to re-emerge as the leader of the French. I was retired as president of the United Press by then, but I called some of our people to find out whether they agreed with me, whether they, too, felt that hunch when the name De Gaulle was mentioned. They did, and they were planning to do something about it, to make sure the situation was covered. It's that sort of prescience, a feeling for future news, that makes it possible for a great news service to cover history as history is made.

Chapter 20

GAINZA PAZ AND PERON

"I AM in favor of freedom of the press," lied dictator Juan Perón of Argentina, while weighing schemes for the suppression of *La Prensa*, the great newspaper of Buenos Aires and one of the great newspapers of the world. Perón had already harassed the other newspaper publishers into line, or closed down their plants. Only *La Prensa* held out against him, maintaining its right to print the news without government interference. Perón had made no secret of his desire to throttle *La Prensa*—and, if possible, its director, Dr. Alberto Gainza Paz. But, meanwhile, he had American visitors in his office, so he poured out the old oil.

With me in Perón's office for the interview were American Ambassador James Bruce and the UP vice-president for South America, Thomas Curran. They weren't much impressed, either.

Perón was set up in pseudo-Mussolini style. To get to his office you had to go through a number of large rooms, and when his double doors were swung open, there he was, sitting at a massive and littered desk, wearing a uniform. Perón had been Argentine military attaché at Mussolini's court, and obviously he had picked up a number of tricks from the master. Like Mussolini, he was a large, pulpy fellow, but taller. He had a kind of skin disease on his face. I was impressed by the shortness of his arms. Later I was told that many of his fellow officers in the army said that he looked like a crocodile, standing upright. Unlike Mussolini, however, he was by nature a salesman, and he tried to charm his visitors rather than awe them.

He greeted me with an *abrazo*, as if we were the oldest of pals, and behaved throughout our talk in a very matey manner indeed. At the conclusion of our conversation, which had been through a translator, he suddenly switched to English, and paraded with considerable pride a limited English vocabulary. I was surprised that he spoke any English at all. He enjoyed my surprise, and was flattered by it. As we traipsed to the door, Perón became more friendly than ever: he put his arm around my neck and escorted me, stride for stride, down the huge length of his office—talking English in my ear the while. This, too, of course, was Mussolini: I had left Mussolini's office in the same affectionate manner thirteen years before. But Mussolini had given you his friendship as a final gesture, after going through the routine of antagonism and suspicion, allowing you to win him over. Perón was not up to such subtleties.

Like the other big figures in the news, Perón had a personal magnetism which you felt in his presence. But it was second-rate stuff. I had the feeling, talking to him, that his heart wasn't really in his work—that is, he wished the going were easier. He was a rather repulsive front man, rather than a driving force. A little fellow inflated like a balloon—weak, but capable of great outrages. To get right down to it, Perón struck me as a fake—though he might be all the more dangerous to the people who had to live under his rule, just because he was a fake. Most dictators commit their worst crimes to cover their weaknesses.

There was one more major difference between Perón and Mussolini: Perón had a prominent wife. So prominent, in fact, that when I saw the red streaks on his face (of the kind usually called liver blotches), the first thought that struck my mind was that Eva had been giving him a pep talk with her fingernails. "Evita" was her husband's supercharger. She was not received in the best homes in Buenos Aires, because her background was shady. But whenever she made a speech—which was fairly often—the whole town had to turn out. I remember one occasion, shortly after we arrived, when the hotel where we were staying was placed in a state of suspended animation by one of Evita's public appearances. All the servants were ordered to go to the Plaza de Mayo, where she was to orate from a balcony overlooking the square. The contingents paraded into the

Plaza for the "popular manifestation"—and, on their way, they were marched past the offices of *La Prensa* to hoot at Gainza Paz. While Evita spoke, business was shut down all over Buenos Aires. And woe betide anyone in the crowd who didn't perform as expected.

Nobody else ever had a career quite like Eva Perón's. There was a lot of curiosity about her outside Argentina (it wasn't safe to be too curious about Evita *inside* Argentina). I remember that I called on President Truman at the conclusion of this Latin American trip, and told him what I had seen in Argentina, Chile, Peru, Uruguay and Brazil. He listened with attentive eagerness to my full report, then asked the question I hadn't answered. He leaned across his desk and said, "What about Mrs. Perón? Is it true she has a past?" I cleared up the Presidential curiosity as best I could.

I arrived in Buenos Aires on an old paddlewheeler, the *General Artigas*, which ferried us over from Montevideo. Dr. Gainza Paz was at the dock very early in the morning to greet us. With Dr. Gainza at the wheel, I was driven in his automobile from the pier to the Plaza Hotel. On the surface, everything looked normal. Traffic was heavy—people were hustling along on the sidewalk, the city looked big and imposing, the hotel was deluxe and very smooth.

The minute you cut under the surface, however, you smelled trouble. Our rooms at the hotel were wired—the first time that had happened to me since Moscow. When we talked under a certain chandelier in our parlor, a faint echo indicated the presence of a not-very-well-adjusted microphone. During a United Press reception in my suite I mentioned this experience to Sir John Balfour, the British ambassador. "Oh, yes," he said genially. "I once occupied these rooms for a while, and we were always careful to stay away from that chandelier when we were talking."

I had a number of meetings with groups of businessmen at the Jockey Club (which was subsequently destroyed by a Perónist mob). And at these luncheons and gatherings they told me of their troubles, and I listened to their discussions of how to slow down the steady encroachment upon them by Perón, his devices and his ukases.

At *La Prensa* itself, the trouble was visible on the service. A parade of very rough-looking characters was marching by the building, shouting denunciations. On Dr. Gainza's desk lay a row of missiles which had been hurled through the windows by mobs at various times—jagged chunks of iron, sizable rocks, any object hard enough to throw through glass. The police made a pretense of protection, surrounding the building with mounted officers attired like elite cavalry, but nobody was ever arrested for molesting *La Prensa* in the days of Perón. Loudspeakers brayed Perónist propaganda around the building at all hours. Across the street, the government operated an "oral newspaper" called *Octubre*, which blasted away to encourage the demonstrators and annoy the people in *La Prensa's* building.

The siege of *La Prensa* by Perón lasted seven years, and was full of incidents—such as a contrived charge of "eluding customs duty on newsprint," though newsprint had been specifically excluded from tariff since 1917. Finally a faked "strike," starting with news vendors whose demands amounted to confiscation of the newspaper's circulation, gave Perón his excuse to suppress *La Prensa*. Of course all the demands were deliberately designed to be unacceptable. The government took over the building and Dr. Gainza's offices, and started issuing a bogus "*La Prensa*." We were asked to continue supplying the UP service to this government organ, and we refused—thus jeopardizing our own existence in Argentina.

When I was in Buenos Aires in 1948, however, Gainza was still publishing *La Prensa*, and those whom Perón hated—the "oligarchs," and the people who had built Argentina, and their descendants— were still holding out against the dictator with magnificent courage. Our ambassador, James Bruce, was, I think, a great help to them. He gave glittering diplomatic dinners, to which he invited what Perón would have called all the wrong people. I attended one such dinner— a perfect diplomatic affair at which men in formal dress and women in evening gowns, wearing jewels, medals, decorations, sat at two long banquet tables. And practically every guest had been selected from Perón's list of people to be liquidated at the first opportunity.

But Dr. Gainza himself held the strongest leash on Perón's eagerness to annihilate his opponents. He kept the attention of the world focused on Argentina and its dictator. He traveled abroad, and by his writings, speeches and public appearances, his talks with publishers and political leaders, reminded the people of the free world that though Hitler and Mussolini had been destroyed, their imitator

Perón was still in power. Every time Dr. Gainza returned home he knew he was going back into graver personal danger, for Perón watched his every move. But he remained serene and even—to all appearances—detached. He never lost his savoir-faire. He was not a man to wax emotional. The peril in which he and his family lived day by day, the never-ending threat to his newspaper, had no visible effect on his demeanor. By his actions and his bearing, he earned the respect of all the world—except the hoodlums arrayed against him.

Once *La Prensa* had been suppressed, however, Gainza could no longer fight effectively within Argentina, and he resolved to escape, to keep the issue of Perónism alive by writing and speaking abroad. If he had stayed, he would have been imprisoned and perhaps tortured to confess to imaginary crimes committed by *La Prensa*. Nevertheless, he felt doubtful about leaving, when so many of his friends had to stay behind—and it was not until Perón had been overthrown, and Gainza had been convinced of the importance of his own work abroad in hastening that overthrow, that he was certain he had made the right decision in leaving Argentina. We in the United Press had known it all along, and had never felt anything but admiration for Gainza's courage and wisdom.

While Perón was still in power, Gainza was unwilling to tell the details of his departure because he wished to protect those who had helped him. After Perón was unceremoniously booted from Argentina, Gainza was too busy reconstituting *La Prensa* to talk about personal experiences. Recently, however, I asked him to tell me the full story of his escape, and he did.

It was on March 21, 1951, that Gainza first discovered Perón would not allow him to leave Argentina. He was about to board a plane for the fifteen-minute ride across the river to Uruguay, where his mother had a ranch, to spend Easter week with his family. *La Prensa* had been seized only the day before by an "Intervening and Investigating Joint Committee" from both Houses, acting under Perón's orders. Gainza needed a rest "after those days of trouble, worries and anxieties."

"To travel to Uruguay at that time," Dr. Gainza says, "all you needed was to have your identification card. I had my identification card, I had my passport, I had all my documents, vaccination certificate, good-conduct certificate, and so on. So I bought the tickets without any problem, because to obtain tickets you had merely to show those papers. And on Wednesday morning around eight o'clock we drove to the airport, which is located on the waterfront. The plane was a flying boat, one of those Short Sunderlands of World War II. Well, we went through the Customs (you had to go through the Customs to get out of Argentina). We went through the Immigration Department. The employees looked at my papers and those of my wife, and they were all in order; and we went into the little boat that would take us to the plane.

"The boat wouldn't move. We waited, everybody waited. The three of us sat there, and suddenly one man, in a white overall, which is the kind of uniform that the customs officers use here, came down the stairs, stepped into the boat, and came to me and said very softly: 'Dr. Gainza Paz, I am sorry, but by order from the police you cannot travel.' I asked him what authority the police had to prevent me from traveling, and he answered: 'I am sorry, but these are orders.' So I had nothing to do but obey, and I got up. My wife, Elvirita, and my son Jorge followed me, and we climbed upstairs.

"When we were climbing up the stairs, the customs officer told me in a subdued voice, 'But sir, there are a thousand ways of getting out of the country. Why did you choose this one?' My reply was that I wasn't trying to get out of the country, that I was just going to spend a holiday and relax a little—two or three days—with my mother at our ranch at La Barra de San Juan. But anyway, when I got up the stairs I saw a man who had that unmistakable aspect of a policeman in civilian clothes.

"It was a plain-clothes man, in fact, and I had the feeling that he was going to arrest me. So, to test the situation, I said aloud, 'Well, since they won't let me go to Uruguay, let's go home.' As soon as I said that, the man ran into the building, obviously to telephone headquarters. I told my son to take care of the bags, and, with my wife, jumped into my car and told the chauffeur in a loud voice, 'Let's go home.' The chauffeur drove off. (He hadn't left the airport because he wanted to see the plane taking off.) I looked back down the straight street we had taken and saw that nobody was following us. As soon as we got around the corner, I told the chauffeur, 'Don't go home,' and gave him the address of my lawyer, Dr. Coll."

At the lawyer's home Dr. Gainza apologized to Dr. Coll for having ignored earlier advice to leave Argentina—because "I couldn't realize, I couldn't believe, that these things could happen in my country." He told Coll that he was now ready to escape, if he could. "The first reaction of any man who is unjustly deprived of his freedom," Gainza says, "is to protect it and keep it, if possible." Coll began calling his friends and Dr. Gainza's friends, but nobody was available, because Easter holidays had begun and people had gone out of town to the country or the beaches. (Easter comes at the end of summer in South America.) Finally Coll found a relative who owned a yacht but had stayed in the city, anyway.

The yachtsman came directly to Coll's house, heard Dr. Gainza's story, and confessed himself unable to help. He had no crew for his boat. But, he said, he knew someone else who had a small boat and could ferry Gainza across the river, and he left to find his friend.

At this point, Dr. Gainza decided it would be unsafe—both for himself and for Coll—to stay at the lawyer's house, and he drove to the home of one of his daughters, outside Buenos Aires. Shortly after his arrival there, his oldest son called, not knowing Dr. Gainza was at the house, to warn his sister to stay away from the family home in the city—because the police had occupied it and wouldn't let anyone out. Dr. Gainza reasoned that if the Perónists had seized his home and placed his servants under house arrest, they might soon search for him at his children's houses, but he didn't know where to go. The invaluable Coll again had a suggestion—an unoccupied suburban house owned by another relative of his, where Dr. Gainza could wait until arrangements were made for a boat.

At four or five o'clock that afternoon word came that at seven-thirty someone would come to pick up Dr. Gainza and take him to the boat. Unfortunately, the men who ran the boat were not willing to take Señora Gainza with her husband, confronting Dr. Gainza with still another difficult decision. At his wife's urging, he decided to leave without her. At half-past seven, Dr. Coll's relative came in a car not his own (to protect him from the police), and took Gainza to a quiet place on the river shore, to hide in an anchored yacht waiting for his rescuers to arrive.

"At eight o'clock," Gainza continued, "I heard the noise of an engine, and a small boat came into the little harbor. The name of the boat was *La Bronca* (which means 'The Brawl' in Argentine slang) —a small sailboat, about twenty-seven feet long, with an auxiliary engine. And in the boat were two men. One was the skipper, Mr. Herbert Michaelsen, and the other was Mr. Pravia, his nephew. Mr. Michaelsen was of Swedish origin, but I think he was an Argentine citizen. He was the manager of an important business in Buenos Aires, and he introduced himself. We shook hands and I told him, 'Mr. Michaelsen, I have no words to express my gratitude for what you are doing.' He answered, 'Please don't do it, because we consider it an honor. . . .' I told him, 'I am deeply moved, and I hope you won't get into any trouble, and of course I will never mention your name so you will be protected from any persecution from Perón.' And he looked at me and said, 'To hell with Perón! I am doing my duty.'

"So we started off at dusk. In this period, in late summer, it is still clear at eight o'clock. And there was a bright moon, a full moon, in fact, which always happens during Holy Week, as you know. So, the night was clear with a slight mist coming from the horizon. Mr. Michaelsen told me that he didn't expect to be searched, but that if during the crossing any patrol boats would come toward us, then I would have to take a life preserver and jump overboard holding in my hand a flashlight. I would stay in the water and would let *La Bronca* proceed her course and be searched. After the patrol boats had searched her and left, then I would flash my light so that they would be able to come back and pick me up. Of course, the prospect wasn't very pleasant, but I realized that it was a good scheme because the boat was so small that I couldn't hide in her anywhere. Well, we started off.

"Fortunately there was no wind, and we found a yacht, which had no auxiliary engine, stuck. They asked us if we could take them in tow and we said, 'Yes, we'll do it.' And under that very innocent attitude we went through the first patrol boat station. There we took leave of the yacht and headed toward Uruguay.

"The skipper asked me if I cared to steer. I said, 'I will do it gladly if I can help you.' 'Yes, please do,' he said, 'because we are going to cook our dinner.' I hadn't eaten anything since breakfast at eight o'clock in the morning. He gave me a night compass and he gave me the bearing. He said, 'Northeast by east 60.' So I steered all the way until my time to eat came, and I was relieved from steering. Then I came back and steered again. . . .

"During the crossing we saw many lights that looked suspicious coming toward us, but after scrutinizing the horizon and trying to see who they were we found that they were only cargo ships and other yachts crossing the river. So, after about five hours of sailing by engine—because there was not a puff of wind—we finally landed at the mouth of the River San Juan [in Uruguay]. . . . Before leaving, Mr. Michaelsen told me that he had asked me to steer because he realized that I looked worried and must have been worried, so he said, 'Those five hours would be very cruel for you, and if you had something to do to keep your attention, that would keep your mind off your worries.' I was, of course, very much moved, touched, by this delicate thought and thanked him a lot, and they went back to their boat.

"This is the story of my escape. . . . My wife, Elvirita, never went home because the police were there, but instead spent the night with our daughter Chiquita, who is married, too, and has her home. The next day she, thanks to the help given by friends, crossed the river in another yacht and joined me in Uruguay. She stayed with me during those almost five years of exile, and we came back on November 30, 1955, when La Prensa had been returned to us."

I saw a great deal of Dr. Gainza during those years when he was fighting Perón by arousing the public opinion of the civilized world. He is tall and aristocratic, smooth-shaven, with a youthful look about him. His English is perfect—and he is a good sport, willing to don a ten-gallon hat and parade in a Texas football stadium to help his cause. I have even seen him in a zoot suit, which he put on to have a little fun with his friends during a tour of the United States. But all those years in exile he never stopped thinking and fighting. He stood for freedom.

Part of his reward for this gallant fight came only recently, in 1958, when he was named president of the Inter-American Press Association. But the greatest part, of course, he had already, gratefully, received—on February 3, 1956, when he reopened *La Prensa* as it had been in the days of Argentine democracy, before Perón. I sent him a message on this occasion:

The reappearance of *La Prensa* after five years of enforced silence and imprisonment under totalitarian dictatorship is a majestic and inspiring triumph for all the peoples of the free world, who owe you a tremendous debt for your indomitable leadership and unflinching determination through the dark years. Lord Grey once said the lights were going out, never to be rekindled in our time. But here is a light that never went out. It burned everlastingly because you never let *La Prensa* be forgotten and it became an instrument of irresistible strength in the final emancipation of the Argentine people. Medievalism has lost a decisive battle. Freedom has won an historic and significant victory. I am honored to join your friends of all lands in extending my felicitations to you, and to Argentina, on this great day.

Chapter 21

KOREA

I WAS on a beach in Bermuda, resting from the strains of a recently concluded telegraphers' strike, when the call came through from headquarters: the Communists had attacked in Korea. In a matter of hours, I was back at my desk. Two months later, I was on my way to Tokyo, and the front.

Tokyo reminded me of London in the Second World War. It was a place to which men could withdraw from actual combat, and find "wine, women and song." But there was one great difference—Tokyo was not in the war. It was not being bombed and rocketed. The Japanese were busily going about their own affairs, and enjoying the economic boom which was a by-product of the United States effort in Korea.

For war correspondents, Tokyo was not so cheerful; in fact, the Correspondents Club at No. 1 Shimbun Alley was often a rather morbid place. Quite a list of reporters had been killed, including Christopher Buckley, whom I had known in Sicily. Some correspondents were talking about carrying suicide pills, in event of capture, and a number were armed—contrary to the Geneva convention, which went overboard in this savage Asian civil war. I saw a famous photographer examining his gun and saying, "I just want to fire those one or two shots before they get at me." The North Koreans didn't play by the rules. They apparently couldn't distinguish between combatants and reporters, and preferred to fire on an unarmed man, figuring him a special case. And many of these newspapermen had been through the Second World War. They were stretching their luck. I soon procured a gun myself, the first since the old police days in Los Angeles.

In Korea, our forces had been pushed back into what was a beach-head similar to the one which preceded Dunkirk. The front ran from the little port of Masan on the left, up to Taegu at the apex of the triangle and over to Pohang-du on the right flank. The entire area occupied by the Allies was half of the size of the state of Connecticut. It was known as the Pusan perimeter. Pusan was the main port and HQ.

MacArthur told me he had received no warning from Washington that the North Koreans might attack. When the blow fell, he had to gather up the household troops—accountants, jeep drivers, chefs, guys who had joined the army to learn a trade, and were in Japan with wife and kids—and throw them into battle. They had fought with unparalleled bravery. But they had been rolled back and back by weight of superior numbers and tanks. Some of them, MacArthur said, were kids who would stay sixty days in the line without changing their pants or brushing their teeth; in danger of death, capture and torture, day and night.

But the time had come to turn the tide. MacArthur exuded confidence. The original North Korean army which had started the invasion, he said, was now pretty well exterminated. Many had been well trained, built up from a central cadre of Chinese civil war veterans. At the beginning, these troops had merely been aided by irregulars and armed peasants who sneaked into rear areas. Now such irregulars made up a large part of the attacking force. But, MacArthur pointed out, a coolie of only twelve or thirteen can be very formidable when equipped with a Russian burp gun and a sack of grenades.

On the Allied side, many of the Korean commanders were graduates of the Japanese war college, and had been in the Japanese army. The war was essentially Asian. But Americans were bearing the brunt of the attack.

The day after I talked with MacArthur I was in Korea in the shrinking beachhead and properly impressed by the country's over-all filth and stink, the primitive appearance of towns and people, lousy roads, naked children, elders in smelly horsehair high hats, women with flat breasts hanging outside their garments (the "Korean plunging neck-line," as our soldiers called it). We arrived at an airfield, or mudhole, between Pusan and Masan, on the left flank. Beyond the field, the Communists had everything. We started off toward Pusan and Fifth Air Force HQ in an antique bus which presently blew a tire. That stopped us completely, because there weren't any spare tires. So we hailed an army truck and persuaded its driver to take us along, using a few bottles of whiskey to reinforce our arguments. As the soldiers hauled me over the tailgate of the truck they addressed me as "Pop." No doubts about rank here. . . .

From Pusan we flew to Taegu, the point of the salient—half an hour in a slowish plane, over deep and terrible mountain gorges, with poison-green rice paddies in their depths. At Taegu the rumble of battle was all around you. The town was in a state of perpetual alert, heightened the night I was there by a report that guerillas were about to attack the airfield.

I was billeted in the Presbyterian Compound. (Schools always end up as headquarters sites in wartime. In Pusan, the army occupied the university, plus a tent city on the grounds.) General Earle E. Partridge, commander of the Fifth Air Force, had me as his guest, which would seem to guarantee a certain amount of protection—but we were told to keep our guns handy, just in case. I slept with mine on my bed table. Sentries were stationed under my window, which had happened to me before—but on this night one of the sentries let loose with an automatic carbine at some suspicious scuffling in the blackout. That was new.

You took your life in your hands when you wandered around a blacked-out Korean town at night. The sentries were in holes where you couldn't see them, but they could see you. There was no warning—just a call of "Halt," at which you halted, and promptly, too. The ROK (Republic of Korea) sentries were considered quite touchy. They stopped you with a grunt, and you froze. Passwords, however, seemed almost too simple. The Americans challenged with "Toll," to which you replied, "Gate." To get past the ROK grunt, you merely said "GI."

MacArthur's landings at Inchon started a few days after my arrival at the front, and I watched the push out of the Pusan perimeter. One

day I found myself in a schoolhouse containing the command posts
of the 8th and 7th Cavalry regiments, which were attacking a hill
immediately ahead. The 7th Cavalry was Custer's old outfit. Now,
of course, the cavalrymen had no horses, though their officers still
carried riding crops, in memory of the good old days. The attack on
the hill had powerful air support. Time after time the planes dived,
there were flicks of lights as the rockets discharged, then heavy explosions reverberating and rumbling among the mountains; rapidly
whacking machine guns and the occasional thump of bombs; then
black smoke plumes showing where napalm (jellied gasoline) was
blazing in enemy positions. The calvarymen inched their way up the
heights, digging in, squirming, running, dodging ahead from shelter
to shelter. The line of fires and explosions, which showed where the
planes were dropping their load, moved slowly up the hill. Finally
the bombs and rockets and napalm went behind the ridge, showing
that the Communists had retreated to the back slope. Artillery got
in on the show, sending shells whispering overhead, thundering into
enemy concentrations. There seemed to be a tremendous effort involved in capturing this one elevation.

A few minutes later, an officer said grimly, "Well, we've got the
hill. . . . Now let's see if we can hold it."

The native population had been cleared out of a wide belt of territory along the front line, to guard against infiltration and sharp-
shooters posing as peasants or refugees. The result was that as you
approached the actual front, along the scowling mountains, you
passed through many deserted villages where there wasn't so much
as a stray dog to be seen. Outside one such "empty" village, at the
edge of a farmhouse compound, our escorting soldier alerted his carbine, and whispered, "I think there's a gook."

The "gook" turned out to be a great-grandmother who had been
abandoned to starve when her family left, because she was lame and
couldn't keep up. She thought we were going to kill her. She moaned
and rocked, holding her hands, palms together, as if in prayer.
The soldiers approached her with the utmost caution, and carefully
examined a little bag of oddments she carried—lest it contain a
grenade. In this war, they said, it wouldn't be at all surprising to find
a great-grandmother booby-trapped. We brought her in.

Among my companions was a distinguished and unusual war correspondent—Tooey Spaatz, now retired after serving as Chief of Staff of the Air Force, and disguised as a reporter for *Newsweek*. Tooey was determined not to be mistaken for an active soldier, and refused to get into any kind of uniform. He wore a felt hat and a raincoat. So did Bascom Timmons, a top Washington newspaperman, who went to the front in his civilian clothes: no fatigues for him.

The Pusan perimeter was small enough so that you were likely to see every newspaperman on the story. Accommodations contributed to this togetherness, too. At Pusan all three news agencies—plus men from a couple of newspapers—were in one tent, sharing one telephone, which rang all night long. You screamed your stories into the phone. If you got your hands on an exclusive story, it was usually exclusive for exactly the length of time required to call it in.

Among the visitors to our tent in Pusan was Randolph Churchill, who had been a commando in the Second World War and had gone out with patrols here in Korea—with the result that he had a wounded leg, and was living on a hospital ship while the rest of us lived in the mud. Churchill wore a uniform of his own design, and chided us for our battle fatigues. "You Americans can look like garage mechanics if you wish," he said. "*I* shall be properly dressed."

I had known Randolph for years. I remember once, after the Second World War, I ran into him in Portland, Oregon, where he was booked on a lecture tour. I invited him to drop in on me at my hotel room in Eugene, Oregon, where I was making a speech to a journalism convention at the state university. Randolph arrived at 3 A.M., well after I had gone to bed, but his penetrating voice soon pierced the wall of my chamber, and when I emerged I found him in the parlor, in a shouting argument with a group of students and visiting newspapermen, about the situation in Spain.

Again, in Rome, in 1948, he and I sat up night after night in the Grand Hotel, comparing notes on the Communist menace to Italy. I had lunch with him in London at his house, which had once been the hunting lodge of King Charles II. Another guest was Sir R. H. Bruce Lockhart, the British secret agent turned distinguished military historian. Churchill apologized because there was nothing to drink but champagne, which he served in antique silver beer mugs. He also apologized for the service, saying that there were no proper champagne glasses in the place. And he murmured further at the absence of gin, which he said he would have preferred to champagne.

After Bruce Lockhart had departed, Randolph got down to the subject he wished to discuss with me. At that time the United Features Syndicate, of which I was president, was distributing his column, and the sales were disappointing—to him and to us.

"The trouble lies with you," he yelled, striding the floor and waving a silver beer mug of champagne. "You are treating my column like a piece of stinking fish!"

But once this was off his chest, he became again the gracious host. I was always impressed by his resemblance to his father, in walk and mannerisms, and even in cadence of conversation. He was never at a loss for a bit of biting sarcasm, and he seemed imbued with an awesome self-confidence. But he wasn't always carrying on. He could be smooth and winning when he wanted to be, with low and cultivated voice, and due deference for the other man's opinion.

He got into so many arguments mostly because he loved to argue—and that tent in Pusan was a good place to find a verbal fight. I shall never forget the sight of Randolph in his special uniform, drinking Scotch and Lister water out of an old beer tin, and arguing abusively with Frank Owen, another Fleet Street correspondent, about everything from the partition of Ireland to the conduct of the Korean War. The rest of us went out for evening mess, and came back to find them still at it, while the tent was coming down around their ears in a typhoon. A group of enlisted men were trying to brace the tent with timbers—with an occasional glance at the two erudite writers who sat in a shadowy corner, rain leaking in on them, talking vigorously with Scotch-filled beer cans in their hands.

These correspondents' bull sessions were productive of much hyperbole and interesting editorial introspection. The men would come in from a day of filth and stink around the fighting, and start talking to take their minds off what they had seen. One session started, I remember, with a well-known writer deep in meditation, from which he emerged to announce that after the war he was going to make his fortune by inventing a perfume that smelled like ordure, and selling it in Korea. He argued that the people must love that aroma: they lived with it all around them.

"The effluvia of the honey cart, that's what they want," he said. "They want it behind their ears and in their armpits. We shall see that they get it, at a reasonable price. It's a natural!"

I came in for considerable and not always well-meant ribbing. They dubbed me "CINCUP"—for Commander in Chief, UP. It isn't every day that the guys on the other end of the wire get the chance to give it back to the boss. But the correspondents weren't all tough guys by any means. Neither were the troops. Men brought up in the soft civilization of today develop a protective armor when they get into situations such as the Korean War. Sometimes it takes over their characters, and they become fascinated by the ugly atmosphere as an escape from the dreariness of everyday work. Sometimes they go back to the wars too often.

Lieutenant General George E. Stratemeyer, commander of the Far East Air Force, rolled out his C-54 (a big cargo plane fixed up as an office) to fly General Spaatz to Taegu. Having known Tooey for years, I hooked a ride. I also procured a lift for Gene Symonds of our Staff, who had jeeped in from Masan the previous night, riding all the way with his revolver in his hand. That was a good precaution, even behind the lines. Symonds was an A-1 reporter, always going to the source of the news. He was doing just that in Singapore, in 1955, when a Chinese mob beat him to death as he left his taxi to approach the rioting "students."

Spaatz thought it was a mistake to put educated, trained American boys out in the field against illiterate coolies, to fight on their terms. He pointed out that all the Americans had at least the equivalent of a high-school education. Many were trained technicians in whom thousands of dollars had been invested. Yet they were being sent out to be ambushed and massacred by the shadowy North Koreans, who fought Indian-style. Tooey thought the job ought to be done largely in the air, where we had overwhelming superiority.

Our army was encumbered, and had to travel on the roads (at least, at this stage in the game). We carried a big transport. The soldiers rode up to the front in trucks. Supplies came the same way. We strung miles of wire, and had an intricate system of telephone communications.

The Communists didn't bother with all this. They could walk up steep mountainsides like flies. They had no evacuation system for wounded. If a man fell, he was left there. One of his comrades might pick up his weapons and ammunition, and go on fighting. The Communist soldier's communications consisted of Russian-style field radios. His rations were a few handfuls of rice. If it became prudent for him to do so, he would bury his uniform, resume the costume of the simple peasant, and go back to his rice paddy. But he usually kept a rifle stashed away handy, so he could indulge in a bit of sniping if opportunity offered.

He could sneak around behind our lines, in or out of uniform, doing quiet murders in the dark. Eventually we learned to trap with trip-wires or neck-wires across likely paths, so we could do a bit of murdering on our own. We were baffled by his camouflage, at first. Whole regiments of his army could advance almost imperceptibly, with bushes for headgear, like Birnam Wood to Dunsinane, in *Macbeth*. His supplies came down the roads in broad daylight, concealed in columns of refugees, many of whom carried heavy burdens of grenades and other ammunition in frames on their backs, or hidden under robes. His tanks, viewed from the air, sometimes looked like peasant huts. But we learned.

We went forward from Taegu now, to the front, and parked on a high ridge which offered an excellent panoramic view of the battlefield. The total number of our troops around that perimeter was about sixty thousand—considerably less than a full house in Yankee Stadium, a fairly small crowd for the Los Angeles Memorial Coliseum. But they had held the beachhead and they were now advancing as the Reds fell back, menaced from behind by MacArthur's Inchon landings.

These thoughts were interrupted by a GI who poked his head out of a foxhole and drawled, "Say, that's a shit-pore place to pahk! WE're gettin' mortah fire aroun' heah. An' you-all ah on the skyline . . ."

On our return to Pusan, Spaatz announced that he was going to visit General Kean, who was holding the left flank at Masan against repeated fanatical charges. I found that Tooey had kindly arranged to take me along. The flight was to be made in two-seaters. Mine was ready, surrounded by a bunch of grinning youths ready to boost me in and strap me into my parachute. I kept wondering what I was doing, heading out on this idiot flight. It's my experience that you go along on such expeditions simply because you don't have the guts to say no. It takes a man with more bravery than I have to decline and quail away from a plane and amused helpers.

"If you bail out," they explained, "first you pull this ring, then you pull that one." All very simple.

My pilot was about twenty-one. We ascended like a bit of thistle-down. His seat was between my knees. As we got going, he shoved a pack of cigarettes at me over his shoulder and lit one himself. Off our left wing I could see General Spaatz enjoying the ride, in his felt hat; peering out one side, then the other. In no time we reached Masan, and Spaatz' plane landed. There was no field. You came in on an embarcadero of flat cobblestones, with warehouses all along one side and at both ends.

The youngster tilted the nose sharply over the warehouses, and we went swooping down the embarcadero between the warehouses and the water. But the wheels didn't touch. The warehouses at the other end came at us very fast.

I could hear the pilot talking to himself: "Sit down, you son of a bitch. Stop flyin'. Stop flyin'."

But it didn't sit down. So he gunned the engine, and we shot up over the buildings with nothing to spare. The pilot showed great aplomb. Didn't even shake his head. Circled the city and tried again.

Down there, miniature figurines, Tooey and a group of officers were watching us. This time the pilot made it, and pulled up alongside General Spaatz and the welcoming party.

"Where you been?" inquired the General. "We're behind schedule."

He hadn't even bothered to wear a parachute.

The next day we "toured" the whole front in an obsolete B-17 with office fixtures—a traveling headquarters. The front was clearly marked with luminous red panels, to reduce the hazard of bombs dropping on the wrong side. Our trucks and jeeps had similar red panels on their hoods. We saw smudges of smoke, like hill fires, and I counted seventeen burning villages. The towns looked like honeycombs, thoroughly blasted out. The city of Pohang on the right flank was all unroofed. The airstrip was deserted, under fire from both sides. Waegwan (known locally as Wigwam) was completely gutted, but only our patrols had gone in as yet. It was a mystery how the "walled city" held out. It had been thoroughly doused with napalm and looked like the surface of the moon. But the Communists were still there, in caves.

A sudden evil red rapid blinking below showed when the enemy had opened up on us with anti-aircraft guns. But nothing came close.

"Once we flush them out of those towns, we can kill them by the thousands from the air," an officer remarked. "But ruins make better defenses against ground attack than the cities did before we knocked them down."

At Kimpo airfield, in the Inchon beachhead, I found Robert Miller, one of our best. He wore a Marine outfit and had a good bristle of beard. Here as elsewhere he had seen plenty of action. Bob landed with the first wave at Guadalcanal. At Verdun he was wounded, and nearly lost an arm. He was in the Palestine fighting, and saw the Moslem-Hindu massacres when India was "liberated." Now he was in the middle of the fighting for Seoul. He was full of vitamins, as usual.

While were were talking, a Navy Corsair fighter, returning crippled, tried to land but went straight into the ground with a heavy explosion and a brilliant plume of bright crimson flames for a funeral pyre. An American pilot had died. The fire engine and those concerned rushed to the spot. The rest glanced for a moment, then went back to showing us some Russian Yaks that had been captured in the hangars, all armed and ready to go.

Now the attack was on Seoul. The city exuded mountains of smoke. The fighting men around the Kimpo field were all holloweyed and wild-looking, including the officers. Behind us there was a crackle of rifle fire from a swamp where a covey of guerillas were entrapped. A force of ROK troops had been assigned to keep after them until they were exterminated.

Shortly thereafter, Tooey Spaatz and I flew back to Pusan again, to meet Syngman Rhee, the fiery President of South Korea. As we rolled along in a jeep from the airfield to Rhee's modest residence, men along the road snapped to attention and gave roundhouse salutes. Spaatz, who was wearing informal attire complete to a slouch hat that needed only a few fishhooks around the band to identify him as a trout fisherman, was surprised and disconcerted at the special attention.

"Who the hell are they saluting?" he demanded.

Then he investigated, and found that our jeep had a four-star plate on the front. His disguise had been penetrated. He was the only war correspondent who got the honors of a four-star general.

Rhee started off his conversation with us in a bland manner, then grew more empathic, speaking with an intensity and fervor surprising from a man with a Buddha-like exterior. "Where is the 38th Parallel?" he demanded. "Show it to me! It is nonexistent. I am going all the way to the Yalu, and the United Nations can't stop me. I will enter Seoul in triumph in a few days.

"I can handle the Communists," he continued. "The Reds can bury their guns and burn their uniforms, but we know how to find them. With bulldozers we will dig huge excavations and trenches, and fill them with Communists. Then cover them over. And they will really be underground.

"The overwhelming majority of the Korean people are not Communists. They were forced into the North Korean army. The actual Communists were a minority in the North at the beginning of the Russian occupation, but the Russians took charge and soon subjected the territory along the Balkan pattern. This is how the Russians operate whenever they get control of a country. You see it all around you. And there will be more. But not here. Once we have reunited Korea you will find that the Russians have suffered one of their greatest defeats in their expansionist campaign. But if we should by an evil accident fall short of that objective, they will push on. Japan is their next target in this part of the world. We must go to the Yalu and restore Korea. Our own Korean army is growing fast, and you Americans are training it splendidly. Our army will be of tremendous help.

"The only reason we have this situation today, with all your American casualties, is that the Russians were permitted to organize the Koreans on their side of the 38th Parallel" (he almost spat out this objectionable phrase) "and make them into a formidable army, while we were obliged to sit back and trust to their good will and fair play."

Rhee talked slowly, with a controlled voice, but with great impact. The year's hadn't slowed him. His eye was bright, his demeanor vigorous. He walked up and down the room as he spoke, burning with patriotism.

There was much whispering about Dr. Rhee. Some people deplored his determination not to settle for half a loaf. There were always persons around, I had noticed, who shrank from the idea of fighting the Russians' fire with our own. Don't do anything rash. If you took the position that the Russian strength was exaggerated, and that we ought to stop the Communists before they grew up to their advance notices, you were regarded as half-witted. I had run into the same attitudes in Shanghai, five years earlier. And now where is Shanghai?

"Rhee is an old Terrorist," I was told.

The reply to that one was, of course, "Sure, but he's *our* Terrorist. We could use more. . . ."

I left with MacArthur after the ceremony in Seoul at which he delivered the Lord's Prayer, and I never went back to Korea. But, like everyone else who lived through any part of that war, I have never forgotten what I saw.

"The 'thin red line' of Balaklava," I wrote from within the Pusan beachhead in 1950, "has been justly celebrated for one hundred years for the stand it made, which probably lasted forty-five minutes. This 'thin green line' of tired guys in fatigues has stood and fought, then retreated to avoid encirclement, and stood and fought again for over two months." I had thought that the magnificent accomplishment of our troops, during those first months of the Korean campaign, would be a source of continuing pride and patriotism in the United States. In fact, however, people tried to forget about it as fast as they could.

One of the most important pieces of information that comes into the offices of a press association is the report on how much of which stories your clients have been printing in their newspapers. News must be, to a large extent, what the editors of the papers say it is. If you are spending fortunes to cover a story, and the newspapers aren't printing what you send, you are simply wasting your money.

Ordinarily, when you find that the papers are not using the stories, you reduce your coverage. During the days of the so-called Phony War in Europe, I put through a "downhold," to bring expenses into line with the quantity of news that the papers wanted to print. But when I found that our stories from Korea were not getting much play, I decided to go the other way. In the summer of 1952, the following message went out to our Far Eastern headquarters:

BAILLIE SUGGESTS QUOTE LET'S REVIVE KOREAN WAR BRING IT BACK TO LIFE NOW IT'S MERELY ANOTHER BORE WAR. AMERICAN TROOPS WHO ARE OUT THERE AND THEIR PEOPLE HERE DESERVE BETTER TREATMENT THAN THIS. LET'S HAVE FIRST PERSON STORIES FROM TROOPS UNDER FIRE FIRST TIME. SUGGEST SCENES DRESSING STATIONS MILITARY FUNERALS EVACUATION WOUNDED BY HELICOPTER BRINGING UP SUPPLIES JUST AS IF IT WERE ALL BRAND NEW . . . SUGGEST DESCRIBE IN INTERVIEW NEW TROOPS ARRIVING OLD ONES DEPARTING WITH BATTLE WON MILITARY DECORATIONS. ALL THIS BATTLEFIELD STUFF SHOULD BE VIVID AND RAW BECAUSE OTHERWISE IT WON'T GET PRINTED. KOREAN WAR WHICH NOW SOMEWHAT FORGOTTEN IS REALLY ONE BIGGEST COSTLIEST DILEMMAS THIS COUNTRY'S HISTORY SO SUGGEST WE REMOBILIZE INTEREST ACCORDINGLY WHILE OPPOSITION IS SLEEPING. LET'S GIVE IT THE WORKS ON NEWSPICTURES ALSO UNQUOTE.

Our push helped for a while, but not for long. Hard as it was to believe, the American people simply did not want to think about their own boys, dug into the foxholes and trenches in the stinking Korean mud. And eventually, as usually happens, the American people achieved their desire.

The boys are still there, holding the armistice line, no longer dying but still sweating out one of the most uncomfortable situations in the world. And except for their own immediate families nobody back home thinks about them from one end of the year to the next.

Chapter 22

EISENHOWER

HE CALLED his book about the war *Crusade in Europe*, and I thought that was just right. To me, since my first meeting with him in Africa, Eisenhower has always seemed The Crusader—a winner of glorious victories, and a gallant loser on those few occasions when he has had to lose. A fighter: ruddy, athletic, abrupt, incisive, impatient of failure. And, like the best of crusaders, he had that special talent for leading men who had almost nothing in common with each other—men of different backgrounds and attitudes, habits and languages—toward a common goal.

SHAPE was, in that regard, a typical Eisenhower operation. The men who formed Supreme Headquarters Allied Powers Europe represented all the countries in the great complex of forces arrayed to oppose the Russian tide. But they were perfectly co-ordinated, all equally dedicated to the same cause. Despite their different uniforms, you could look on them as members of a single army. It was the greatest Foreign Legion ever formed—because Ike's talent for leadership had formed it.

I saw Eisenhower's office at SHAPE after he had left it, and General Alfred Gruenther, his friend and successor, pointed out to me the scuffed place in the carpet which marked the spot where Ike swung his golf club while dictating letters and reports, many of them no doubt of the utmost international significance. Now that Eisenhower had gone on to be President of the United States, the worn spot in the carpet had almost the status of a holy relic. Visitors examined it with awe.

But you can put too much stress on the fact that Eisenhower has shown this astonishing ability to lead very assorted groups of men. It seems to imply that he can get along with anybody, that he does not cherish his own views or fight for them. In fact, Eisenhower leads by conviction, strength of purpose, and energy. The public build-up of the Eisenhower legend, both during the war and during the political campaign, stressed his geniality, which is real enough. But, like any career soldier who has risen to the top, Eisenhower is also a tough customer. He is a slugger. His personality hits with tremendous impact when he takes off the wraps—which he does best in face-to-face conversation, or in small groups. And his supply of energy—at least until the time of his heart attack—was apparently limitless.

I sat beside Eisenhower at a Gridiron Dinner, where he told me he regarded Bradley as the greatest general of the war, and I saw him on business several times while he was Chief of Staff. I met him again on November 30, 1949, when he was president of Columbia University and guest speaker at the annual St. Andrew's Dinner in New York. The United Press had asked the general's office at Columbia for an advance copy of his speech, and to our surprise the word came back that there was no advance. At the gathering of guests of honor just before the banquet, Eisenhower descended upon me to find out what the UP wanted. "What's all this about an advance?" he demanded.

"General," I replied, "you are making the principal speech, and by giving an advance to the press you will get much wider publicity for what you have to say."

"I'm not going to say anything important," he told me. "Just going to respond to a toast, make a few remarks and tell a couple of stories, that's all."

This was interesting in itself, because Ike was already being mentioned for the Presidency, and we had thought he might use this occasion as part of a political launching ceremony. Obviously, there was no such thought in his mind. But St. Andrew's is the annual feast of the Scots, and the audience was to be almost entirely Scottish. I told Eisenhower that, and added, "These Scots have paid twelve-fifty a copy for their tickets. They have come here expecting a speech from you. You can't get away with a couple of funny stories and sitting down."

He swept my advice aside with a friendly laugh, and went on shaking hands with the guests. He was wearing white tie and tails, and enjoying himself to the hilt. He seemed the embodiment of bounding health and happiness. The idea of saying something serious was far from his mind.

The dinner was a spectacular affair, with bagpipes and haggis. Field Marshal Lord Montgomery made an unscheduled appearance and uttered a few extemporaneous remarks, turning to Ike occasionally as if to see how he was doing. Then it was Eisenhower's turn. Seats were hitched up closer, as the audience waited to see if Ike would say anything of political significance.

He started out, as he had said he would, with a funny story and a tale about searching to see if he had any Scotch ancestry anywhere. He said he had put the Columbia history faculty on the job, and they had failed him. The geographers, he added, had been unable to find a single Loch MacIke in the whole country. It was all very much off-the-cuff and casual. Then he said that he was not, however, a stranger to Scotland. He said how much he had enjoyed staying at Culzean Castle in Ayrshire, where apartments had been presented to him by the people of Scotland in appreciation of his leadership in the war; how he was a freeman of the city of Edinburgh, a burgher in the town of Maybole; a member of the Royal and Ancient Golf Club at St. Andrew's; an honorary member of the Pipers' Band of Ayrshire; an Honorary Doctor of Edinburgh University.

"But more important to a soldier," he declared, "I have been privileged to be the comrade on battlefields of the Fifteenth, the Fifty-first and the Fifty-second Highland Divisions."

He had his audience. The cheers and applause rang out again and again. Obviously, here was a man who could inspire crowds and get them out of their chairs . . . especially when not restricted by paraphernalia and gadgets, microphones, stop watches, glaring lights. When he indicated that he was almost through with what he had to say, the crowd wouldn't let him stop. They wanted more. Cries of

"Speech! Speech!" came from the galleries.

So, without any notes, he rolled on, and made one of the best orations of his career—man to man, wholly human, without any worry about reporters who might be taking it down. The audience had caught the contagion of his enthusiasm, and rolled along with him. His personality filled the room.

Then he switched from humorous sallies to deadly seriousness, and began to lay down the law in his most forceful manner. His obvious earnestness silenced the laughter as he began to speak of Scottish characteristics which had influenced life in the United States.

"Of course," he said, "there were in our early days many Scotsmen who came to America. The fact that we have much Scottish blood in the country would scarcely need to be argued here, but I think more important were those elements of courage, spirit, a defiance of oppression, a readiness to face nature and wrest from it a living, and above all, simplicity—simplicity of character, which means truth, a denial of the virtue of duplicity, of pretense, in order to secure a claim for popularity. That was America long before even the writing of the Declaration or the writing of the Constitution. . . .

"Seemingly, somewhere along the line we have lost some respect for mere thrift and independence. . . . Now we recognize the degree to which we have changed, when we come to see that the definition of a Liberal is a man who, in Washington, wants to play the Almighty with our money.

"We seek an illusory thing called 'security,' and what Scotsman, born any time in historical times, at least after the melting of the several races the previous speakers have told you finally made the Scotsman, has the word 'security' in his adventures? . . .

"Whence does that thought of security spring? Possibly the basic instinct of self-preservation, and if there is anyone that can show us how we can finally defeat the attack of the Grim Reaper, then I will say possibly security is attainable. But until that can be shown, I do not believe that security, in the sense we may live in slothful indolence and ease and stagnation, can ever be achieved unless we do it, gentlemen, as slaves of someone who directs us. . . .

"Possibly we have become too regardful of things that we call luxuries. Possibly we like to wear fried shirts too well—I don't know.

Maybe we like caviar and champagne when we ought to be out working on beer and hot dogs. Whatever it is, the thing that has happened to us, gentlemen, is of the spirit.

"This country still has broad acres, and in spite of all the waste and all the exploitation, we have great forests, great mineral resources. We still have more land per capita, more fertile land per capita, than is discoverable almost any place else in the world. We have the greatest industrial fabric. . . .

"I believe that I found in the dinner this evening just a bit of symbolic courage, let us say. We had haggis. I understand it is made from liver and lights and oats. Now, we have much in common with people who speak our language . . . we are all of the same breed, we believe in the same things, and that whole group . . . has a sense of value that places one thing above all else: the freedom of the individual, the dignity of the human, his mastery over the state and not his subservience to it. . . . If, to preserve that, we have to eat nothing but liver and lights and oats, let's do it gladly."

This St. Andrew's Society address went almost unnoticed by the press. The UP sent out a story about it, but the story received little play. Eisenhower had tremendous personal popularity and prestige—but, of course, he was only a private citizen, without so much as a political ambition to lend importance to his views. But the St. Andrew's speech showed the way his mind was working. A couple of years later, when Eisenhower entered the Presidential race, researchers began frantically digging around among his ignored speeches to find clues to his purposes. And seven years after the St. Andrew's speech, in his Second Inaugural Address, Ike returned to the same theme—the need for sacrifice if we hoped to achieve our ideals.

My first experience of Eisenhower as a Presidential candidate was on July 28, 1952, when I visited his political headquarters at the Brown Palace Hotel in Denver—where, a third of a century before, I had heard the crowds calling up the great stairwell for President Wilson, who was trying to seize a few minutes' sleep upstairs. Eisenhower and I were alone in his office, and he made me a speech which was probably better than anything he delivered in the campaign. What galvanized him into action was my more or less offhand comment that there was no doubt the Democratic slogans would be "Don't Let Them Take It Away" and "You Never Had It So Good."

"As a lifelong army man," I added, "you understand fully the implications of the last one."

"Don't let them take it away!" Eisenhower exclaimed. "Don't let them take away *what?!* Don't let them take away graft and corruption? Don't let them take away the fear of war that is always hanging over your neck; don't let them take away the squandering and profligacy in Washington and directed from Washington that runs your taxes up. . . .

"You never had it so good! You never had such a big national debt, such tremendous taxes, such government expenditures, such fear of the future, such high prices, such interference in your private affairs! The whole idea of 'Don't let them take it away' is that the administration is in some way doing it for you; and that if you don't have the government acting as a crutch, you will collapse. Whereas the administration is, as a matter of fact, interfering with the natural development of the country. America is just on the threshold of greatness. Tremendous things lie ahead. Nothing can stand between the people of this country and the inheritance which is theirs."

Energy was shooting out of him with very high voltage indeed, and the few hairs he had left seemed to be standing on end. We turned to his more immediate problems, and he expressed impatience at the politicians around him. He said he was tired of being told that if he didn't do this, that or the other, he would be "sunk."

"They want you to accept all their propositions," he said. "If they have five, they want you to take five; if you take four and turn down one, they say, 'We are sunk if you don't do it the way we say.' In the army, men used to tell me: The infantrymen are tired—we are sunk. The planes are grounded—we are sunk. Our communications are severed—we are sunk. We are out of ammunition—we are sunk. But it generally got around to 'Go ahead, you bastards, and win the battle regardless of being sunk . . .' And they did so."

Ike thought the Republicans had missed the boat terribly by taking the negative side on all important issues, and allowing the New Dealers to claim the credit for pulling the country out of the hole. He was anxious to attack. He was voluble, enthusiastic, and full of fight. He felt that he had made a considerable personal sacrifice in standing for the Presidency. But now that he was in it, he was determined to win. Defeat was unthinkable.

In the months directly after Eisenhower's election, we of the press went to work on him to win him to the idea that there should be the freest possible news coverage of his administration. He listened, and made up his own mind. Our first triumph came when he made his trip to Korea, in line with his campaign promise, to gain a firsthand impression of the war. Orginally, he did not plan to take representatives of the press and radio with him on the trip. This seemed to me to involve a question of freedom of information, and I sent a letter to the President-elect, arguing that he had an obligation to take with him at least a representative group of correspondents. Merriman Smith, our White House man and dean of the correspondents' corps, carried the letter in by hand. Other personally delivered letters of which I was informed were sent by Roy Howard of the Scripps-Howard Newspapers and Frank J. Starzel, general manager of the Associated Press. Eisenhower changed his mind, and took the press with him to Korea.

On January 6, 1953, a few weeks before his inauguration, I met with Eisenhower in New York to speak with him specifically about the problem of the Presidential press conference, and how he intended to handle this now venerable institution. It was quite obvious that he was skittish about the idea of press conferences. He said he thought it was time to restore some dignity to the Presidential office, and that the President should refrain from engaging in catch-as-catch-can with various leftists, curve-ball throwers and mischievous people who asked questions just to make trouble.

I told him that he seemed to have handled his press conferences very successfully upon his return, and that I had sat in on a few of his wartime meetings with the press overseas, which had always been a great success. Eisenhower admitted that the press had proved itself trustworthy during the war. He recalled that he had revealed details of the Sicilian invasion to the press corps in advance of the landings, and that there had been no leaks—which was fortunate, since the Germans had two divisions in Sicily, and if they had learned our plans "we might have had a very bloody nose." He could remember only one instance when a reporter tried to sneak out via a circuitous route a story that had been blocked in Algiers. The story went as far as Gibraltar, he said, "and since I was in command there also, of course, it was caught." He laughed heartily at the recollection. He did not believe, however, that his wartime experiences with the press were necessarily a good guide to what he should do as President. "Remember, Baillie," he said, "I always had the censorship behind me."

There were reporters clustered around outside his room while I spoke with him, and I knew that when I emerged I was going to be asked what Eisenhower had decided to do about press conferences. I told him that, and pressed him to give me something I could tell the boys. He then said that he saw no reason for having regular press conferences on the old basis, and that he thought the Presidential press conference had become a lazy man's way of covering a story. The reporters, he argued, should go and get their story from the department involved, and not depend on the President's more generalized knowledge of the subject.

I pointed out to him that it would be very difficult to abolish the press conference, which had become a kind of national tradition, and I added that I had seen all kinds. I told him about Hoover's press conferences, when all questions were submitted in writing, and the President just chucked those he didn't want to answer into the wastebasket—and you weren't supposed to say anything about your question if he didn't answer it. Eisenhower seemed to have a somewhat higher opinion of this procedure than I did. He expressed a certain distaste for answering questions from representatives not only of the "hostile press," but also of the actual "enemy press."

But, he added, he had Jim Hagerty taking cross-sections of opinion as to how to conduct press conferences, and he was studying a number of suggestions. One of these suggestions, he said, was that a select group of ten reporters should be appointed from the White House press corps, men of responsibility, dependability and experience, who would meet in the hall before each Presidential press conference, examine the questions their fellows reporters wished to ask the President, and decide which should be asked and which should be discarded. I told the President-elect that in all candor I would have to advise against such a procedure. In the first place, I thought that nobody would want to serve on the committee of ten. Eisenhower replied that people would have to learn how to take responsibility, a statement with which I agreed. But, I argued, even if newspapermen did accept appointment to such a committee, they would be hard put to decide whether or not their colleagues' questions were pertinent. Anyway, I told him, the first result would be a big hassle among the press themselves before every press conference—plus charges from some of the newspapers that the President was setting up a censorship committee to protect him against unwanted questions.

Eisenhower listened to my arguments, but I did not feel that I had convinced him. Nevertheless, I pressed him once again on the question of what I should tell reporters when I emerged from our meeting. He said, "Well, just tell them that when I get to Washington there will be press conferences."

I said, "Well, then I should tell them that they will be on the regular basis, General, because that's what they'll be asking."

He said, "No, don't tell them any more than that—that there will be press conferences when I get to Washington. You can then go on and tell them that we reminisced about the old days. . . ."

Then, for my personal information, Eisenhower added that if he did have traditional press conferences he would go the whole hog . . . abandon the usual restrictions on quoting the President directly . . . put the entire scene on television. "And," Eisenhower said, "I will want to answer every question. I hate to say, 'No comment.' "

In the end, again, Eisenhower went along with our arguments. His press conferences have been the biggest and the most successful in the history of the Presidency, eclipsing even those of Franklin Roosevelt. He has accepted and answered all (well, almost all) questions—and answered them directly, for quotation. No head of state in the history of the world has ever been cross-examined as Eisenhower has been at his press conferences. And it is a safe bet that no head of state has ever shown the tolerance and patience he has displayed even under the most grueling barrage of questions.

President Eisenhower has always listened to advice—though he has always made up his own mind after hearing it. One of the ways in which he obtained advice—or at least learned what was thought by people of some circumstance outside his immediate circle—was by giving occasional "black-tie" stag dinners at the White House, during which conversation was free and easy. The first of these which I attended was on November 6, 1953. There were twenty others present. We assembled in an anteroom where drinks were served, then proceeded to the State Dining Room. At the table, the conversation covered a wide range, and was such as might have occurred at any gentleman's table where the guests were considered more or less well-informed and were invited to air their views. Ike made no attempt to dominate or preside, but he listened with interest whenever anything of interest was said. There weren't any arguments. The Presidential presence seemed to exert a restraining influence on those who under other circumstances might have taken the center of the stage.

After dinner we went to the Red Room, where—as at any party—people formed small groups to continue their conversations. The President drifted from group to group, joining in whatever conversation was going on. He covered a wide range—nuclear physics, the attitude of the public toward the atom bomb and the H-bomb, golf, fishing, football, farm prices, and so forth. The President had no trouble participating in any conversation, no matter what the topic.

A year and a half later I attended another of these White House affairs. A few days prior to this occasion, I had sent General Eisenhower a recently published book on the Battle of Gettysburg. The minute I entered the anteroom he came forward most cordially, shook hands, and said, "Baillie, have you read that book yourself?"

I said I surely had, and he launched into a discussion of the battle which was clearly about to lead me beyond my depth. I was saved by the bell: the arrival of a new group, whom the President rose to greet. In the Red Room after this dinner, the pattern was different. Instead of roving from group to group and participating in many different conversations, the President seated himself on one side of the room, and stayed put. Inevitably, all the guests gravitated toward him, and soon he was the center of the whole crowd. Instead of the President's joining in what his guests were saying, his guests came around to question him. He seemed much more inclined to do the talking himself—and did so, while the clock on the mantel tinkled the quarters. He surged right along, oblivious to the lateness of the hour and the fact that he had to be up and at his desk very early the next morning. He discussed issues and conditions, and answered questions in a casual manner which reminded me of Woodrow Wilson's impromptu bull sessions with correspondents in the club car of his train. But Eisenhower has a temper, too, and some questions can irritate him. He showed this irritation once or twice, the signal being a slight raising of the voice and an answer beginning, "My friend . . ."

Look out for Ike when he says "my friend" in that tone of voice.

From what Eisenhower said that night—and from other evidence, too, of course—I gathered that his brother Milton and Secretary of State Dulles were his two most influential advisers. He referred regularly to information he had received from them, or to their opinions. But the President was still willing to listen to anyone who had anything to say—and unwilling to be swayed by anyone without good reason. He can be a very stubborn man when he feels the interests of the nation are at stake.

I remember before a Gridiron Dinner early in the President's first term, I remarked to him that his administration seemed to be "going over big with the people." Eisenhower, who was about to enter the ballroom to a flourish of drums and bugles, turned to me and said with considerable vehemence that with prayer and earnestness and honesty his administration deserved to be successful, although *honest* mistakes might be made—and that if he and those with him couldn't accomplish what was best for the country, nobody could. He seemed very steamed up at the idea that anyone could even suggest any other view of his administration.

From what I have seen of Eisenhower over the years, and from my conversations with him, I do not feel that he has been able to carry into effect the entire program he brought with him to political office. Large parts of that program, in my opinion, he hasn't even been able to propose, because the politicians around him were too cautious to support it. But I don't think the President has quit on his ideals. I don't think Eisenhower ever quits—he was built to be a fighter, to the very finish

Chapter 23

THE LESSON:
FREEDOM OF INFORMATION

I STOOD on News Nob, the observation hill at Yucca Flat, and the planes came over at 30,000 feet. A loudspeaker called the countdown; "Bomb away." I thought, Christ, here it is, At 10,000 feet the bomb imploded, and we saw it.

Pictures don't convey what an atom bomb looks like. It roils and seethes with a life of its own, turning every poisonous color you can imagine. It has such tremendous vigor—the genie in the bottle, and someone let it out.

We felt a blast of heat, as though someone had opened and closed a furnace door, saw the shock wave rippling toward us across the desert floor, and braced ourselves against the benches and desks to be ready for the shove when it hit us. The sound was nothing much: a sharp crack rather than a big boom. The burst went up in a mushroom cloud of opaque fumes, and when the gas cleared away we could see that the bomb had sucked up the floor of the desert.

Then, ten minutes later, the bomb was gone. Off in the distance, the remains of the explosion looked like any other cloud—nice, white fluffy cloud. In the gambling houses of Las Vegas the gamblers were cursing: the thump had "cocked the dice." Everybody knew about the atom bomb . . . what I had seen was just another "test."

But it is possible to imagine a world in which the atom bomb had never been used as a weapon. A world in which the Japanese had been defeated by conventional armaments, and the atom bomb was still Top Secret. How different—how infinitely more dangerous—the international scene would be if only a few men in Washington knew that the United States had a stockpile of atomic weapons—and only a few men in Moscow knew about the Russian counterparts. Such circumstances seem farfetched today, when the question of banning atomic tests is a major item of international discussion. But there are many countries in the world where an effort would have been made to keep the existence of The Bomb a secret for as long as secrecy could possibly be maintained. In the United States, it was understood that as soon as practical the news would be released. As it was at Hiroshima. The bomb could not play its role as a guarantor of peace and security unless the whole world knew of its existence. . . .

Gibbon said that history is the chronicle of the crimes and follies of mankind. This book, as contemporary history, turns out to be more a chronicle of The Mistakes of the Mighty. Its theme might be stated as: "If only they had known . . . if only their information had been better."

Wilson, unwilling to believe that the people of America would not support the contribution of American troops to an International Police Force . . . Hitler, challenging Juggernaut out of his ignorance of what Britain and America were like . . . Mussolini, obsessed by the notion that he could make himself the new Caesar by securing the garbage concession at Hitler's banquet table . . . Edward VIII, seriously proposing the outdated notion of a morganatic marriage . . . Chamberlain, announcing that German planes would never bomb London, proclaiming that "Hitler has missed the bus" . . . Roosevelt, compromising the independence of the Eastern European countries to persuade Stalin to attack Russia's old and obvious enemy, Japan . . . Chiang, asserting that the unification of China would be "much easier" now . . . The Communists stumbling into war in Korea because they thought the Americans would not fight . . . MacArthur, not allowed to attack the enemy in its privileged sanctuary, bulling ahead toward the Yalu and near-catastrophic defeat . . . Perón, discounting the Argentine love of liberty, running up bills that the nation could never pay. . . .

Some of these great mistakes were the result of faulty judgment—but many others were, simply, failures of information. It will be objected that dictators do not make rational decisions on the basis of information. But even dictators are limited in what they can do by the attitudes of the people they govern. When the people have accurate information, they are almost automatically protected against the worst mistakes of their leaders. The greatest imaginable force for peace and progress would be a worldwide free press, free in access to all the news, free in publication of all the news. This earthly paradise will not arrive in my lifetime or in yours—but it is a goal worth fighting for.

The United Press was founded in 1907 by E. W. Scripps, essentially to guarantee an unrestricted flow of news to additional papers which he planned to start. At that time there was no other full-scale wire service competing with the Associated Press, which was beginning to look more and more like a monopoly—dangerous not only in itself, but in its implications. You couldn't get the AP service just by paying for it. The AP was a club, and the publishers who already belonged to the club could blackball any new applicant. As a challenger, Scripps knew he would find himself blackballed, out in the cold, in many cities where he planned to start newspapers.

In launching the UP, however, Scripps had higher goals than the mere servicing of his own newspapers. His press association, he proclaimed, would not be a club—it would be a service. Any newspaper that wished to buy the service could have it, even though the paper was published in competition with Scripps' own. By making his news service available to all, Scripps helped new papers get their start, and gave struggling papers a chance to prosper and expand.

The fact that all newspapers had equal access to the UP service did not mean, however, that the UP had equal access to all news. Any paper that wishes to belong to the Associated Press, for example, must give all the news developed by its reporters to the AP *exclusively*. Today, in many newspapers, the AP and UP teletypes sit side by side. But if an AP member paper digs up an important story for sent out on the UP wire. Internationally, at the time the UP was started, the restrictions were even more severe. The AP was a member of a great "cartel," which included the national news services of Europe. By the terms of its "exchange-of-news" agreements with the other members of the cartel, the AP automatically, without any effort on its part, received stories about what was happening abroad. No such reports were available to the UP, which was forced to establish its own very extensive staff of foreign correspondents.

As an upstart, the UP had to be a fighter for freedom of information. But the fact that we weren't in a cartel—and couldn't just pick up the news stories dug up by all the newspapers we served—helped us more than it hurt us. We had to be quicker on our feet, and we had to present the news in a more lively manner. Therefore we could give the men who worked for us the chance to put personality in their copy. Some of the best reporters in the world joined up just because the UP was a more exciting place to work. Finally, the members of the "cartel" had divided up the earth among themselves, and posted No Trespassing signs in their own countries. The AP could not sell its service in Britain, for example, because its arrangements with Reuters gave the British agency exclusive rights in the United Kingdom (and elsewhere, too). But these No Trespassing signs meant nothing to the UP; we "didn't belong." We were free to solicit sales for our service in all the nations of the world. Our foreign bureaus could become not merely sources of news, but also sources of revenue.

The strength of the UP position was soon visible abroad. Twice while Roy Howard was president of the UP, Baron Reuter, head of the British agency which was an indispensable part of the cartel, approached him with the suggestion that Reuters might switch its American affiliation from AP to UP, if Howard was willing to join the "club." Howard refused. Later, when Karl Bickel was president of the UP, the Baron's successor at Reuters, Sir Roderick Jones, tried again. And again the UP declined. By this time, the UP was operating everywhere, both gathering and distributing news in countries from which it would have been barred had it joined the consortium. The cold facts of the situation reinforced the UP's desire to maintain its freedom.

Meanwhile, Kent Cooper had become general manager of the AP, and was proceeding to shake his agency loose from the cartel—an accomplishment which he described in his book *Barriers Down*. The Supreme Court of the United States also helped liberate the AP from its ancient shackles by ruling that the blackball procedure, through which established papers had been able to deny AP service to new papers in their cities, was a combination in restraint of trade and violated the antitrust laws. (The court's decision, however, left the AP free to continue its rule that member newspapers must deliver their own stories to the AP exclusively, even though they *receive* news from both AP and UP.) Now the AP was free to solicit members as the UP solicited clients. For the first time the two press associations were truly competitive with each other, and the AP could join the UP in its worldwide fight for freedom of information.

When I became president of the UP in 1935, much of the pioneering work had already been done. Howard had opened up news sources and outlets in Asia, South America and Europe, and had done front-page reporting himself in the process. Bill Hawkins, his successor, had strengthened and expanded UP connections in South America and Europe. Bickel, my predecessor, had campaigned the world to secure fresh sources of news and revenue.

Then the war came, and—like everybody else—we began to plan for the wonderful new world we would make when peace returned. The old news cartel was shattered forever. The UP began a campaign to establish, as a cornerstone of postwar freedom, an agreement for international reciprocity in the gathering and selling of news. All agencies should be free to operate in all countries, without government control and without restrictive contracts. As the legal foundation for this reciprocity, we proposed a basic list of Four Freedoms of Journalism:

1. News sources—particularly official sources—competitively open to all;
2. Transmission facilities competitively open to all;
3. Minimum official regulation of news content;
4. Equal access to all news sources for all newspapers throughout the world.

One of the reasons for my trip to London in 1944 was to secure adherence to these principles by the principal British publishers and by the governments of the allied powers. I spoke to representatives of the governments-in-exile of Belgium, the Netherlands, Norway, France and Czechoslovakia, and exchanged cables on the subject with the governments of Sweden, South Africa, Canada, New Zealand and the Philippines. All of them went along with us. Eduard Beneš, president of Czechoslovakia, was especially enthusiastic. He received me in his shabby little London office, heard my proposals, and said his government accepted them "definitely and positively. My country will be a leader among nations insisting on a free press and radio to keep the people informed about events inside and outside their own country.

"Free people must have an independent press," he added. "They must be informed honestly and fearlessly." His face was aglow with optimism. He had no presentiment of what the future—and the Russians—would bring to his country.

The year Czechoslovakia fell, 1948, was also the year in which we made our greatest effort to win worldwide agreement to our basic principles. Under the auspices of the United Nations, representatives of fifty-three countries met in Geneva in an International Conference on Freedom of Information. Carlos P. Romulo—smiling, urbane, adamant—was the chairman of the conference (he is now Philippine ambassador to the United States). The American delegation was headed by William Benton, later Senator from Connecticut, and included several distinguished publishers and advisers from the State Department. My executive assistant Robert L. Frey and I were on hand as consultants to the delegation, though no other American news agency was represented.

To say the least, the conference was a disappointment. We soon found we could vote down the Russian bloc—which of course had no idea of emancipating its press—but we could not handle opposition from nations we had thought were on our side. The French, for example, had an idea about an international press card and courts of honor to try those charged with violations of ethics. An obvious result of such a system would be to give governments a new way to pressure reporters and keep them from sending stories the governments didn't like. It would also give reporters who had been roasted by their home offices for being late with a story a chance to get even by bringing unfair charges against the man who had scooped them. In the end, the conference adopted three draft treaties—an American proposal, and parallel proposals by the British and French delegations. These were all shipped to the United Nations in New York, where they still moulder in some pigeonhole. They have become so loaded with amendments that they would probably damage the cause of Freedom of Information if they were adopted. So let 'em wither. It was a good try.

During the course of our postwar fight for journalistic freedom, we found we were picking up a number of supporters who spoke approvingly of a "free and *responsible*" press. It was encouraging to find more and more people learning that the news doesn't merely arrive at their doorsteps like the morning milk but comes to them through the effort and drive, the planning and energy of reporters, press associations and publishers. But I could see little difference between their notion that the press should take a vow of chastity and the French notion that courts of honor would be a dandy disciplinary device. Both are just ways to restrict freedom.

Of course the press must be honest and responsible. Otherwise it fails. A newspaper's reputation for accuracy and dependability is its most valuable asset. The shores of the journalistic netherworld are littered with the wrecks of papers that lost public confidence. I realize that there are always some obstreperous and freakish papers which are tolerated for their entertainment value, so long as they don't get too reckless. But the existence of such papers is a cheap price to pay for freedom from the sort of restraint that is always implied when canons of "responsibility" are laid down by the parties in power.

Nobody is arguing for unrestricted license. Obviously, there are times when information must be kept secret. But such cases are clear-cut, and newspapermen gladly accept the restraints which are put upon them when they accept credentials giving them access to secret happenings. When I returned from London in 1944, I knew all about the V-2 rocket, but I was quite willing not to talk about it until one of the warring governments released the information. You don't need codes of ethics to maintain simple decent behavior.

The history of the United Press is packed with incidents from our continuing fight to eliminate censorship and restrictions on the news. I had a hand in several of them myself, arguing with the Allied Control Council about the importance of admitting reporters to the executions that followed the Nuremberg trials, and convincing Eisenhower that he should take the press with him on his 1952 trip to Korea. My successor, Frank Bartholomew, was responsible for breaking up what was probably this decade's most brazen attempt to muzzle the free press. Bart spotted in the fine print of the agenda for the Korean truce negotiations at Kaesong a provision that reporters and photographers from United Nations countries would be barred from the scene. (The Communist reporters, however, were to be admitted!) He immediately dispatched a written protest to the UN Commander, General Matthew Ridgway, who moved in promptly to avert this disaster. Without Bart's careful attention to detail, and forceful reaction, the free world might have received through Communist channels all its information about the Korean negotiations!

The UP's most famous triumph in this never-ending war came back in the 1920's, when the United States Senate was still holding secret votes on the confirmations of Presidential appointees. Paul Mallon of our Washington bureau developed a source of information in the Senate, and began putting on our wire the roll calls on all important nominations. We believed that the people had a right to know how their Senators had voted on appointments. The lid blew off on President Hoover's controversial nomination of Senator Lenroot of Wisconsin to be a federal judge. Great care was taken to keep the vote private. Yet Mallon published it, as usual. There followed a Senatorial investigation, to which Mallon was haled as a witness, to divulge—under the threatened penalties of contempt—the name of the man who had told him. Supported by UP general counsel Paul Patterson, general news manager Robert J. Bender and president Karl Bickel, who accompanied him to the hearing room, Mallon stood his ground. The Senatorial inquisition backfired, and the Senate changed its rules and abolished executive sessions on Presidential appointments.

It is the courage and determination of men like Bartholomew and Mallon that make possible the free flow of important information. Somebody is always trying to dam the flow, to hold back the news, and the reporter who uncovers the facts does so at his peril. The courts have not always recognized a reporter's claim of privilege in refusing to identify his sources. (As I write, the most recent case of this nature, a contempt case involving Marie Torre of the New York *Herald Tribune*, has just been lost in the Supreme Court and she has been jailed.) Only the force of public opinion, behind the idea of a free press, has enabled reporters to withstand the constant pressure of governments to distort the news.

We have made little progress since the war. "Public relations officers" have blossomed in government departments and in private industry, sometimes serving legitimate functions, sometimes working to manufacture fake news and restrict access to real news. During the war it was easy for government departments in Washington to mark information "Top Secret" and keep it out of the hands of the public. This habit has been hard to break. Scarcely a week goes by but some officious lackey tries to restrict a story, ostensibly because it violates secrecy, actually because he does not like what the story says. The Secretary of State has taken it upon himself to say where American reporters may and may not go in looking for news. Some government officials have developed an elaborate technique of calculated leaks, by which favored reporters receive special access to big stories. These bad habits cut across party lines. They are part of the disease of big government, which always wants the press to act as official mouthpiece rather than independent examiner.

The only man who can do anything effective to fight these restrictions on freedom of information is the man in the field. It's important that he have backing from professors giving lectures and spokesmen haranguing international meetings and publishers writing editorials —but the weight of the job always rests on the reporter at the spot. (In a dictatorship the man on the spot may be the newspaper proprietor—like Gainza Paz, who kept the flame of *La Prensa* flaring for years, until all the world knew of the agony of Argentina under Perón.) That was one of the reasons I traveled so much when I was president of the United Press, so that I could bring my own brand of pressure to bear in person, man-to-man, where reporters were being denied access to the news.

This is the meaning of the free press—which has nothing to do with passes to the ball game, or immunity from traffic tickets. Freedom of the press means news: real news, gathered and written by reporters of the highest ability and personal rectitude, free of illegitimate government interference or special "guidance" by public relations experts, free of restraint by those who have an interest in giving out a distorted view of what's going on in the world.

To me, freedom of information is the greatest modern cause for which a man can fight. I've never for a moment regretted that I gave my life's work to this fight.

But the fight goes on. The crusade continues. All over the free world, as you read, reporters are digging out the news, overcoming obstacles. Some newspaper books end with "30," the telegrapher's code for end, finish. This one doesn't. Instead of "30," I believe that at this point I should say:

"TO BE CONTINUED."

INDEX

291

Date Due

Demco 293-5